L M S LOCOMOTIVE DESIGN AND DEVELOPMENT

THE LIFE AND WORK OF TOM COLEMAN

For Matt and Josh.

The next generation falls under Stanier and Coleman's spell.

L M S LOCOMOTIVE DESIGN AND DEVELOPMENT

THE LIFE AND WORK OF TOM COLEMAN

Tim Hillier-Graves

PEN & SWORD
TRANSPORT

AN IMPRINT OF PEN & SWORD BOOKS LTD.
YORKSHIRE – PHILADELPHIA

First published in Great Britain in 2018 by
PEN & SWORD TRANSPORT
An imprint of
Pen & Sword Books Ltd
Yorkshire - Philadelphia

ISBN 978 1 52672 162 4

Typeset in Palatino by Aura Technology and Software Services, India.
Printed and bound in India by Replika Press Pvt. Ltd.

Pen & Sword Books Ltd incorporates the Imprints of Aviation, Atlas,
Family History, Fiction, Maritime, Military, Discovery, Politics, History,
Archaeology, Select, Wharncliffe Local History, Wharncliffe True Crime,
Military Classics, Wharncliffe Transport, Leo Cooper, The Praetorian
Press, Remember When, Seaforth Publishing and Frontline Publishing.

For a complete list of Pen & Sword titles please contact

PEN & SWORD BOOKS LTD
47 Church Street, Barnsley, South Yorkshire, S70 2AS, England
E-mail: enquiries@pen-and-sword.co.uk
Website: www.pen-and-sword.co.uk

Or
PEN AND SWORD BOOKS
1950 Lawrence Rd, Havertown, PA 19083, USA
E-mail: Uspen-and-sword@casematepublishers.com
Website: www.penandswordbooks.com

CONTENTS

ACKNOWLEDGEMENTS

One of many influences on my childhood fostered by my uncle - the wonderful world as seen through the eyes of the *Meccano Magazine*.

Does the writer find the story or the story the writer? It should be a simple answer unless you believe in some mystical quality in life. I don't,

VOL.XXIV. Nº5   MAY 1939

MECCANO MAGAZINE

THE NEW "CORONATION SCOT"

6ᴰ

but I am still left wondering how Tom Coleman came into my sphere. It wasn't a natural or easy route, but depended on many random elements of chance coming together. From childhood, I knew of his work, but the names of all the locomotives that caught my eye were preceded by the name 'Stanier'. But this is a universal epithet hard earned by any leader of any team of designers, no matter from where they come. But this generic heading set me wondering, at an early age, how any one person could design, construct and build such complex machines. Of course, no one person could, unless a super being capable of covering all the myriad issues involved in a scientific creation of great significance.

And so I began looking beyond the multi-talented and resolute Staniers to of this world, to see who supported them. With this I was led to Tom Coleman, a man as resolute as his leader, with immense gifts that drove the Stanier revolution to an unequalled level, but who chose the cover of anonymity to disguise all he did. As he gradually emerged from his self-imposed shadows, this book was born, but it might never have reached fruition without the help and support of many people – some now long departed so not to

enjoy the fruits of their labours. First amongst them are my late father and uncle who fed my interest at an impressionable age, helping me cultivate an understanding of engineering and develop a passion for history. The many items they collected and the opportunities they gave me to meet individuals or see their designs shaped my life and provided the basis for this and other works.

But behind them there are a number of other people who were more directly involved in Tom Coleman's world. I was even privileged to meet some, though often too young to understand their significance. They are – Roland Bond, Ernest Cox, Laurie Earl, Alfred Ewer, Sir Harold Hartley, Dr Frederick Johansen, Eric Langridge, Mike Lemon, O. S. Nock, Robert Riddles, Joseph Smith, Sir William Stanier, Bill Starvis and Bishop Eric Treacy. Permission to use material they held and their memories are greatly appreciated.

We are privileged to have many fine institutions in this country that preserve our heritage and support the historian. The National Railway Museum (NRM), the National Archives (NA), the Institution of Mechanical Engineers, the Solent Sky Museum and the Churchill Archive Centre provided many primary sources of material for me when writing this book. This work was often presaged and supported by many individuals who stepped in to salvage historic railway material on the point of its destruction, sometimes taking the law into their own hands to do so. Much of this remains in private hands, although a lot has found its way to the NRM. In due course, the research for this book will be donated to Search Engine at York so that future generations can make use of this material.

A number of official documents are quoted in this book. My thanks to the NRM and NA for permission to include this material.

Last but not least I thank my good friend John Scott Morgan, who encouraged me to write this book, and to Pen and Sword Books who have turned my rough draft into such a wonderful production.

History is often about new interpretations as much as newly discovered material. Nothing will ever be completely explained and new truths can be hidden around many corners. So no work will ever produce the final word on a subject or find universal agreement. All a writer can do is attempt to reach an unbiased view of all the material available at one point in time, presenting a picture and an interpretation that best reflects what may have happened. I hope this book might lead to more evidence being uncovered so allowing Tom Coleman's story to continue. I also hope that this work gives this singular and gifted man the belated recognition he deserves.

Who could be a boy in the 1950s and early '60s and not hope to own a train set and be the happy child in the picture.

FOREWORD

Tom and his youngest grandson, Mike, in 1946.

Being the younger son of a very successful engineer, I have throughout my life been intrigued by the careers of both my paternal and maternal grandfathers. In both cases, they passed away when I was in my teens and being of tender age it is quite clear that not much information was taken on board. This, subsequently, has proved to be a matter of regret, particularly as I was aware that both my grandfathers had exercised substantial roles within the railways and my father became a qualified engineer in Crewe Works.

From a very young age, railways always played a part in everyday life, whether by way of pure interest or circumstantially within my family. It was deemed a great pleasure to travel by train and I was always the first to put my head out of the window and return to my seat with a rather smutty face having not only enjoyed the views but also the sensation of a massive steam engine powering along the tracks. Even the inevitable vapours were a treat. During this period in my life it was a pleasure to build up a small OO gauge railway with engines built by Hornby. As you may imagine, I was never short of advice about technicalities concerning my model railway!

During the period when my parental home was in Shropshire, in the early 1960s work took me to London so each weekend became a delight not only to be with my family but to travel from Paddington to Wolverhampton Low Level station and back by train, normally powered by steam. Father would greet me and say that I had a dirty face again and then would proceed to have a natter with the driver. To him this was a matter of course.

The reflections concerning my ancestors and the substantial impact they had on the family have only in recent times been brought to the fore following a letter I received in October 2016 from Tim Hillier-Graves who kindly informed me that he was in the process of writing a biography about my maternal grandfather (Tom Coleman) which would also include reference to my paternal grandfather (Fred Lemon). This came as a great and pleasant surprise, particularly as I had only a very limited knowledge of their achievements within the railway world. During my business career, a few people in engineering companies have requested my thoughts on the family railway connections and I have been woefully lacking in valuable

One of life's lighter moments in the months before war was declared.

Tom's close and loving family: Daughter Helena Marion (though known as Marion by all her family), son Reg and wife Harriet.

response. Family matters are one thing but to have learnt so much from Tim's writings, especially about Tom, has been a great privilege for me. He has thoroughly established and substantiated the role Tom Coleman played in the design work he produced which, hitherto, has not been disclosed. Tom would never have 'blown his own trumpet' so it is with immense thanks to Tim for the disclosures he has made. Not only do I feel proud of my grandfather for all things he did but I am happy that his massive contribution to United Kingdom transport has been recognised and will be remembered. This book is a wonderful testimony to his life's work.

Michael Lemon

City of Chester in all her glory encapsulating all Tom's great skills as a designer.

INTRODUCTION

I can no longer remember when I first heard Tom Coleman's name. His presence as a locomotive engineer just seemed to creep into my consciousness via a few meagre references, spread over many publications. In some the word 'shadowy' was used to describe his life and work. Yet William Stanier would later say that all that had been for the LMS would have been impossible without his Chief Draughtsman. Even allowing for Stanier's invariable habit of deflecting praise to others and playing down his own achievements, this is an exceptional tribute. But even the words of this most reflective and respected engineer have failed to encourage others to uncover more details about Coleman's life, beyond the most basic facts.

Designers are often linked by name to their creations – Caxton's Press, Wren's St Pauls, Mitchell's Spitfire and many more. And railway history is dotted with the same references – Gresley's A4s, Bulleid's Pacifics, Churchward's Stars and Stanier's Princesses. But such expressive links do not describe the creative process or give merit to the team sitting behind these great creators, who will be largely forgotten even when the leader is as modest and generous as Stanier. And here we face a dichotomy. In building up the image of a team member we can diminish the contribution of the great engineers, and may, in the process, create new myths which fail to recognise the contributions of many others. But in Coleman's case, I believe this is justified. He was a man of extraordinary talent and Stanier's praise was, in fact, hard earned. So this book seeks to turn a light on his life and take him out of the shadows as well as explore the nature of leadership and team dynamics in the creative world of design.

At one stage 'Coleman's Coronations' was suggested as

Bassett-Lowke caught the spirit of the 1930s in their catalogues.

a title for this book; it seemed to present a truer picture of the real origins of many fine locomotives that the LMS produced during Tom's tenure as Chief Draughtsman. Would this changed perception weaken Stanier's reputation in any way? I don't think so, because his greatness had many facets. He was much more than a locomotive engineer; he was a leader and manager of unparalleled skill and accomplishment. But as many have observed, he was a production engineer, not a design engineer. The difference is an important one. Both are essential for success, but each has a distinctive part to play in design, construction and operation.

Stanier and Coleman came from each engineering camp, yet found a way of working together that drew the best from each of them. Perhaps it was a marriage made in heaven, or, if not, a random chance of time and opportunity that profoundly affected locomotive development. And in this story, we find all the elements of this remarkable relationship coming together, with many apocryphal stories that have grown and been embroidered slowly stripped away. In so doing we come to recognise the many influences that shaped the creation of all these superlative locomotives and what these two great men achieved together.

When researching someone's life it helps if that person left behind a store of papers, diaries, letters or books to guide historians; the apparent absence of such an archive, in Coleman's case, has proved a stumbling block. Here we have a man of great repute but little evidence to prove it, beyond the

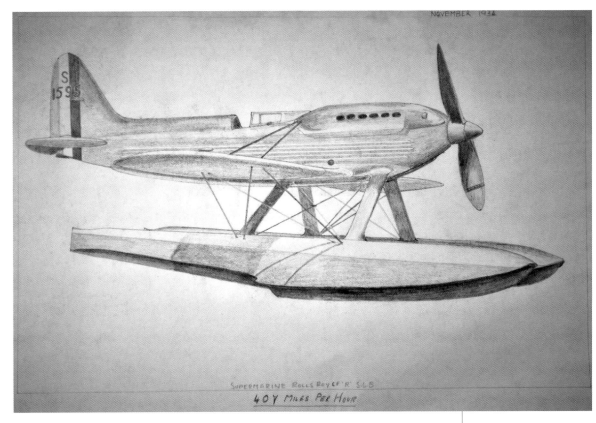

occasional reference to his work by contemporaries.

It seems that Coleman was a very private man, who did not seek the limelight, even shunning any attempt by his senior colleagues to draw him into professional bodies, where his specialist skills and wisdom could lead others. He was, in fact, the perfect 'back room' man and this persona seemed to fit his character and temperament like a glove. But even in the shadows, great skill and achievement is often hard to disguise and impossible to deny. Like it or not, he may have escaped recognition in his lifetime, but William Stanier, an astute and perceptive man, left a tantalising clue to Coleman's great talent, leaving it there for

others to find and follow. Would he have appreciated this attention? Probably not. There are many for whom any invasion of privacy, no matter how well intentioned, is distasteful and Tom Coleman seems to have been cast firmly in this mould. But to ignore such a man is wrong because the part he played in designing so many iconic and unequalled locomotives should be recognised. And the benefits accruing from his work did not simply profit the LMS, his employer, but the whole country; his designs doing so much to support the war effort over nearly six years of the most dire conflict. So, this book may see him 'backing into the limelight', but better that than be ignored and forgotten.

Tom's drawing of R. J. Mitchell's Schneider Trophy winner - the S6B. The links between Coleman and Mitchell were a feature of their lives and work.

The arbitrary nature of chance will always play a significant part in any life. Coleman, or so it seemed for a long time, left very little to show that he had played such an important role. But in the years following his death, when steam locomotion was being eclipsed and removed from the country's consciousness, a few far-seeing people sought to preserve what they could. In some cases, they even retrieved material just before its destruction, occasionally with the agreement of local managers happy to be relieved of a problem. Sadly, a great deal was destroyed, but by this 'accidental' route some survived. Today we frown at such wanton destruction, but then it was simply a case of pragmatic expediency. Yet amongst the papers that have survived, many echoes of Coleman's work can be found if you look hard enough.

Whilst this was happening others sought out the leading champions of this dying science before they too passed into silence. My late uncle was one of them. By chance he met Tom Coleman at a railway exhibition and this led to occasional meetings and a period of correspondence, until illness intervened. Although not a 'railwayman', my uncle was fascinated by locomotive engineering. In the years following a war which had seen him in combat across North Africa, through Italy, then from D Day to May 1945, in France, Belgium, Holland and Germany, he found some peace of mind by immersing himself in the gentler, more placid world of railways.

It is hard to say why these two men, of such vastly different ages, should find so much in common, albeit briefly, although a mutual interest in football provided one connection. But Tom Coleman's son, also a railway engineer, had died in tragic circumstances so he may have found contact with a young man of similar age comforting. Whatever the reason, this late blooming friendship meant that Tom had the opportunity to record some of his memories.

And there was another source that appeared out of the blue to enhance this story even further and

The Black Five - the LMS's premier work horse. 842 were built.

The 8F Class of which 852 were built. A peacetime and wartime success.

on a more personal level. I made the acquaintance of Mike Lemon, Tom Coleman's grandson. And here the story deepened in a unique way, allowing me to see Tom in a new light – as a family man, as well as an engineer.

By these diverse routes, good fortune has enabled me to present a fascinating picture of this singular man and his outstanding locomotives, many of which are still with us today. Will this be the final word on this exceptional engineer? I doubt it very much, because the random chances that came into play allowing me to discover much about his life may still throw up new information leading to better interpretations.

Whilst this book is primarily about Tom Coleman, it also highlights other largely forgotten people who worked together to create these masterpiece locomotives. There is Frederick Lemon (Mike Lemon's other grandfather), the Superintendent of Works at Crewe, whose hard work and dynamism ensured that the construction of so many of Stanier's locomotives, including the Princess Royals and Coronations, were completed successfully. Then we have the scientist Frederick Johansen, who, whilst working for the National Physical Laboratory and then the LMS, did so much to develop aerodynamic principles that affected locomotive and

aeroplane design in the 1930s. And it was this work that brought him and Tom Coleman into contact with R.J. Mitchell, then developing his masterpiece, the Spitfire. A link that Coleman and Mitchell had first made in Stoke-on-Trent early in the twentieth century when both were fledgling engineers.

And so we have a story which goes beyond the simple epithet 'Stanier's locomotives' to explore the true complexities of scientific discovery and design and to see how they are woven together to create dynamic, aesthetically pleasing machines.

I am old enough to have seen the Coronation Class working on the West Coast Main Line and have

A high speed blurred image of a Coronation rushing past. Here 46223 thunders through Tamworth in the early 1950s.

The lightweight diesel multiple unit experiment of the late 1930s in which Tom Coleman played an active part.

very clear memories of being taken to Euston by my father and uncle, when very young, to see them in action. Later, I would follow them by myself as they reached the end of their lives, noting their decline and taking as many photographs as my pocket money would allow, aided by gifts of film for birthdays and Christmas. But a basic Kodak camera could only record a hazy, poorly focussed impression of these locomotives especially if moving at speed in the foggy conditions that seemed to follow me and my friends around London.

It is hard to understand, now, how misty it could be. As an avid follower of trains and Tottenham Hotspur, one trip to London and then White Hart Lane in January 1964 summed up how bad these conditions could be. Spurs met Chelsea in the third round of the FA Cup and played in conditions so poor that it was difficult at times to see beyond the halfway line from behind the Spurs goal. A cheer went up, but it was not until the players returned to the centre circle that we knew for certain they had scored. Only later, when reaching Waterloo Station on the way home, and buying a copy of the *Evening News*, did I and a friend know that the scorer had been Terry Dyson.

Earlier in the day we had stood in one of our regular haunts overlooking Willesden Sheds hoping to see engines in action. Usually a wonderful sight, but on this and many other occasions barely visible, through the bank of swirling smog that seemed to enhance the wonder and power of those last few Coronations before they were withdrawn and scrapped. We saw two, but this was the last time I saw them in action. Their wraith-like image on that foggy day will stay with me always.

My father and uncle were schoolboys in 1930s London when Stanier's career was at its height and the results of his work found a ready audience through magazines and periodicals. Such was his impact on young minds that on returning from military service, and trying to pick up the threads of their disturbed lives, both found consolation and hope for the future in their boyhood dreams of locomotives. Who can blame them? After all those years of death and destruction anything that could revive a sense of normality was worth striving for.

And boyhood fancies once shaped rarely change. No matter how poorly your team plays or the things that fascinate you perform, they remain rooted in your consciousness and will continue to tantalise and fascinate. And so it was with their interest in the two great pre-war rivals – the LMS and LNER. When Hornby Dublo began manufacturing again, in the late 1940s, amongst their early products were a red Duchess and a blue A4 Pacific. My father and uncle bought one each in nearby Ponders End and were able to dream of building huge layouts in the years to come. But the demands of life, career and family meant that the dream stayed largely unfulfilled, although it remained an aspiration for the rest of their lives, revived, occasionally, by visits to exhibitions.

Even towards the end of their lives the Stanier-Coleman locomotives were outstanding no matter how far maintenance standards slipped.

Then I arrived in 1951, to be stirred then captivated by their interest. A North London boy, lucky to be growing up in a time and place capable of feeding my fertile imagination. Not for me the ersatz appeal of today's highly polished preserved mainline steam locomotives, with their attractive, but heavily sanitised allure, but a harder time where great endeavour was commonplace and the power and aesthetics of industrial might were evident every day. So strong is the impression that I can still visit, in my imagination, Euston, Kings Cross and Waterloo, and be drawn back into that imposing world to see and smell a time now long past; a world that beat to the power of steam. And the two Hornby locomotives my father and uncle bought in those optimistic days after the war are of that time and a treasured inheritance for that reason. Together, my father and uncle created a desire to understand the work of these great engineers, and this has led me, along many unplanned and unsuspected routes, to Tom Coleman.

One final note before the story begins. My life was profoundly shaped by my family whose lives bequeathed me a rich legacy of knowledge and experience. The standards they lived by and the courage they always showed, no matter how dire the circumstances, in peace and war, are a cornerstone of everything I do. Nearly all are gone now, but new generations have taken over and they too demonstrate these same traits. My youngest child has also fallen in love with Stanier and Coleman's greatest achievement, in this case *Duchess of Hamilton*, though still entirely unaware of his family's inheritance and the origins of this exceptional locomotive. When older, I hope he finds and follows the rich threads contained in this book and discovers his own family history.

Steam and diesel together at Euston. Old technology about to be replaced by the new.

Chapter 1

A VICTORIAN CHILDHOOD

s it nature or nurture that shapes a life? Does talent find a natural outlet or is it simply a matter of luck that allows it to develop? Does the instrument find the child or the child the instrument? The possibilities inherent in all lives and the element of chance we face shapes who we are and what we do. But, in truth, these are questions without answers, and we all have to accept that some will discover and develop real talents whilst others, who may be equally gifted, do not find an outlet and may remain unfulfilled. And quite often that person's gene pool gives no clue that these talents were growing through the generations. A descending line of general workers or artisans of different trades may suddenly produce someone of outstanding skill in the arts or science or the business worlds in a way which is puzzling to the interested bystander.

There are so many examples of this random selection leading to great achievement that it has become commonplace and accepted without query. But biographers will still begin their search of another's life by asking this question, looking for cause to explain the effects. This is nowhere more apparent than a life producing much but which has

remained largely undiscovered; the story of Tom Francis Coleman is just such a case. Other writers and contemporaries who survived him have occasionally hinted at his exceptional talents but, despite this, he has still remained a figure barely visible today. Even the limited information about his birth has, up to now, been wide of the mark. Born in Endon, North Staffordshire, has been the usual starting point, but, in reality, his mother, Helena, gave birth to him at home in Horton, Gloucestershire, on 28 May 1885. His father, a local teacher, and his mother married two years earlier and he was their first child. The young baby was called Tom, after his father, followed by Francis, his mother's

Tom and his mother, believed to be when he was christened.

Horton, Gloucestershire, at about the time Tom was born there in 1885.

Tom photographed in Lower Street, Shere, during the early 1890s.

The Coleman home in Shere.

second name. Two years later a brother, Reginald George, was also born, in Gloucestershire.

The story of how these two young boys came into being is one steeped in the social upheavals that were part of Britain's Industrial Revolution. This swept away so many of the long-established ways of life, which had revolved around the rural economy for centuries. Migration away from the countryside into towns and cities, where manufacturing had come to dominate so many aspects of existence, was commonplace as the march of industry became an irreversible stampede. And it fed on a workforce driven by poverty and aspiration for better lives. Yet exploitation, common in the countryside, simply spread to these new areas of work, driven by the need for profit and lack of any true legal protection.

Since the late eighteenth century, the Coleman family had led a peripatetic existence, seeking work where they could find it. Tom's great grandfather, William, was a farmworker often moving to find employment, whilst his grandfather, Harry, became a horticulturist working on estates around the country. It was during 1854, whilst living in Hampshire, that his eldest son, named after his father, was born. Their second child, Tom senior, arrived in 1860, after the family had moved to Warwickshire. Sometime later he became a florist in Lancashire, although by then he and his wife, Eliza, lived separately. This must have been a difficult time for the family and we discover Tom, described as the head of the family, and his mother living in Bankfield Road, North Meols, near Southport, where he had become an elementary school teacher. In those days, education was a profession open to only a few – graduates from university or bright pupils recruited as trainee teachers by their old schools. It is unclear which route Tom senior took, though the few records still existing suggest he attended university. Whichever path he followed, it seems he possessed ambition and looked for better posts and promotion. A move to Gloucestershire followed in 1880, to take up a position at a Parochial School. It was here that he met his future wife.

Helena Francis Alberta Merrett was born in Bristol during 1866, the eldest child of Frank and Louisa. Her father was a brush maker, who moved his family to Wotton St Mary in Gloucestershire to take up the post of Overseer to the Poor, later becoming a Poor

Rate Collector in Gloucester. These were tasks of great responsibility, with the high levels of poverty and vagrancy that existed in Victorian Britain, and this gave his family some status in the community, allowing Helena and her two brothers to be educated to a better standard than the majority of the population. Frank's father, George, hailed from Cork, in Ireland, and became a gardener, rising to become 'overseer for a land owner'.

Later in life he took up the role of Poor Rate Collector and it seems likely that his son 'inherited' this post when George retired, following the death of his wife, Sarah, in 1874.

Young Tom and Reginald, growing up in rural Gloucestershire, had the benefit of educated parents and lived in an environment well away from the industrial grime of the cities. But it also seems that their mother and father were aspirational, seeking to improve their lives whenever possible. So in 1890, the family moved to Shere, in Surrey, where Tom senior had found a post in the local school. It was a promotion and the post entitled him to live in the School House, where the young boys could enjoy their growing love of sport and the benefits of countryside living and fresh air. It seems that young Tom had also begun to display some of the skills that would become central to his career – construction and drawing – but he was also developing an interest in photography, sponsored, it seems, by a number of amateur camera men and women living in the village. On several occasions, he or his brother would pop up in their work, happily posing and keeping still whilst the photographic plates

slowly developed. And so their lives continued in this rural idyll until January 1897, when the family moved to Endon in Staffordshire, where Tom senior became headmaster at the Parochial School in the village.

Endon sits on the edge of the 'six towns' of Burslem, Tunstall, Hanley, Stoke, Longton and Fenton. Together they formed a substantial industrial centre served by an ever-expanding railway system and canals, still a major support to the local economy, though in decline as more traffic moved by rail. The transport system and the natural resources of the area meant that pottery became the biggest industrial concern, but coal mining, iron and steel production and heavy engineering were not far behind. Each of these towns had

distinctive characters and dialects, and rivalries were not uncommon, but the rapid expansion of industry and new construction broke down ancient barriers, and in 1910 the 'six towns' came together as the City of Stoke-on-Trent.

Arnold Bennett, a son of Hanley, would, through his fictionalised accounts of life in the 'Five Towns', as he re-titled them, leave a vivid description of the area when Tom and Reginald lived there. He did change the names of each of the towns, but it is easy to match fiction and fact:

'He stood on the steep-sloping, red-bricked canal bridge, in the valley between Bursley and its suburb Hillport. In that neighbourhood the Knype and Mersey Canal formed

The *White Horse* public house with Tom and Reg getting into the photo of a local cameraman on the bank of the Tillingbourne.

the western boundary of the industrialism of the Five Towns. To the east rose pitheads, chimneys, and kilns, tier above tier, dim in their own mists. To the west, Hillport Fields, grimed, but possessing authentic hedgerows and winding paths, mounted broadly up to the sharp ridge on which stood Hillport Church, a landmark. Beyond the ridge, and partly protected by it from the driving smoke of the Five Towns, lay the fine and ancient Tory borough of Oldcastle, from whose historic Middle School he was now walking home. The fine and ancient Tory borough provided education for the whole of the Five Towns, but the relentless ignorance of its prejudices had blighted the district. A hundred years earlier the canal had been obtained after a vicious Parliamentary fight between industry and the fine and ancient borough, which saw in canals a menace to its importance as a centre of traffic. Fifty years earlier the fine and ancient borough had succeeded in forcing the greatest railway line in England to run through the unpopulated country five miles off instead of through the Five Towns, because it loathed the mere conception of railway. And now, people are inquiring why the Five Towns, with a railway system special to itself, is characterised by a perhaps excessive provincialism. These interesting details have everything to do with history of each of the two hundred thousand souls in the Five Towns. Oldcastle guessed not the vast influence of its sublime stupidity.'

At this time, Stoke was no different to many other urban conurbations all expanding rapidly and randomly to meet industrial needs, with many resisting these changes. And these towns and cities were often grim places to live for all but the wealthiest in society. For the rest, their only hope lay in getting the best education possible, acquiring professional training and finding safe employment. Only this would allow them to rise above the mass and gain even slightly better lives. Tom and Reginald were luckier than most and today would be seen as being middle class, and benefitting from the opportunities this can offer.

Living near such a large industralised area must have intrigued the two young boys, who were more used to the countryside. Endon, although a farming community, was only separated from the 'Six Towns' by a few miles and would have suffered from drifting pollution generated by all the coal fires in factories and homes. Endon had its own station, so trips into the city would have opened up this new world to them. Strange sights, sounds and smells would have played on their imaginations and the buzz of this novel environment must have affected their perception of life. Both were now in their early teens and aware that in the very near future they would leave school and this strange place would reach out and absorb them. Their thoughts are not recorded, but the choices they faced would undoubtedly see them training to work in one or more of the local industries.

No matter in which age you live there is always a rite of passage to

Gomshall & Shere Station - one of Tom's regular haunts and where his early interest in trains was cultivated.

Industrial Stoke at the time the Coleman family moved there in the late nineteenth Century

But occasionally the smoke and grime were blown away and the industrial strength of the city could be clearly seen.

Tom's stepmother overseeing a class at Endon Parachial School in the early 1900s,which he attended for a while.

be negotiated as childhood ends and adulthood begins. All a parent can do is encourage a child, support and cajole them through education and offer mature advice to the fledgling as they choose a career. With Tom, who had grown into a tall, robust, self-assured young man, the course of his life might have been easier to plan. Well-spoken and well educated, by the standards of the age, he had begun to develop a natural gift for design and construction, stimulated by his parents and now awakened by all he saw around him in Staffordshire. Railways had caught his imagination and like many children he was fascinated by all aspects of life on the line.

Whilst living in Shere, Tom and his brother had often wandered to their local station and small marshalling yard to observe all that went on there. He was an avid reader of books and magazines and had begun a lifelong practise of cutting out articles and pictures of locomotives, pasting them into albums and scrapbooks, two of which have survived. He noted unusual details, aspects of performance and colour schemes, sketching outlines of some engines and adding additional features. The move to Endon only intensified this interest and the North Staffordshire Railway became his new stamping ground, with the London and North Western Railway only a short bike ride away.

This emerging passion had another outlet in Stoke with the railway works there, and as his time at school came to an end he and his parents discussed professional openings in that industry. As a school master, Tom senior was aware of the employment opportunities locally and encouraged all his pupils to seek careers. Now his own sons, as they came of age, drew some benefit from their father's researches and contacts. Engineering apprenticeships were highly prized and companies were able to select only the best candidates and some pupils from Endon had already taken this path into work. And now it was Tom's turn to apply and Kerr, Stuart Ltd, locomotive builders, became his main target.

This company only came into being during 1881, when James Kerr opened an engineering business in Glasgow. A partnership with John Stuart two years later was followed by the purchase of one of their sub-contractors, Hartley, Arnoux and Fanning, in 1892. Although specialists in building equipment for the pottery trade, they had expanded into the locomotive business. They had constructed twenty-one engines for Kerr, Stuart in their California Works, which stood between the Trent and Mersey Canal and the North Staffordshire Railway main line in Fenton. This acquisition meant that Kerr, Stuart expanding business had a more substantial manufacturing base, so they could begin constructing locomotives on a larger scale.

In the years before Tom joined, as an apprentice mechanical engineer, they were known for designing and constructing locomotives and rolling stock for 'off the shelf' sales, as well as working on commissions from around the world. In this they found a niche market and began

In his collection Tom seems to have had a preference for express engines - here an LNWR 4-cylinder compound.

Another picture from Tom's collection - place, location and photographer are unidentified.

to profit from it. As a company, they could not compete with the major railway firms and they were lightweight by comparison to locomotive works such as Swindon, Doncaster and Crewe, but their reputation for engineering was excellent and their apprenticeship schemes were sound, attracting many fine students during the early years of the twentieth century.

Apprenticeships were supposed to start when a young person reached the age of 16; nevertheless, this regulation was often infringed, one presumes with the agreement of a child's father eager to get his offspring settled in a secure billet. Industrial Britain had begun the slow march towards civilised management of its workers, but exploitation was still rife and safety and health were often compromised for the sake of profit. Life, as the First World War proved in no uncertain terms, was cheap in the early part of twentieth century.

Tom, just short of his fifteenth birthday, began his five year engineering apprenticeship in 1900. However, he did look and sound much older having faced a toughening process helped by his sporting activities. His family's move to Staffordshire meant that he had greater access to football and there was a plethora of amateur teams eager to recruit young players as the national sport began to take root all over Britain. Stoke was something of a hotbed in football's development and such a sturdy, competitive person as Tom found a ready outlet for his energy and talents in the game. When not playing, he followed both local senior league teams – Burslem Port Vale and Stoke Football Club. Though not the most successful outfits at the time, their grounds attracted large crowds and passionate support, which encouraged lesser teams to form and compete.

As a teenager, Tom began making an impression in the area, being noted in local papers as a 'strong and agile centre forward [who] headed powerfully and scored many goals, always keeping defenders on their guard'. By all accounts he was not shy in tackling older, bigger players and often captained the teams he played for, showing himself to be a determined, capable leader, cajoling and encouraging in equal measures. And it seems he revelled in being a team player, giving credit to those he believed deserved it, but castigating others he felt had fallen short of expectation. In time, he would come to the notice of Burslem Port Vale who actively tried to recruit him as a professional footballer, but becoming an engineer had become his key goal in life and there was little that could deflect him from successfully completing his apprenticeship. Yet football would continue to be a passion, with cricket gradually becoming something else to pursue in the summer months, when the soccer season was closed.

It seems that Tom senior was transferred to Hanley High School as temporary Head for a time and found amongst his pupils a young Reginald Mitchell. Like Coleman's eldest son, Mitchell showed great interest in engineering and would, in 1911, join Kerr, Stuart as an apprentice. It was part of Tom senior's duties to advise young students on future careers and effect introductions with potential

Henry Ivatt Snr's 4-2-2 A4 built in 1898, based on the Stirling 7' 6in 'singles`, appears to have been a particular favourite of Tom's.

employers. Being well versed in the virtues of such a career, and having seen his son growing to maturity under Kerr, Stuart's guiding hand, it is likely that Tom senior played a part in the young man's employment by the company. It is also rumoured that, before accepting an apprenticeship, Mitchell and Tom junior met to discuss the sort of training he might get.

There was another link though. Both young men were eager to supplement what they learnt as apprentices, and then as qualified engineers, by attending the same evening classes at the Wedgewood Memorial Institute, established in the 1860s to offer the citizens of Stoke greater educational opportunities. Technical drawing, mechanics and mathematics were key parts of their studies, to which Tom added creative drawing and photography. Although they passed through their apprenticeships a few years apart, Tom, it seems, remained aware of the progress being made by the very talented younger man, as contact years later suggests.

Tom's first year as an apprentice at Kerr, Stuart was passed in the Erecting Shop working under a charge-hand in one of the 'gangs' building a locomotive. He learnt basic skills, but also acted as 'skivvy' to the workers there, fetching tools, making tea and cleaning up the constant mess produced by heavy industry. The work was dirty and hard with little respite or sympathy, but was designed to toughen up the new recruits and sort out the wheat from the chaff. It was unsympathetic and sometimes brutal, but those who survived tended to do well later.

From the Erecting Shop, he progressed to the Boiler Shop, the Forge and the Foundry, gradually increasing his skills and knowledge of locomotives and engineering. Finally, he moved in to the Drawing Office, at which he had cast envious eyes ever since beginning his training. Fired up by what he learnt at evening school, and at work, he felt that this was his natural environment and remained there for the remainder of his apprenticeship, gradually taking on some basic design tasks given to him by the qualified draughtsmen. This included some drawings for two 3ft gauge 4-6-2T locomotives for the Londonderry and Lough Swilly Railway in Ireland, later named *Aberfoyle* and *Richmond*, and 2-8-0 tender engines, of the same gauge, for use in Mexico. Tom kept several of his drawings and photographs as souvenirs, clearly proud of his first efforts at design work.

Tragedy is never far below life's surface and on 29 March 1903, as Tom immersed himself in this new life, his mother died, at home with her husband by her side, having contracted tuberculosis some years earlier. Grief is immeasurable even when expected, its long term affects impossible to understand and the reality of recovery infinite. All he, his father and brother could do was struggle on, meeting each day's challenges as best as they could. But it seems that the loss of his mother took an insular, family orientated young man and increased his sense of privacy still further. Death of a loved one, though terrible, does not always have negative effects and it can often translate into a determination to succeed or to make yourself the best you can be.

If so, his mother would surely have been proud of all he would achieve.

By now the boys were becoming increasingly independent and looking outwards to a wider world, so making the burden their father had to shoulder a little lighter. Life goes on even in the direst circumstances and three years later Tom senior and a fellow teacher, Elizabeth Ann Dutton, married, a son, Harry, arriving in 1906. Tom and Reginald's reactions to their father's new life are not recorded, but one hopes they were able to view these changes with as much objectivity as can be mustered in

The entrance to the Wedgewood Memorial Institute which opened in the late 1860s. Both Tom Coleman and R.J.Mitchell benefitted hugely from its work.

these circumstances. No matter how much they may have wanted to see their widowed father find new happiness, the sense that their much-loved mother no longer counted, or was being forgotten, can be difficult to bear. One thing is certain though, there would have been scars to be borne and difficult adjustments to be made.

By the time his father had begun his new life, Tom had completed his apprenticeship with Kerr, Stuart and was considering his future. Employment within the company was not guaranteed and may not have provided him with the challenge he sought. By now he realised that the shop floor was not for him and he saw a future in design beckoning. As it turned out, Kerr, Stuart could not offer such a post, but the North Staffordshire Railway could and in mid-1905 he successfully applied to be a draughtsman with them.

In some ways, a move to the NSR was a major step up. Though considerably smaller than the nearby LNWR, it had more substantial facilities and offered greater opportunities than Kerr, Stuart. They were also much sounder financially. His old employers seemed to be facing a constant battle to survive and were more vulnerable to the effects of market forces and poor management. They survived until 1930 when some dubious investments damaged their liquidity and the company was wound up, its 'goodwill' being bought by the Hunslet Engine Company.

Apparently, Tom Coleman kept in touch with his old colleagues and, as his reputation grew, he was offered posts in their Drawing Office several times, but it seems likely that he saw this as a retrograde step at this stage of his career. But when he looked back at his time with Kerr, Stuart he felt that it had given him a better grounding in locomotive design than many of the larger works could have provided. Attitudes within the big companies were often dictated by tribal loyalties and beliefs, each in its way capable of blocking creativity and any developments that did not fit in to pre-conceived patterns. At Kerr, Stuart, with so many different customers, each

Kerr, Stuart advert of 1904.

This 2ft 6 in gauge loco was produced by Kerr, Stuart draughtsmen assisted by Tom. It, plus others, was built in 1905 for the Bowater Paper Mills in Kent.

job could vary enormously, so engineers had to think in a much broader way if they were to understand and meet client needs effectively. In a later age, this would be called 'thinking outside the box', where new and radical solutions or variations of existing practices had to be considered frequently.

When he joined the LMS, on its creation in 1923, Tom would bring this open mindedness with him to the often entrenched attitudes inherited through each of its constituent companies. He was not Crewe, or Derby, or Horwich or St Rollox, but he was a free thinker, open to new ideas without the inheritance of bias so many retained from their parent companies.

The NSR had come into being during 1845 to promote new lines around Staffordshire, Cheshire, Shropshire and Derbyshire. As Arnold Bennett recorded, the rapidly developing Manchester to Birmingham line, which was absorbed by the London North Western Railway, was being built too far to the west of the Six Towns and offered the area little support as industry expanded rapidly. At the same time, the Midland Railway was being developed too far east, with its operating centre at Derby. In reaching agreement over routes, the NSR decided to acquire the Trent and Mersey Canal Company, an unusual addition, but politically sound because it removed one area of opposition to their development plans, then being considered by Parliament. If their intention was to run this business down it proved to be a stillborn wish. By the time Tom Coleman joined the company in 1905, the canal was still in use and

required considerable support, as he was soon to discover.

With opposition removed or stifled, the North Staffordshire Railway Bill was passed into law on 2 July 1847, with most lines being completed by 1852, although new construction continued, in fits and starts, until 1910 when a final short section of track was built between Stoke and Trentham Park.

The heart and guts of any railway will be its works, where rolling stock is designed, constructed and maintained. This was nowhere more apparent than on the NSR, which established its workshops in the mid-1860s on a twelve acre site to the west of Stoke Junction, between the Trent and Mersey Canal and the company's roundhouse. It was a cramped location, becoming more so as the works were developed to meet an ever-growing workload.

When Tom arrived in 1905, it employed around 450 men, with another 400 working in the carriage and wagon shops nearby. And in their Drawing Office he found a

variety of tasks underway reflecting the diversity of the company's interests – rolling stock, both broad and narrow gauge, machinery, buildings, bridges and any other work demanded by company officers, including support for their canal system, which stretched for more than 90 miles. If he was expecting to focus solely on locomotive work he would have been surprised, but this diversity meant expanding his knowledge rapidly, giving him an excellent grounding in many areas of railway management.

The locomotive works consisted of two Erecting Shops, the larger for engines, the smaller for tenders, but each had three roads serviced by electric overhead cranes. Adjacent to these buildings were the main fitting and machine shop, the tool and gauge store, a newer machine shop and the boiler house. An engine room sat in the midst of all these shops, providing power to drive each shop's machines through overhead shafts and belts. The main offices, including Tom Coleman's

Tom also assisted in the design of two 3 foot gauge engines for the Londonderry & Lough Swilly Railway Co in Ireland.

Port Vale FC in 1907 or 08. Tom stands to the left of the goal keeper - a strong and imposing figure.

Kerr, Stuart of Stoke - a day to day scene that became common to Tom when he started his apprenticeship there in 1900.

new workplace, were situated in a two-storey brick building near the main entrance to the site.

By any standards the business was a compact, self-contained one, and their new recruit settled down to his new life eager to build on the knowledge he had accumulated. The NSR suffered from the usual ills of any business, lack of funding and the stresses of internal politics, but it seemed to offer those with ambition a ready outlet for their talents. It also encouraged continuous learning and placed emphasis on sporting activities outside work. In this Tom was well ahead, though. His love of football had not diminished with the passing of the years and had survived the increasing focus of his engineering career. He eagerly looked forward to the start of each season and playing for his local team in Endon and occasionally turning out for Burslem Port Vale's reserves as a full back. The Football League team were constantly looking for new players and continued to see in Tom someone who might be encouraged to make the step up from amateur to professional status in time.

On a couple of occasions, he also played for the Codridge Church team, part of the North Staffordshire Church League. Whilst their first team were winning their league championship and a local challenge cup in the 1906/07 season, he turned out for their reserves. Fired up by success they then sought to move up a level and applied for membership of the North Staffordshire Federation League.

Meanwhile Burslem Port Vale and Stoke, the two local teams of note, were facing an uncertain future and would, in 1907 and 1908 respectively, be forced to resign from the national Football League when driven into liquidation by the parlous state of their finances. Someone's misfortune can be another's opportunity and Codridge Church discussed and agreed a takeover of Burslem's ground, re-naming themselves Port Vale in the process. And so, by this speculative route, Tom's football career would take a step upwards.

By all accounts he was a talented, very resilient player who could, if he had so wished, have made a name for himself at a higher level. But pay for footballers in those days was modest. Most careers were over by 30, with prospects beyond that poor, especially in a job market where competitors might have been learning a trade since the age of 15. Although the game clearly drew Tom, his practical nature and love of engineering would

Burslem Port Vale's ground when Tom played for the team. It seems to have suffered from a slope so typical of many grounds at the time.

Endon Cricket Club in 1910. Tom, back row to the left, nonchalantly leans against the door frame cigarette in hand.

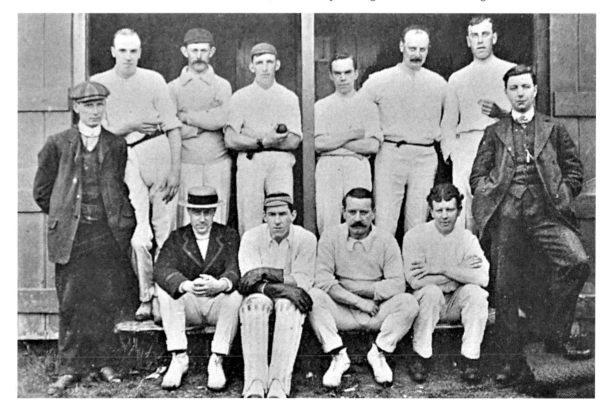

have steered him away from a few brief years of sporting glory. But as an amateur he could enjoy both for a time, encouraged by his managers at Stoke Works.

After a good start in the Federation league, Port Vale's ambitious board applied for membership of the North Staffordshire and District League and recruited new players to help them make this step up. Tom had become a player of some note locally and was engaged by the aspiring club in time for the 1908/09 season, in which he played 42 times. But until January, their form had been poor, with the *Staffordshire Sentinel* providing a caustic running commentary. In a disastrous run up to Christmas they were bottom of the league, but on 5 December they beat Congleton Town. The paper reported, 'Yes, it is true. Port Vale have won a match at last!'

Struggling to survive, and with poor gate receipts, the club

sought backers and this allowed a consortium of Burslem Port Vale's former investors to buy into the new club. They quickly established themselves, dominated the team's management, brought in some former Burslem players and changed the team's tactics. But success still eluded them for a time and it was not until Tom was moved from full back to centre forward that things changed. The improvement was dramatic and by the end of the season he had scored nineteen times in eight weeks, four times on three occasions, as the team moved up to 8th place in the league. Such form suggests this might have been his best position, but, with the departure of Nixon, their centre half, to Manchester, he moved back into defence for the next season.

By now, the team were playing to crowds of many thousands and were signing professionals from top league clubs, such as Joe Brough from Spurs, to help boost their

performance. Tom remained in midfield and continued to perform well, still scoring occasionally, as the team began to climb the table. But the 1909/10 season ended in some disarray. With a championship in the offing they needed one point from their last match to clinch the title and it was a derby game away to local rivals Stoke. Sharp practice and sport are never far apart and Port Vale decided to 'sign' four talented amateur players for this one match. One of them was Dickie Roose, the former Stoke and Welsh international goalkeeper. Vale were 2-0 up when the home crowd could stand no more of this 'injustice', rushed on to the pitch and carried Roose away, with the aim of throwing him in the River Trent. A Stoke player was knocked unconscious and other players roughed up quite badly, leading the referee to abandon the match. It seems that Tom was in the crowd, dropped to make way for one of Port Vale's four temporary players, in this case Chapman, the England amateur captain. Such is the nature of sport and the desire to guarantee success that if the team had been left unchanged they would probably have beaten Stoke and won the championship. There was some compensation though, when the well-established players beat Chillington Rangers 3-2 in the more prestigious Staffordshire Junior Cup before a 12,500 crowd paying record receipts of £211 9s 2½d, with Tom scoring the winning goal.

Success in football always draws interest from bigger clubs eager to recruit up and coming players and before the start of the new season a small exodus took place at Burslem. Tom, being 24 and in his playing prime, had drawn the attention of

During the late 1920s Tom visited Ireland and took this photo apparently of one of the two L&LSR 4-6-2T engines he helped design.

various teams around the country, but any formal approaches to turn professional were rebuffed and he continued as an amateur with Port Vale for one more season. In 1910/11, he played thirty-two times for them and scored nine times, though injured and missing a number of matches; one of eight regular players who suffered serious injuries in the late stages of the season. Despite this, they finished in second place, even though a goal had been disallowed when the ball passed through a hole in the net.

With such success, and supported by ever increasing numbers, they sought a return to the Football League's Second Division, but a bureaucratic mix up meant that the opportunity was missed and they agreed to play in the Central League instead. It was still a major step up, because the league was populated by reserve teams from the major clubs in the North East and so called for a higher level of professionalism and obligation from players and staff alike. After all, even when playing against the second teams from Manchester United, City, Liverpool, Everton, Bolton and Burnley, a greater sense of commitment is essential, and there is a need to travel further afield to play.

Faced with a choice between football and his burgeoning engineering career he chose to focus on industry and not the playing field. It was a momentous decision that would have important consequences for railway history and the success of the LMS and, in time, its contribution to a country hard pressed by war. But there may also have been another reason he concentrated on his

work for the North Staffordshire Railway. He had met and married a young Hanley woman, Harriet Ethel Scarratt, the second child of William, an ironworker, and Alice his wife. In his last season with Port Vale they had set up home in Alder House, a large six room property in Endon, very close to his father. Inevitably, work and family needs increasingly dominated his life, to the detriment of other interests. Tom would still play football and cricket occasionally, gradually switching from one sport to another, as joints and muscles reacted to the constant hammering absorbed on the soccer field, but it was a reducing commitment.

Much later, when a few of his fellow engineers came to record very brief memories of Tom, he was described as a rough diamond. It is interesting to think why this was so. Was it a true description or simply the self-serving comments of lesser men resentful of his abilities? He was a keen footballer and to some this denoted belonging to a coarser element in society, but he

was the educated son of educated, middle class parents following a career of great professional worth and understanding, who had moved easily between country and city living, and through different levels of society. Today he would be called well rounded and be regarded as more perceptive for the variety and depths of his experiences than others. But the engineering world in turn of the century Britain was not for the faint hearted and everything about Tom spoke of strength, discipline, education, determination, understanding and creativity. Team sport at the highest possible level would be a natural part of such a person's life, a metaphor for all he stood for and wanted to achieve.

As the new decade dawned, he was well established in his engineering career with the NSR and had begun to understand the creative edge in his personality. And the undiscovered years ahead would see him pursue and grasp any opportunity he could to develop and exploit his great skills to their limit.

In 1905 Tom joined the North Staffordshire Railway as a junior draughtsman and worked in this office for the next 20 years.

A scene that would become a familiar to Tom on a daily basis - the Loco Erecting Shop at Stoke Works.

When with the NSR Tom acquired this drawing of the Vulcan de Glehn engine.It seems he was impressed by the layout and concept.

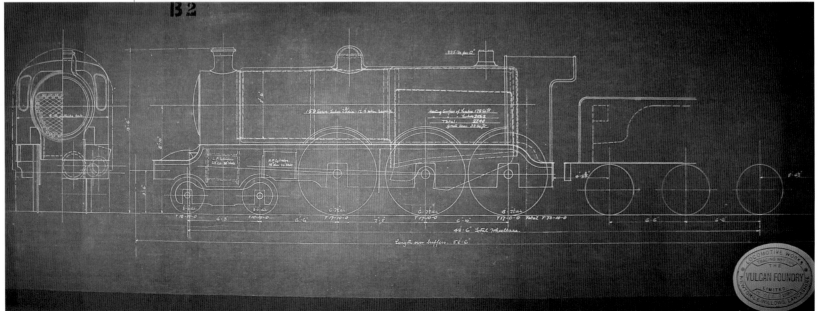

Chapter 2

FLEDGLING DESIGNER

As the years passed and he gained knowledge and experience of mechanical engineering, Tom thought deeply about his role as a draughtsman. Gradually, he developed a keen appreciation of the skills required to undertake his work successfully. He realised that he had to acquire a wide range of competencies across a number of disciplines to function properly, even though as a junior he might only be focussing on one element of a design. In some ways, it was a role in its infancy, embracing many engineering and aesthetic subjects that would now be provided by a wider, more diverse team of specialists. So to fully understand the role of a draughtsman in the first half of the twentieth century, when science and engineering were still in an embryonic stage, it is best to see them as Design Engineers, a later title that better describes the work they did.

Later in his career, when it had become clear how essential the Drawing Office role in design was, a paper was read to members of the Institution of Locomotive Engineers in Manchester. In it, the author, A.E. Howell, set out to describe modern production and costing methods that should be applied to locomotive engineering. Copies were circulated to many staff

involved in this work, presumably to provide a good example for them to follow. Howell described the role of Drawing Offices in this process in very simplistic terms:

'Upon an order being received by the chief draughtsman it is handed over to the leading draughtsman, who after going through the specification, draws up the list of drawings required

and allots the necessary drawing and sketch numbers.

'After having obtained the time limit set by the production department when the drawings must be ready in sequence, he sets his men on to the various key or arrangement drawings, having a watchful eye upon the requisitioning of all parts requiring the longest time to procure or manufacture, such as

The NSR in 1906 and the sort of engine the company were producing in the first few years of Tom's time at Stoke Works - engine No. 15.

special forgings, steel castings, all in relation to the order of building. A schedule giving particulars of all quantities and sizes of every individual part is put in each drawing as well as a separate copy filed in its appropriate section, the whole comprising a complete schedule of every part of the order.'

A shorter description of a complicated, creative process would be hard to find. But these were days in which education could hardly keep pace with the changes taking place in society, let alone the industrial world, which, for the most part, still managed learning by watching, listening, then copying.

In the absence of a more structured instructive programme, budding engineers learnt as the best they could, relying upon their instincts and the ability of trained men to guide them effectively. And the more conscientious supplemented this meagre fare with evening classes.

The key to a designer's role will always be a detailed specification, no matter in which field they labour. For early twentieth century locomotive engineers, these could be very broad statements of requirement indeed, allowing draughtsmen a certain amount of leeway in developing solutions. As Howell emphasised, there had to be a clear procedure in place, but beyond that, the Chief

Draughtsman and his team had freedom to experiment, investigate and develop options. And so a broader picture of a design engineer's role gradually emerges. They had to be aware of all current developments in their field, whether it be from within the engineering community, or elsewhere, and seek to invent new solutions if necessary. This was a process greatly helped by the work of the Institutions of Mechanical Engineers and Locomotive Engineers. They allowed designers to analyse options and look for better ways of improving efficiency and performance.

This mix and match arrangement, which married the best of established practise with new, occasionally untried concepts, lay at the centre of the designer's work, with their freedom to manoeuvre limited only by a company's desire to gamble or not. But within this framework, draughtsmen had to apply much more than engineering principles. Function and form sat together. The engine had to be efficient and effective to meet or improve upon the specification, but aesthetics were also important. Product branding was still in its infancy, but it existed and in a privatised world the look of your business could have immeasurable benefits. It may have been a small part of the designer's work, but it was there nonetheless. And my experience of engineers is that the look of their creations was of great importance to them. As Tom's career would show, he was blessed with great engineering skills, but also an artist's eye for shape and form.

At the North Staffordshire Railway, Tom had John Adams

John Hookham
the NSR's Works Manager, who became Loco Supt in 1915 following Adams' death. Hookham retired in 1924.

as Locomotive, Carriage and Wagon Superintendent, assisted by John Hookham as Works Manager, with Arthur Tassell, the Chief Draughtsman. These three experienced, enlightened men were responsible for recruiting him, then ensuring that he had every opportunity to develop his skills in the years ahead. Adams' pedigree could not have been better. He was the third son of William Adams, who had risen to become Locomotive Superintendent of the London and South West Railway and an engineer of great skill. John inherited his father's gifts and benefitted from extensive education in Britain and Belgium before being apprenticed in 1877 to the Great Eastern Railway. He was based at the Stratford Works in East London where William was Locomotive Superintendent.

When his father moved to the London and South Western Railway's Works at Nine Elms, near Waterloo Station, a year later, his son followed him there to complete his apprenticeship. For a period after qualification he became a fireman, then driver, before spending a year with Tannett, Walker and Co of Leeds, who were specialists in hydraulic engineering. Having such an experienced parent, who understood career needs very well, his guiding hand can be seen behind John's gradual progression. A move to Brazil, as Superintendent of the Donna Thereza Christina Railway, in 1887, was followed by an appointment as assistant manager of the South Eastern and Chatham Railway Works at Ashford. This, in turn, led to his appointment with the North Staffordshire Railway in March 1902.

Hookham, three years Adams' junior, began his career with a five year apprenticeship under William Kirtley at the London, Chatham and Dover Railway's Longhenge Works, before becoming an assistant draughtsman there. This was followed by periods in the drawing offices at the Nine Elms Ironworks and then the Glengall Ironworks of Millwall, working on marine engines and barges. During 1891, he returned to the LCDR, at Longhenge, as assistant draughtsman, then spent a short period at the South Eastern Works at Ashford in Kent, when this company began sharing operations with the LCDR in 1899. A year later, he followed John Adams to South America, replacing him as Superintendent on the Brazilian railway, though there was a gap of some months between their appointments. Nationalisation of this company only two years later brought Hookham back to Britain where he became the NSR's Works Manager under Adams, succeeding him in 1915 when the older man died on 7 November.

Arthur Tassell left school at 16 and began his engineering apprenticeship at Tonbridge Running Shed, before moving to Ashford Works to complete this qualification. His proficiency as a draughtsman led to his employment in the company's Drawing Office when his apprenticeship came to an end in 1897. Throughout his career he sought to enhance his abilities and continually attended evening classes to achieve this. He became a strong advocate of higher education and encouraged his staff to improve their skills through

this route too. He even became a lecturer in Machine Construction and Drawing, so strong was his belief in continuous learning, and ran special classes for NSR staff until 1915.

Before becoming Chief Draughtsman at Stoke in 1902, he was a senior draughtsman at the Hyde Park Loco Works, Glasgow, for a year. He was well known and respected by both Adams and Hookham, who actively campaigned to recruit him when they became the NSR's Superintendent and Works Manager respectively.

John Henry Adams, the NSR's Locomotive Superintendent from 1902 to 1915.

Arthur John Tassell.

introduction of the 4-wheel bogie to engines and carriages. But apart from these changes, his time as Superintendent was not noted as a period of great design innovation on the NSR.

Hookham, on the other hand, demonstrated his ability as a design engineer from the first, even though constrained by the NSR's budgets. Amongst his projects was a 4-wheeled battery powered shunting locomotive that was successfully employed by Thomas Bolton and Sons at their Oakamoor works, from construction in 1917 until the mid-1960s. This was followed by a 4-cylinder 0-6-0 tank engine which appeared in 1922. In this design, he altered the crank arrangement to restrict the cylinders acting in pairs. By re-setting the cranks, Hookham was able to get the engine to achieve eight exhaust beats per revolution of the wheels, which increased torque and reduced the disruption in the firebox. He also introduced such things as a new type of feed-water heater, oil firing and soft iron packing for piston rod and valve rod glands, which, by all accounts, improved wear and sealant qualities. It was a development that found wider application across the railway world.

Tom was fortunate to have these talented engineers in charge when he became a draughtsman with the NSR in 1905 and was at a fledgling stage of his career. And probably even luckier to have Hookman directly responsible for him, rather than Adams, as Works Manager, in terms of his development as a designer. He was, it seems, more a scientist than an engineer, and possessed very advanced analytical

skills and a better understanding of the many principles that underpinned physical science. These abilities would have made him a better guide for those such as Tom, who were eager to reach a deeper understanding of the ideologies and doctrines of their profession.

This is not to say that Adams' role in development was unimportant. His drive, knowledge of production methods and his broader management skills complemented Hookham's more specific design abilities and gave young draughtsmen the balanced picture they needed to flourish as engineers.

However, Tassell's role in Tom's development was probably the most crucial of the three. As Chief Draughtsman, he had day to day responsibility for his work and progress. As an educationalist and seasoned lecturer, he actively encouraged his staff to develop their skills at all times and ensured that the NSR supported their endeavours by forming their own evening school. Undoubtedly, Tom benefitted from this patronage and it is clear from surviving records that Tassell was impressed by the younger man and actively sought to advance his career.

Every new draughtsman had to start at the bottom, picking up the more mundane tasks delegated by senior colleagues as they learnt their trade. It could be frustrating at times, especially if the newcomer was a quick learner and possessed great skills. But it was a good grounding nevertheless. Most, in time, took on more detailed work and quite often this was accompanied by time on the

Adams and Hookham were perfect examples of the two complementary sides of locomotive engineering. Adams was very much a workshop man and a moderniser who had an excellent understanding of production techniques and processes. He effectively re-organised Stoke Works, equipping it with new machinery and improving production flow. This allowed the company to build and maintain all its own engines and most rolling stock, reducing its commitment to outside contractors. Whilst he was in post there were improvements to tender axle-box bearings and the

footplate, a practice encouraged by Adams who had learnt much from this experience himself. Assessing locomotive performance was a developing art and designers relied heavily on the opinion of drivers as well as more scientific measurements. Under George Churchward's guiding hand, the GWR was showing the way ahead in this type of analysis, even building a rolling road to test locomotives in a controlled environment. But other companies were well behind in these developments and were struggling to find adequate ways of evaluating outputs, though dynamometer car tests were becoming more commonplace.

From 1905 onwards, Tom often took the opportunity to ride on various locomotives, recording in fine detail different elements of their operation. Luckily, a number of his reports have survived intact. These show a man immersing himself in all aspects of engine running – route, timings and reasons for delays, weather conditions, loads, performance components, comments made by the crew and anything else that sprang to mind. The depth of his analysis demonstrated the level of commitment he felt towards understanding all aspects of locomotive operation. Such is the power of a strong analytical mind determined to get to the root of a problem and there seems little doubt that he believed this task essential to his work in advancing engine design. It was a practice he would follow throughout his career, no matter how far he rose.

A view of a machine shop at Stoke Works. With belts and confined working spaces it was inevitably noisy and dangerous. Caps did provide some protection against being scalped.

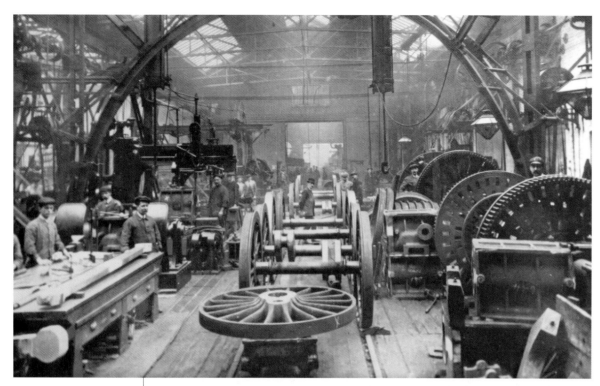

However, his interest in the construction of new locomotives was equally well established from the earliest, fostered in part by his time with Kerr, Stuart, but also an interest in the improvements Adams brought to the production process. But whilst footplate crew seemed content to have a 'manager' on the footplate assessing their performance, shop floor workers often resented this interest. The relationship between capital and labour was still very one sided, though worker's rights were beginning to be recognised and fought for. As a result, industrial relations in the railway industry were changing rapidly and even in the NSR disputes were becoming more commonplace in the years leading up to the First World War, as a national pattern of agitation

The wheeling section of the NSR's Erecting Shop. The bowler hatted figure amongst the wheels is said to be John Hookham.

No 9, an M Class 0-4-4T, built in 1907 at Stoke Works and withdrawn in 1936.

and unrest spread. So officers such as Tom were advised to be circumspect when observing construction and maintenance work going on in the shops.

To understand how Tom developed as an engineer and designer it is best to follow the work being undertaken by the company at the time. Some production records still exist and the locomotive building programme is well documented, plus Tom kept copies of a few drawings he had worked on. The picture is not complete, but is as clear as it is ever likely to be and reflects the variety of work the NSR's Drawing Office tackled under Arthur Tassell.

It seems to be a general principle that newcomers were set to work on interesting, but basic tasks. This kept them busy and allowed them to develop their competencies without constant supervision. In this way, they could have a degree of independence and be in no danger of slowing more important tasks. In his first few months Tom was tasked with surveying the workshops and producing updated drawings of layout, post the modifications implemented by Adams. At the end of this project, he presented his work to the Chief Draughtsman, then the Works Manager, who would scrutinise the results, delivering a summary of their views, suggesting additional tasks and then signing off the work as completed to their 'entire satisfaction'. Other similar tasks followed before the trainee moved onto more advanced work. In Tom's case, this meant preparing updated engine diagrams and drawings of various items of workshop machinery. But with the canal

network on the railway's books, the Drawing Office were often called upon to prepare illustrations of structures and machinery connected with their infrastructure. And this work became a regular feature of Tom's life, culminating in a major design project in 1917.

The Trent and Mersey Canal Company owned a section of waterway known as the Caldon Branch which ran from Etruria to Froghall Wharf. To speed the transfer of limestone from nearby quarries from rail to boat, a new basin was built at Endon. The needs of wartime production drove a need for more and more limestone, and the NSR decided to improve supply by installing new crushers at Caldon Low Quarry and a new

mechanical chute and hopper at the basin. Tom is recorded as the designer of this equipment, which was built in Stoke Works and worked successfully until the 1930s, becoming known locally as the Endon Dip. As a resident of the village, he must have taken a much closer interest in this project than the other draughtsmen at Stoke.

Variety was the key to work in the Drawing Office and whilst many of these non-standard tasks must have held their interest, they could also prove to be a distraction. They were locomotives designers principally and would have regarded work designing new engines or modifying existing stock as their main purpose. And in the drawings that have been preserved,

A Class L built in 1913 on a Stafford local.

we see Tom working on dome and regulator modifications to various classes, blocks for springs, petticoat pipes, modifications to frames and so on. One development of some significance on which he also worked was the use of the Belpaire boiler system invented by a Belgium engineer of that name in the 1860s. From 1910 onwards, this design featured in most newly constructed locomotives and Tom became something of an expert in its application. These boilers had a greater surface area at their top, which improved heat transfer and steam production.

In conjunction with this, the NSR also investigated the introduction of superheating elements developed by Wilhelm Schmidt in Germany in the late nineteenth century. The GWR under Churchward became great aficionados of this system and by 1909 had introduced their own version – development work that greatly influenced other railway companies. And the benefits were only too obvious. By superheating steam generated by a boiler, thermal efficiency would be improved, heat loss reduced and lower rates of water consumption realised. The key issue which remained unresolved was the temperature level to be achieved by superheating. The laws of thermodynamics suggested it should have been the highest possible, but many locomotive designers believed that too high a temperature only wasted energy and so decided to adopt a minimum essential policy for a given task. It was a debate that ran on for some time and became a major issue later when William Stanier became CME with the LMS and Coleman his Chief Draughtsman. Stanier preferred to keep the temperature low and Coleman, who by this time had become a specialist in the field, argued long and hard for the maximum achievable. But this debate was still a long way in the future when the NSR adopted superheating in 1910.

Gradually, as his reputation grew, Coleman was tasked with more important tasks, with a small team under his control. With Hookham and Tassell's support, he began taking a leading role in designing the H1 0-6-0, which came into service during 1910/11, the K Class 4-4-2T in 1911/12 and the C Class 0-6-4T in 1914/15. Though the number constructed of each type was small, they represented a big outlay in time and resources for such a small company and its team of designers. But as they enjoyed the fruits of their labour, the old world they knew so well was about to come apart as a hapless tumble into war shook uncomprehending minds. The world was about to descend into disarray and a generation of young men, from many countries, would soon become the innocent victims of an industrial genocide committed by intransigent, feckless leaders.

The railways would be swept up in this maelstrom, their industrial might absorbed and exploited for the war effort. Peacetime plans were immediately placed in abeyance as the Government sought to harness all effort in fighting a war some mistakenly believed would be over by Christmas 1914. How wrong they were, but hope will always seek to triumph over reality; a hopeless wish for calm and normality when the world has gone mad.

The impact on the North Staffordshire Railway was not

Another engine which Tom helped design was the K Class 4-4-2T which were constructed in 1911 and 1912. The loco here is seen in Stoke Station.

immediately apparent. Traffic increased as the British Army moved onto a war footing. Soldiers and their equipment were transferred to front line service and others to training centres, but Staffordshire was not, for the most part, a major rallying point for these efforts at this stage of the war and industry was far from being organised to support the conflict. The mass movement of munitions and other equipment from factories to the frontline was far from being a reality just yet. So life on the NSR went on, for a time, as though the country was still at peace.

For Tom and Harriet, the war would bring many extra worries, particularly as they now had two children, Helena, though called Marion by the family, had been born in the Spring of 1911, whilst Reginald arrived in January 1914. Although Tom's position with the railway might have been deemed a reserved occupation and prohibited him from fighting, his own conscience and public pressure may have prevented this happening. No record of his thoughts seem to have survived and one can only wonder at the struggle he and many others faced in trying to decide what was right and what was best for his family. It seems to me that a man who had displayed such determination and courage on the football field would have wished to serve his country, but being a realist would also have been aware of the pressing nature of work and family commitments. Many of his fellow workers on the NSR did sign up or were conscripted later and by war's end nearly a thousand had seen service.

His position remained unclear until January 1916, when the reality

of heavy casualties and the scale of the war began to hit home. Volunteers for service were still coming forward, but the number had slowed to a trickle compared with the mass rush to the colours of the early months of the war. So in January 1916, to ensure that the mincing machine could be fed, the Government introduced a Military Service Act, which presumed that all men between certain ages were deemed to be conscripted. They could only avoid call up if they were in a reserved occupation or had some other qualifying reason, which tribunals would then consider and judge. In this case, reserved was deemed to cover men doing work of 'national importance' – farmers, coal miners, shipbuilders, railway staff who kept the system running and employment in any other heavy industry essential for the effective conduct of war.

There is no evidence to suggest that Tom served in the forces, so

we can assume that he was one of the 1900 or so NSR employees who 'attested', as the Act described the process of release, and remained in reserved occupations. In his case, a very sensible outcome. People with his skills and level of productivity were far more important to the war industry than anything he could have achieved in front line service. One suspects that he may have found being a non-combatant irksome, but his wife and family less so, eager in their wish to preserve the life of a loved one in the face of near certain death or disfigurement in the trenches.

For those remaining on the railways, many peacetime tasks gave way to wartime schedules. In the workshops, maintenance of railway stock continued, albeit on a reduced scale, but new construction virtually came to an end as many factories around the country were directed into war work – weapons,

In 1914 the new C Class 0-6-4 tank engine appeared - 8 being built at Stoke Works. It was another engine in which Tom was involved.

New Class F No 2048 built in 1916. The 0-6-4 configuration was unusual and intrigued Tom, particularly its use of a 4-wheeled trailing truck.

ammunition and other goods to War Office specifications. This was nowhere more apparent than at Stoke Works where only fifteen new steam locomotives – 0-6-4 tank engines of the C and F Classes – were built between the beginning of 1914 and the Armistice, a level of work that was insufficient to keep the Drawing Office fully employed, even when staff numbers reduced due to the call up for active service at the front. To fill in time, other work was injected, including the design and construction of the 'Endon Dip' and the 0-4-0 battery powered shunter for the Oakamoor Copper Works in 1917. Tom led on the first project and was also closely

linked to the latter, working closely with the NSR's electrical engineer, A.F. Rock, to come up with the design, which had the looks of a converted truck. Nevertheless, it began his association with alternative technologies to steam and the presence of several drawings in the papers he left suggest that the work was of interest to him.

Peace, when it came, did not immediately release the railways from war's constricting hands. Until the Peace Treaty was signed, at Versailles in June 1919, a resumption of fighting was still possible. So the country remained on a war footing, though

this reduced in scale month by month, as servicemen and women clamoured for release.

During this period, Stoke Works slowly returned to normal; women who had been employed to replace men going to war were themselves released to make way for survivors. But the going was not easy, especially when a flu epidemic spread quickly and killed indiscriminately, bringing a new level of horror to the lives of those already blighted by war.

In December 1919, at only 43 years of age, Arthur Tassell died leaving a widow and daughter of only 10 to survive as best they could. Though the date of his promotion is unclear, it seems that Tom became Chief Draughtsman early in 1920 after acting in this role for a period following Tassell's death. Although comparatively young at 33, he had proved his worth to John Hookham, who himself had been promoted to Locomotive Superintendent in 1915. Just before Tassell passed away his long-held wish to be elected a member of the Institution of Mechanical Engineers was granted. Such was the depth of respect in which he was held that his application, sponsored by Hookham and supported by many leading engineers of the day, including Robert Thom, notable later for his great achievements under Nigel Gresley on the LNER, ensured a successful outcome. Sadly, notification of this was only received by his widow a few weeks after passing away.

In 1919, a new triumvirate of senior managers was completed when Henry Ivatt, returning from France having served as a Major on the Director of Transport's staff, became principal assistant to Hookham and Works Manager. Born in 1886, his father, also Henry, was a locomotive engineer and designer of note, ending his long and active career in 1911, as Superintendent of the Great Northern Railway. Henry junior attended Uppingham School, then followed in his father's footsteps, beginning an engineering apprenticeship at Crewe in 1904. He and Tom were contemporaries who would spend the rest of their careers with the NSR, the London, Midland and Scottish Railway and British Rail. Ivatt would, in time, rise to become the LMS's last

Chief Mechanical Engineer. It has been said that this link helped and hindered Tom's work as a designer over the next thirty years. If so, their time together on the NSR did not shape their professional association particularly, because the ever-creative John Hookham guarded his relationship with the new Chief Draughtsman very closely.

The years that followed were more a time of mend than make. After four years of heavy use and reduced maintenance, the railways all over Britain were in a parlous state. Investment was essential, but unlikely to be forthcoming in a country crippled by debt as well as the physical and mental injuries inflicted on a war-weary population. A struggle lay ahead to heal these wounds to society and its infrastructures. The NSR

in 1919 presented a microcosm of this bigger picture and, like most industrial concerns at that time, it was slow to recover. For the next four years, Hookham and his senior team did their best to breathe life back into the engineering side of the company. But with revenues reducing, the capital outlay needed to restore the railway to something near pre-war levels easily exceeded net receipts.

Yet by 1920, with many men back in service, the locomotive, carriage and wagon workshops had caught up with the maintenance backlog. A remarkable achievement, thanks mostly to Hookham and Ivatt's leadership, and the commitment of their staff. But this fantastic effort meant that new construction of locomotives was held in abeyance for a short time. To provide some new motive power, Tom led in

The 'Endon Dip' as designed by Tom, under construction at Stoke Works.

The 'Dip' in place and operating.

The Rock-Coleman designed battery loco of 1917.

procuring two new 0-6-0 tank engines from Kerr, Stuart and these came into service during 1919. He had always maintained a link with his old company and he recorded that they again offered him a senior post that year. Though declining the offer, the possibility of his loss may have spurred Hookham into confirming him as the NSR's Chief Draughtsman.

In-house construction of locomotives began again in 1920 and, over the next three years, seventeen new engines appeared – four M Class 0-4-4Ts, twelve L Class 0-6-2Ts and one D Class 0-6-0T. A small number, but enough to keep the Drawing Office and workshops busy. Within this programme, the 0-6-0 tank engine became the centre of attention, exploring, as it did, the capabilities of 4-cylinder drive.

Hookham and Tom Coleman were innovators and scientists by nature and had a strong belief in the need for experimentation and evaluation. They both believed that improvement was possible and new ideas should be considered, whether it be for steam or any other form of locomotion. They were not hidebound traditionalists and looked to the future always, but they were also pragmatists who were keenly aware of the limitations imposed on them by business needs.

Long after his death, some of Tom's contemporaries declared that he had only been interested in steam development, but in reality, all the evidence points in the other direction. He may have been fascinated by steam, but he was a modernist by nature and was intrigued by change. In truth, his interests were very broad indeed. But for most of his career he was in a business that was risk averse and steam was deemed to be the only show in town, its technology being well established and the means of its power cheap and plentiful. The railway companies believed they could make money from following a traditional path and so limited their designers to improving upon what was known and understood. Diesel and electric alternatives were being developed from the late nineteenth century, but whilst steam was cheaper, other options were held back, except in exceptional circumstances often driven by safety needs – steam locomotives in an underground or explosive environment are not a good idea. In time this would change, but for most of his career, Tom could only work on locomotive programmes driven by company needs and accountants' assessments. So steam dominated in Britain well into the 1950s, long after he had retired.

Amongst his papers can be found many examples of his interests in other power sources from the 1920s onwards. Research by Herbert Stuart in the UK and Rudolf Diesel in Germany, investigations by General Electric and the Baldwin Works in the USA, developments on the London Underground system and early work on above-ground electric schemes in the UK and overseas, all feature large. And his work for both the NSR and then the LMS, though tied to steam, was informed by a desire for experimentation and development of other concepts. I suspect that if he had been born twenty or thirty years later, he would have happily embraced new technologies

and developed locomotives more appropriate to the age.

In 1922, as work on the 4-cylinder 0-6-0 tank engine came to an end and testing began, Tom wrote a short article for Hookham to present for publication by the Institution of Locomotive Engineers in their Journal:

'This engine is of the 0-6-0 type, and has four cylinders driving on to the intermediate axle. The four piston valves are each actuated by a gear of the Walschaert type. A special feature is the disposition of the cranks, ie the outside pair and those of the crank axle inside the frames are set 90 degrees apart respectively, but each outside crank is set at 135 degrees relative to the corresponding inside crank on the same side of the engine, so that there are eight exhaust beats per revolution of the wheel.'

Tom completed the article with two photographs he had taken and a drawing prepared specially for the publication. These are quite rare items of his work. He was not noted for self-publicity and seems to have avoided any attempt at encouraging him to do so by suggesting that he present the findings of this work himself. Earlier in the year, he had gone a little further by helping John Hookham prepare a detailed paper for the Institution entitled, 'Comparison between super-heated and non-superheated tank engines'. With the example of his recent advocacy of Arthur Tassell, in seeking election to the Institution of Mechanical Engineers, still fresh in the mind, one wonders if he

also encouraged his new Chief Draughtsman to follow suit. If so, his efforts proved fruitless as Tom resolutely avoided membership of this or any other professional body. One can only wonder why he was so reticent in doing so. It may simply have been that he was not naturally a 'club' man or that he felt unsuited to these types of institutions, by education or expertise. If so, he clearly undersold himself and may even have lacked an appreciation of the depth of his own engineering and design skills.

Andrew Rock - Tom's fellow designer of the battery powered 0-4-0 shunting locomotive.

His involvement in John Hookham's paper is obvious from the first, with descriptions of testing and evaluation which were emblematic of Tom's approach to work. The influence of the older man in encouraging his development, as well as the depth of Tom's appreciation of the subject, is also apparent. It was a subject which would continue to tax his mind as the need for effective superheating grew in importance with the gradual emergence of very high-performance steam locomotives in the 1930s. For the moment, though, the paper is interesting and underpins Tom's growing belief that superheating would only be truly effective on high speed, non-stop trains, operating over long distances:

'The railway is one of fairly heavy gradients. The passenger traffic consists for the most part of trains stopping at all stations, and there is nowhere a run of more than 20 miles between the stations with the fastest trains. The goods and mineral trains are frequently light, and in many cases a good deal of shunting has to be done at stations en route. The greater part of the traffic is worked by tank engines, and the policy for the last 20 years has been to substitute tanks for tender engines as the latter were scrapped.

'It was found that most of the running was done at temperatures ranging from 550 deg to 620 deg F, but the drop in temperature is very marked and rapid with the closing of the regulator.

'It appears that where a stop is of four minutes or more duration, the temperature of the header elements drops to only 50deg or 60deg above the normal temperature for saturated steam, and thereby is lost most of the advantage possessed by superheating or preventing condensation in cold cylinders at starting.

The experiments prove that economy in fuel and water is obtained by superheating, even in unfavourable circumstances … and the results obtained were better than expected … But it is not enough to show a saving in fuel without putting on the other side the cost of obtaining that saving, for it is evident that no advantage is gained by saving on coal bills, and spending more than the saving in first cost and maintenance.

'So far as figures are available they point to the conclusion that the superheater tank engine costs in overhead and maintenance charges about £60 a year more than the other (non-superheated) engines of the same class. At the present price of coal, which may be taken at about or above £1 a ton, this means a saving of 60 tons a year before there is any advantage to be attributed to superheating – this we may call 10%, and any saving above that figure is clear gain. As the economy figure never falls below 14%, and reaches 20% mostly, a case appears to be made for superheating.'

Although his work and the needs of a growing family filled his days, Tom`s interest in sport had

not diminished entirely. Now approaching his late thirties, when football prowess tends to diminish, other sports began to take its place. The NSR unknowingly supported this when they bought the Staffordshire Cricket Ground and its facilities near Stoke Station in 1920. They were ever conscious of the need to improve industrial relations in those post-war years when employees were becoming more strident in their demand for better working and living conditions. There was not a huge amount they could do on pay, with the country's economy struggling to survive, but social issues, such as encouraging sport and other outside activities, was a fairly low-cost way of doing so. By 1921, the company had formed an Amateur Athletic Association, which soon had about 600 members and catered for many sporting and

Henry George Ivatt, son of a famous engineer who would rise to become the LMS' last CME.

NSR L Class Oil Burning Loco, 1921. Converting locos from coal to oil was a common feature of a loco design up to the 1940s. It interested Tom, but never achieved widespread acceptance.

communal activities. Tom soon took advantage of these new amenities, becoming wicket keeper in the company's cricket team, playing eighteen times a season in the North Staffs and District League.

As the railway world appeared to be returning to normal, in the early 1920s, a cloud was on the horizon. During the war, parliament had placed all companies under central control. With such a plethora of businesses and management structures it was essential that all their activities be co-ordinated. A Railway Executive

was formed, with members drawn from the principal companies and government, and it was given wide ranging powers under the Regulation of Forces Act. This remained in place until August 1919, but was then extended by two more years when the Railway Act was passed. The extension was largely sponsored by a growing belief that the pre-war system had been inefficient, whilst unification during the conflict had brought many benefits. As early as 1917, this belief had manifested itself in the creation of a Railway Advisory

Panel to consider the future of the whole system. They soon reported that:

'It became clear that, in view of the changes that had resulted from the War, especially in the economic basis of the industry, it would be impossible for the railways to revert to pre-war conditions.'

This was a view supported by a Select Committee set up in April 1918, but their recommendations went much further. They concluded

NSR's Cricket Team in about 1921. Tom front row with wicket keeper gloves on.

The 4-cylinder tank engine under test. In 1924 it was rebuilt as a tender engine.

that permanent unification of the companies was essential, in public or private hands, if the country was to get the best service from its railways. But the wartime structure did not provide a workable long-term solution, though.

The debate rambled on, under cover of the two-year extension, and in June 1920 a White Paper was published which proposed that all the companies be grouped into six or seven new, privately run organisations. There then followed an eleven month period of consultation with interested parties before a grudging agreement was reached, during which it was decided that the number of new companies be limited to four. These changes were written into law by the 1921 Railway Act, and a commissioning date of 1 January 1923 was set. Workers within the industry must have followed these developments with great interest and concern. Some may have agreed that change was essential, but, inevitably, it would have been viewed as disruptive and profoundly unsettling to those affected. The old order was passing, but tribal loyalties would inevitably be invoked and be hard to suppress. Yet the more discerning could see opportunities arising in this new, bigger world, Tom amongst them.

Chapter 3

THE EXPLOSION BEGINS

Uncertainty can be destabilising and transformation rarely takes place without enquiry and resentment. Some embrace change and find it invigorating, but most see only negative impacts when long recognised ways of working, and a well-established pattern to life, are lost or disturbed. Change is stressful, even when unavoidable. And it seems that only the gifted, the astute and the ambitious see the possibilities that can be found and exploited in an unsettled world. Amongst the NSR's 6,300 employees there were some who fell into this category, but the rest would have suffered the corrosive effects of a Government policy conceived for the best of reasons, yet not fully understood by the people whose lives were so profoundly affected by it.

Sudden change, which reduces the time to think, may be better than a long drawn out affair. If so, the grouping of so many companies into four new businesses, in January 1923, had the benefit of being quick. But because it was so speedy structural changes were slower in taking effect as new managers struggled to make sense of the many diverse organisations coming together under their control. This

was nowhere more apparent than in the biggest of the four new organisations - the London, Midland and Scottish Railway - which merged eight constituents and twenty-seven subsidiary companies into one, including the North Staffordshire. New structures would take time to form and there would be infighting as different factions fought to have their views and working practices accepted by the others, and this would become bitter and acrimonious as the months turned into years. If the Government believed that the LMS would quickly work effectively, they would be sadly surprised and eventually realised that more

drastic action was required to improve its performance.

The LMS inherited 7,790 miles of track and 10,346 locomotives on its formation, with many classes and types tailored to meet each company's specific needs and operating conditions. And the position with other rolling stock was little better. With only 192 engines, three steam railmotors and a single battery powered loco, the NSR was a minnow alongside the bigger concerns in the group and, inevitably, would only have a small voice at the 'big table' in debates over the future. And for the first three years, the old North Staffordshire team continued to

One of Tom's last acts with the NSR was to oversee the conversion of the 0-6-0T 4-cylinder engine into a tender loco. Neither was particularly successful.

work as though still independent, maintaining its own engines, rolling stock and system, with only minor tasks coming their way from its new partners. To say that the LMS was rudderless would be wrong, but it probably had too many hands on the tiller to allow effective control.

Some believed the company to be too large and that improvement could only be achieved by breaking the LMS down into a few groups, based around Derby, Crewe,

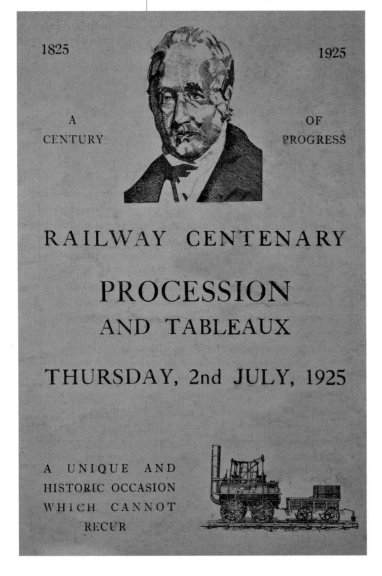

Tom's souvenir of this event in 1925 which he attended with his wife.

1825   1925

A CENTURY   OF PROGRESS

RAILWAY CENTENARY

PROCESSION
AND TABLEAUX

THURSDAY, 2nd JULY, 1925

A UNIQUE AND HISTORIC OCCASION WHICH CANNOT RECUR

Horwich and St Rollox, the principle centres of work. But having decided on the new national structure the Government were unlikely to sanction such a change, so the commitment to a single company for the London, Midland and Scottish region continued. And what a colossal business it was, retaining some 230,000 people, making it the second biggest employer in Britain behind the Post Office. It had a transport network without equal in the world and a depth of business interests that went far beyond its vast railway system into hotels, canals, docks, shipping, aviation, road transport and more. With all this going on, it was small wonder that the NSR should not feel the hands of its new masters for a while. But change could not be delayed for ever and many at Stoke Works must have felt the sword of Damocles hanging over their heads, whilst waiting for the LMS to decide how best to operate in the future.

Much later in his life, Tom recalled the feelings of uncertainty that surrounded these events:

'It seemed quite likely that Stoke Works would shut. It wasn't difficult to see that the LMS had too many workshops and needed to streamline them. There were also too many Drawing Offices and we were probably the smallest, so stood little chance of remaining open. Derby or Crewe seemed our most likely destinations. But it took some time for this to become clear and we occasionally heard whispers of changes taking place. Rumour and conjecture became a way of life whilst we waited to hear … The amount of work we did in

the Drawing Office declined rapidly and it was difficult to find enough tasks to keep the draughtsmen busy.'

Josiah Stamp, who was appointed company chairman three years after its creation, to help clear up the many difficulties created by grouping, touched on some of the problems the LMS faced in creating a fully functioning, profitable business:

'It had to preserve uniformity of treatment and yet keep individuality, spontaneity and resourcefulness. Tradition was its strength, yet capacity to adapt itself to changing needs was the test of its life. With staff so scattered and so diversified in function, organisation had to achieve cohesion. From the highest officer to the lowest rank, staff had to be made into one team working together for the good of the railway industry and for trade and commerce generally. The work of the various departments was subject to the overriding necessity for harmonising working of the whole.

'But organisation for standardized performance is one thing – organisation to absorb, control and utilise a constant stream of change, both human and technical, is far more difficult and important. And it was not merely a question of fitting in an alteration at an appropriate point in time. The railway evolved, partly consciously, partly empirically, as a co-ordinated whole – touch one part and all other parts were affected and

Tom whilst serving at Horwich. He was a very enthusiastic car owner, with a particular liking of sports cars with soft tops.

required adjustment … Railway equipment had to be adjusted to the needs of the community and also its "wants" - not always the same thing – and had to be kept in line with industrial improvements as they had gradually evolved, and with all the shifts of industrial life. More so than ever has this been necessary since the amalgamation of 1923, when standardisation of equipment and practises became imperative if economical management were to be effected and costs reduced.

'On amalgamation it was apparent to us that the multiplicity of types of engines of various constituent and subsidiary companies forming the LMS would be a bar to economic progress unless some standardisation were carried out.'

The sprawling mass of Horwich Works.

George Hughes, the LMS's first CME, who remained based at Horwich for his entire tenure.

Josiah Stamp.

And the problems the company faced were not simply those created by trying to squeeze all these diverse organisations into one cohesive group. The First World War, although over, continued to cast a very dark shadow. A war-weary nation, the loss of so many young men, the lasting effects of mental and physical wounds, a depressed economy and a railway system in severe need of investment were problems largely beyond the LMS and any other company to resolve. As time passed, there would be a lessening of these malign influences, but the residue would last into the next world war and far beyond. But all the directors could do was re-organise, rationalise and seek improvement where possible,

and try to overcome the restrictions placed on them by lack of funds and the need to be profitable.

Until Stamp's arrival in 1926, it seems that real progress towards these goals was simply beyond the ability of those placed in charge three years earlier, a position not helped by extensive infighting, different factions seeking domination of others amongst the constituent companies and the lack of strong, positive leadership. Some believe that turmoil is necessary for change. It can allow the toughest, most effective to battle to the surface. But when the participants are equally matched, have only parochial self-serving views and lack a wider, truer perspective, change is likely to be disjointed and ineffective.

Whilst all this was happening, Tom and his colleagues at Stoke Works marked time. Gradually, signs of change emerged and it was to his individual benefit that the NSR was not influential in the debates that were taking place. The North Staffordshire was too small to be sullied by past allegiances so could be seen as a pool of experienced staff to be absorbed, without controversy or argument. As the LMS gradually formed, and created a new workshop structure around Crewe, Derby, Horwich and St Rollox, the best staff from the other absorbed companies were transferred, Tom amongst them.

Undoubtedly in these early years, senior managers would have assessed staff they had inherited and moved allies or the best into positions where they could exert the greatest influence or do the greatest good. Some would be marginalised or let go, others moved sideways and a few would be promoted into more senior positions. It wasn't a quick process or one untouched by politics or self-interest, as one would expect in an organisation riven by internal struggles fought by rival factions, but at least it began the process of evolution that would eventually see a great number of very effective managers and designers promoted or recruited into positions of authority.

From the beginning, the main struggle for dominance was between staff from the old London and North Western Railway and the Midland Railway. They had developed different ways of meeting the operational conditions each faced and strongly believed that their own policies should be applied across the LMS. Such an approach, whilst understandable, proved unworkable in such a diverse organisation. Sir Guy Granet, the new Deputy Chairman, was a 'Midland' man of some standing and his strong, some say unyielding, character ensured that division would continue. Unfortunately, his Chairman, Baron Lawrence of Kinsgate, seemed unwilling or unable to rein in Granet's bias. But in some quarters, it was hoped that the appointment of George Hughes, from the LNWR, as the new company's first Chief Mechanical Engineer, with Sir Henry Fowler, from the Midland Railway based in Derby, as his deputy, would patch over the differences. But this wish seems to have been stillborn. Fowler was, by all accounts, a good deputy, but his backing was counterbalanced by other appointees who seem to have been far less helpful.

James Anderson, a strong advocate of Granet and all things Midland, became Superintendent of Motive Power. As an engineer of some note he could have become the CME, but Hughes and Fowler were ahead of him in the pecking order and this may have been a bone of contention in their subsequent relationships. If so, his behaviour when appointed might be explained. By slow degrees, Anderson began to dictate locomotive policy, a role usually the preserve of CMEs in all companies, and neither Hughes or Fowler seemed able to stand up to him. Granet's promotion to Chairman in 1924 only exacerbated the problem. And so Midland ideas dominated and locomotive requirements were decided by the user, who should have stated a requirement, and not

the designer, normally tasked with meeting that need. In this case the Derby influence decreed a small engine policy, which was guided by weight restrictions on structures over much of the network. However, the other companies were not affected in the same way and could take bigger, heavier engines.

Sadly, Hughes and Fowler were men better placed to consider conditions over the entire system, by inclination and outlook, but found the influence of Anderson and Granet difficult to counter. They may have been limited themselves by their own professional doctrines and beliefs, but they were more open to alternative ideas. They realised that such a varied and difficult network needed a fleet of standard, interchangeable engines, but also larger and more powerful locomotives, which could offer greater efficiency, economy and pulling power. And Hughes also embraced such developments as long travel valves, larger bearings and the Pacific configuration, then an ever-increasing influence on locomotive design worldwide. Partly through frustration at being unable to move the company forward in the direction he thought fit, and Anderson's constant meddling, Hughes relinquished the CME post in 1925, to be replaced by Fowler.

So in its early years the LMS was handicapped by a whole host of problems – limited and biased management, lack of resources, an infrastructure in need of huge investment to restore it to pre-war conditions and a plethora of rolling stock, with little commonality of type. Small wonder that Josiah

Stamp later felt it necessary to give such a detailed description of the many problems the company faced and the path that should have been taken from day one if it were to succeed. His words about a unified, dedicated team strike an honest note and add a revealing obituary to the failings of his predecessors. By 1926, with improvement still a distant and, to some, an unobtainable goal, a change of focus was essential.

How companies are managed will always undergo review and

James Anderson was thwarted in his hope of becoming CME at some stage and became the LMS's Chief Motive Power Supt instead, in which role he thwarted both Hughes and Fowler.

change. New techniques appear, are considered and tried in an attempt to wring the best from an organisation. If specialists in a field seem unable to achieve objectives, then management is broadened to include other skills. And this is the concept that underpinned Stamp's arrival, sponsored by Wilfrid Ashley, the Minister of Transport, whose growing concern over lack of progress in the LMS brought things to a head. There seems little doubt that he selected Stamp to shake up this failing company. Here was a

Sir Henry Fowler, Deputy CME from 1923 and succeeded Hughes in 1925.

well-connected man of exceptional ability as an economist, with a keen understanding of taxation, banking and industry and a political sense unequalled in Britain at that time. He was also a moderniser and a broad thinker capable of looking beyond restrictions or biases imposed by lesser men. And in Ashley he had a friend and advocate who shared many of his views and ambitions, even to the extent of forming the Anglo-German Fellowship together a few years later.

With Granet's agreement, grudging or otherwise, a new senior structure was imposed on the LMS early in 1926. Stamp was appointed President and given responsibility for selecting a small group of executive managers, each heading up a particular area of work. For the first few months, Stamp looked closely at the organisation and considered its shortcomings, reviewed possibilities and proposed a new structure. On 1 January 1927 it came into being, a key part of which was Granet's removal and Stamp's elevation to Chairman as well as President.

Whilst all these changes were taking place, Tom continued as Chief Draughtsman at Stoke Works, performing solidly and efficiently, taking on any tasks delegated to him. He was eager to see life in the other works and further his career, so when the opportunity arose, he visited other drawing offices and soon became a familiar face to his new colleagues. He also continued his analysis of locomotives, riding on footplates or in carriages as part of his job or simply for pleasure. There was now a wider range of engines to view; those absorbed by the LMS and those running

in the other regions. A holiday to the West Country in 1925 had seen him breaking off from leave to visit Swindon, and see the latest developments there with his young son, and keeping extensive notes of four engines he rode behind; a Class 3150 tank engine, *Polar Star* and two Castle Class engines, *Chepstow* and *Carmarthen*. There is no evidence that he made contact with the GWR's design staff during his holiday, so his interest was restricted to 'lineside' examination. But it added much more information to his ever-growing library of facts and figures and his broadening understanding of engine design.

During this period, he was offered posts at Horwich and Derby, but these would have meant reverting to leading draughtsman, which he felt was a retrograde step. Nevertheless, by staying at Stoke he felt increasingly frustrated at the low level of work that came his way and, as an ambitious man, this gradually became more irksome.

In seeking to learn about the organisation he had inherited, Stamp visited many centres of activity, but his main focus of attention was on the locomotive side of his business. He quickly realised that rationalisation and standardisation of type, though long desired, had barely begun and, even to his layman's eyes, locomotive development lagged far behind the company's rivals and maintenance processes were inefficient and too costly for the output achieved. And so he tried to revitalise these areas of work. His CME was encouraged to look closely at the design and production teams, seek rationalisation and promote young talented men, who would be less hidebound than their seniors. But such a transformation can never be achieved overnight, even by ruthlessly culling those seen to be hindering progress. Change has to be managed in such a way that current work is managed effectively whilst new staff and systems are imbedded. Some, at senior level, did depart, but for most of the organisation things would only change slowly and imperceptibly. Although supremely self-confident, Stamp was a pragmatist and realised he lacked allies in 1926 so he had to try and coerce some managers of questionable ability and loyalty to change their ways. As he gradually strengthened his position, there would be significant adjustments, but this was still some years in the future when he took office.

As the organisation evolved, the four principle Works settled into a pecking order of sorts, with Crewe and Derby the principal centres of operation and Horwich and St Rollox being of secondary importance. Staff changes took place as men reached retirement age or new posts were created, and in 1926 Horwich needed a new Chief Draughtsman and Tom's name came to the fore. There are no records of other candidates or interviews taking place, so we must assume that he was selected on an informal basis, based on reputation and the advocacy of keen supporters. This was not an unusual way of doing business then and some would call it an 'old boy network' coming into play. But it had the benefit of speed and based selection on experience,

rather than the random chance inherent in promotion by interview. Whichever course was taken, Tom was selected and took up his new post on the same day in January that Stamp was made Chairman; two new brooms about to radically alter the way the company ran its business and designed its fleet of locomotives. Other important changes would take place and William Stanier's arrival in 1932 would be of the greatest significance, but the changes in

John Billington and wife in 1910. A gifted engineer who offered skilled and intelligent support to Hughes.

1926/27 marked the moment when the revolution truly began. There were many difficulties to overcome and these were not all related to performance, modernisation or a new locomotive strategy. These changes took place against a background of severe industrial unrest across Britain.

Long festering sores initiated by poor living and working conditions, coupled to the increasing strength of trade unions, empowered employees to pursue action by dispute and withdrawal of labour. For the most part, Government and employers only had themselves to blame when this happened.

Edward Gass became Chief Draughtsman on the untimely demise of John Billington in 1925. He retired the following year to be replaced by Tom Coleman.

For decades, they had ignored the clamour for improvement and had been tardy in their reforms. Then came the wholesale slaughter on the Western Front, which finally broke down the misguided and wholly inappropriate view of worker's rights that had prevailed for centuries.

1926 and the General Strike witnessed the explosion of this bitterness. Though of limited success, it set a standard of opposition that warned employers of greater difficulty ahead if progress was not made. In employing Stamp, the LMS had someone who could see the future more clearly than most. In setting out his principles of cohesive operation and effort, he recognised the balance to be drawn between good business and good management. Just as well that he did because, if this level of strife had continued, the LMS could not have survived let alone met the challenges grouping had set them. No longer could there be an unbridgeable gap between capital and labour.

Employee relations were better at Horwich than most other establishments at this time and had been since the Lancashire and Yorkshire Railway decided to base its premier workshop there in the 1880s. Its original Works at Miles Platting, Manchester, had proved insufficient for its growing needs and the company identified, then bought, 736 acres of land on a site near Bolton, where space to expand existed. Construction began shortly afterwards and within three years the new Works opened, employing upwards of 1,500 people. At its core was an Erecting Shop more

than 500 yards long and 40 yards wide. Adjoining this were Fitting, Paint, Millwright, Joiners, Tin and Coppersmith Shops, an Engine Shed, a Brass Foundry, offices, a Mechanics Institute, housing for workers and staff facilities. All this was supported by extensive internal broad and narrow gauge railway systems. By the time Tom arrived, most of these facilities had been extended and he took over a Drawing Office employing sixteen or more draughtsmen and tracers, all working in a long, single, well lit room.

Tom's predecessor as Chief Draughtsman at Horwich was Edward Gass, where he had been since recruitment as a leading draughtsman in 1888, when 27 years of age. But he himself had only inherited the post in 1925 when John Billington had died suddenly at 52. In writing notes in preparation for his book *Locomotive Panorama*, E.S. Cox, a later associate of Tom's, described life working for both men when amalgamation took place:

'J.R. Billington, for whom I was to work more closely than for any of the others until his untimely death in 1925, was in charge of locomotive design. Of humble Fylde coast parentage, and of short stature and slight build, Billington had a brilliant academic brain. From an early age he had marked himself for recognition by gaining distinction in the educational field and would go on to become a lecturer at the Horwich Mechanics Institute. As Chief Draughtsman he controlled not only the steam locomotive office, but also the electrical design office, in which it must be said his greater personal interest lay, sponsored by the L and Y's development of electric trains. He was a hard task master and did not suffer fools gladly. He could be sharp and acid on occasion; however, he was a born teacher and loved to impart his knowledge to those who would listen at work or in the classroom. If he had lived he might have reached a more senior rank.

'Edward Gass, the leading draughtsman, was his deputy. Of incredible thinness, his bow ties and spats produced a natty appearance not general in the office as a whole. A competent but not original designer, he was a kindly man with very little sense of humour and I fear some of us at the junior end were a sore trial to him.'

Horwich Drawing Office - Tom's domain.

When George Hughes became the LMS's first CME, he chose to make his HQ at Horwich, where he had been the Lancashire and Yorkshire's CME. Remaining there was seen by many as a major blunder, as well as most inconvenient. The seat of power was at Euston and the main centres of operation were increasingly at Derby and Crewe. One can only assume that he trusted those he had recruited and trained at Horwich and drew strength from this unity. It also allowed him to stand apart from the rivalries and infighting elsewhere, hoping to be untainted by politics and conflict. This would prove his undoing, because being remote from these battles meant becoming side-lined and, possibly, irrelevant.

But for two years he pursued this way of working, and John Billington became a major support to Hughes within the LMS and not just at Horwich. As Cox went on to relate:

'Billington, promoted Technical Assistant to the CME in April, used three members of the Drawing Office to undertake what would today be the work of a Development Section, namely to cover all technical investigation, forward scheming and relations with other departments which the large combine demanded … In this trio, consisting of Frank Stubbs, Arthur Phillips and myself, my job was mainly concerned with the new locomotive projects … By the end of 1923 there had been slight stirrings, but thereafter, until Hughes' retirement in 1925, active work proceeded on a 2-6-0, a 4-6-2 and a corresponding 2-8-2, and a Garratt.'

Though understandable, isolating himself at Horwich meant that anything Hughes and his local team came up with would probably struggle for acceptance. Yet his understanding of need was clear and his ideas would prove quite sound, as Cox re-counts:

'The need for a more powerful express passenger engine for the West Coast Main Line was self-evident. The former LNW engines, badly run down during the war, were suffering from various disabilities, and could only be brought to work the easier schedules by dint of much double-heading and special means of identifying units which were in a reasonable state of repair. It was natural that the appearance of Gresley's first Pacific in 1922, closely followed by Raven's version on the NER, should turn the CME's mind towards something similar for the LMS. As a result, a tentative diagram was produced and some calculations made as to possible performances. Thereafter a long silence followed, and it presently became apparent that a quite different solution was being contemplated in the South.

'The Midland had always followed a policy of small engines and light train loads. The new hierarchy therefore visualised splitting up the West Coast services into separate portions, each capable of being worked by a Midland type 4-4-0 compound …The traffic did not prove amenable to this treatment.'

It has been said that Billington was the true driving force behind the plans that Hughes devised and his sudden death encouraged the CME to take retirement. It may be true, but I think greater emphasis should be placed on the level of opposition he faced from Euston and Derby in developing a sound locomotive policy. Either way, the departure of these two engineers meant that

Horwich would never play such a significant role in engine design again. In such circumstances, it is small wonder that Edward Gass stayed for such a short time as Chief Draughtsman and was probably happy and relieved to hand responsibility over to Tom Coleman. Being a 'fly on the wall' to hear the conversations that took place, as one handed over to the other, would have been most revealing. Much later Tom simply recorded that:

'My predecessor was most circumspect about the years at Horwich when Hughes and Billington had tried to guide the LMS to look more broadly at its locomotive policy. When I took over I made a point of looking at the drawings and specifications

2F Dock Tank. Tom's first design as Chief Draughtsman at Horwich. It became known as 'Coleman's Baby'.

they had prepared. The 4-6-2 was of particular interest, but there were many other priorities to concern me so I couldn't pursue the ideas they had begun to develop just then. However, when the opportunity came to see the new LNER Pacifics in operation, I took it travelling on a number of Gresley engines, on the footplate twice at the invitation of Robert Thom at Doncaster, who I came to know through Fred Lemon at Crewe.'

In taking up his post at Horwich, his long association with the NSR, Stoke and Endon finally came to an end. Commuting daily to his new work place was unrealistic and so his family moved with him to Lancashire; a new home and a new school. Tom had grown used to being mobile when young, but it was a new experience for his family. However, at 16 and 13 respectively, Marion and Reginald were growing into independent souls, gradually developing their own lives, so the change may not have been as difficult as it might have been. And their family connections with Staffordshire had reduced significantly during their lives. Their uncle Reginald had married Hilda Stevenson and moved, with his family to Souris, in Manitoba, Canada, some years earlier and grandfather Tom, having retired in 1922, was considering moving to another area, so changes in family affairs were a matter of course when this new life at Horwich beckoned.

Now 41, with thinning hair and knees showing the strain of playing competitive sport over many years,

Tom had to become a spectator. But Lancashire could boast many good clubs to watch, should he feel the need, and Bolton Wanderers, who won the FA Cup three times in the 1920s, became an obvious attraction. In the summer, cricket at Old Trafford in Manchester would be an adequate substitute. Apparently, Tom looked back on his own playing days with some pleasure, and, occasionally, wondered how far he might have developed if he had followed his heart years earlier and become a professional footballer. If so, the chances were that he would now be wondering about the future and not be about to begin the most active and dynamic phase of his

engineering career. Regrets there may have been, 'but too few to mention', is, hopefully, a theme that defines all our lives though.

Although the Horwich Drawing Office no longer had the kudos of a CME on site, it was still a very active office and the Works was still a major influence in the LMS. And few, if any, expected their new Chief Draughtsman to do anything else than support the company, keeping any reservations he might have had about locomotive policy to himself. But it must have been apparent to him that the Midland influence was in danger of failing the company. Even with the strong, more resolute figures of Josiah Stamp and Henry

Tom was always a keen collector of photos and information and amassed a great deal of material. Here we see 5973, a Claughton 4-cylinder 4-6-0, undergoing test in the late 1920s.

Fowler in charge they seemed unable to widen this restricted view.

In setting up his new executive group, Stamp sought to create a balance between railway and business expertise. He was a realist and experience gained whilst a director with Nobel Industries had demonstrated to him that an imbalance that favoured one group over another would undoubtedly fail. But in choosing John Follows as Vice President of Railway Traffic Operations in 1927 he appears to have made a questionable decision. Follows was a Midland man through and through, having served that company from 1890 to 1923 in various senior positions, latterly as its Superintendent of Operations. On grouping, he was promoted to be the LMS's first Chief General Superintendent and then Vice President, where he supported John Anderson in directing locomotive policy with a Midland bias. And they would stay in post for some years, resisting, but not always stifling alternative views.

Fowler, when he became CME in 1925, chose to base himself at Derby, and gradually drew together all the design proposals

under consideration by the Drawing Offices under his control. In doing this he was trying to honour Stamp's primary directive of producing a fleet of standard locomotives capable of meeting the diverse needs of the LMS. Not surprisingly Hughes' and Billington's forward looking work at Horwich was a key part of this exercise. Fowler even tried to resurrect a Pacific design, but with as much success as Hughes, when faced with strong resistance.

When rejected, both 4-6-2 proposals went back to Horwich for filing, but, ever conscious of the need to preserve ideas for possible future use, Tom very astutely kept these proposals in his archive for the remainder of his career. When recalling these events years later he remembered that:

'The drawings were at an early stage and barely gauged or represented the needs of such an engine. If Hughes or Fowler had been allowed to build one or two and tested them then they would have understood the theories better and made changes. When design work commenced on

the first two Princess Royals, Herbert Chambers (then the LMS's Chief Draughtsman) and I did consider the earlier proposals in some detail, but took very little forward.'

If Anderson and Follows had been persuaded to build these Pacifics, when the LNER were advancing their designs in leaps and bounds and stealing a march in the process, the story of Coleman's career may have been entirely different. But their poorly considered resistance led directly to an explosion of exceptional engineering design later. But it was a distant future no one could predict with any certainty when Tom began working at Horwich. It would rely on several other random elements of chance coming together to ensure success. But, unintentionally, these two men set in train a course of events that would profoundly affect the company and railway history.

Although the first two Pacific designs were rejected, Fowler did at least manage to get other, more powerful designs built, though not of his own volition. This step change was partly sponsored by a growing acceptance that existing designs lacked power for the difficult sections of the West Coast Main Line, but also a reaction to developments on the GWR and Southern Railway where new breeds of 4-6-0 locomotives were dominating key, long distance services. At the same time, the GWR and the LNER had, in the spirit of competition, begun comparability trials to prove that their latest designs were superior to the others. In some ways this was a meaningless exercise, because their regional systems weren't in

From Tom's photo album. In 1929 Henry Fowler in conjunction with the Superheater Company produced an experimental high pressure steam locomotive named 'Fury'. Although not involved with its development Coleman was interested in the concept and would, in time, lead on rebuilding the engine to a more conventional form.

competition with each other, but the kudos arising from success had a broader publicity bonus. During 1925, in trials over routes in both regions, two separate GWR Castle Class 4-6-0 engines outperformed the LNER's A1 Pacific 4474 *Victor Wild* quite convincingly and this high-profile success grabbed the attention of the LMS's senior managers.

The Castle Class first appeared in 1923. Derived from the earlier Star Class, it had four cylinders and long travel valves and seemed capable of outperforming all its rivals in all conditions. It was without doubt a thoroughbred, as Tom himself had witnessed when on holiday during 1925. Such was its impact that the LMS contacted the GWR in 1926 to arrange the loan of one engine to see how effective it would be on the West Coast route and No 5000 *Launceston Castle* duly arrived. It seems that this was arranged by Guy Granet, following discussions with his close friend, Sir Felix Pole, the GWR's General Manager. It is hard to imagine how Pole justified this to his CME, Charles Collett, especially after the LNER's comparability tests. There must have been a natural desire to maintain confidentiality over their developments, but the loan went ahead nevertheless.

By November, when the last run was made, the design had once again shown its true class and easily exceeded the performance of anything the LMS could produce. It was rumoured that Anderson and Granet were so impressed that they tried to order fifty engines from the GWR and, failing to do that, obtain drawings from Swindon on which they could base an LMS version. The truth of this is hard to establish and to compound the mystery Fowler and Richard Maunsell, the Southern Railway's CME, and an old friend and colleague, are rumoured to have had a similar discussion concerning the SR's new Lord Nelson Class 4-6-0 locomotive, that appeared in August 1926. It is reported that Maunsell was only too happy to do so and Herbert Chambers began a period of dialogue with staff at Waterloo over its design. With Derby and the other Works loaded to capacity, Fowler and Chambers initiated a bidding process to find a company able to take on the design and construction task.

A bid from North British won and an order for fifty engines was placed in December 1926, with delivery of the locomotives beginning nine months later. The Royal Scots, as the class were called, had arrived and probably reflected a realisation that the LMS could ill afford to continue with its small engine policy any longer. But it was still a small start as the remaining, less than ambitious, programme for 1927 confirms – 100 Class 4 freight engines, 28 passenger tank locomotives, 50 Class 2 4-4-0 passenger locomotives and 10 Class 3 4-4-2 Tilbury tank locomotives.

Did this one step signify that reality was dawning on the Follows and Anderson cabal that change was inevitable, or was it simply a sop to appease a president growing increasingly frustrated at the slow pace of change? As a top economist, it is safe to assume that Stamp could read a balance sheet and would have seen little or no improvement in company finances as the decade came to an end. There were other reasons for this, of course, in a country still in a severe and soon to worsen depression, but you build for the long term not simply the next financial year. And

Royal Scot Class no 6168 *The Girl Guide* appeared in October 1930, one of the last engines of this class of 70. She was rebuilt in 1946 to a pattern decided by Coleman when rebuilding 6399 *Fury*.

it was here that Stamp was looking and engine performance was simply undermining efficiency and profitability. The time was rapidly approaching when major change was unavoidable.

So when Tom walked into the Drawing Office at Horwich in January 1927 it was this programme of work the company were pursuing that would absorb him. But there was a residue of old tasks too, left to him by Hughes, Billington and Gass, and some newer ones assigned by Fowler, principal amongst them being the design and construction of a new 2-6-0 class of tender engines, an 0-6-0 Dock Tank and the 3F 0-6-0 tank engine that had begun entering service since 1924 and would continue until 1931.

He would also get involved in other projects initiated by his CME, occasionally acting as advisor or sounding board. He had a growing reputation as a manager and engineer, elements that had been spotted by Fowler, who approved his transfer to Horwich. A senior manager in a large organisation has to operate on trust, relying upon the integrity of subordinates for delivery and support. In a company riven with internal conflict this was even more important and Fowler found in Tom a man of infinite skills, but also great honesty. And so his role spread beyond the immediate confines of Horwich to become one of the CME's close advisors in this unpredictable and, occasionally, hostile world.

On the design side, it was the 2-6-0 tender engine and the Dock Tank that would hold Tom's main attention for the next few years, supplemented by personal involvement in Fowler's other work on the 4-6-0 classes. There was also a growing interest in the Lancashire and Yorkshire Railway's electrification system, sponsored in part by his own involvement with development of the NSR's electric powered shunting engine in 1917. Although he tends to be remembered as a steam man, his interests were much wider. Amongst the papers he collected and preserved were a great many dealing with early electric schemes and the L&Y's work in these fields is well represented. He clearly took the opportunity to study the work that had been undertaken, travelling on the electrified lines around Liverpool and Manchester on many occasions. He may well have been captivated by steam, but he also seems to have realised that the future of railways lay elsewhere.

The new 2-6-0 class was an interesting development and demonstrated Hughes' and Fowler's determination to build a locomotive capable of meeting one of the company's most pressing needs – a strong and versatile mixed traffic engine, with wide route availability. Starting from scratch tends to attract a level of risk that is unacceptable; it is best if possible to build on known designs and in reviewing the work of the various companies now under the LMS's control, Hughes had come across a 2-6-0 design by the Caledonian Railway. Loosely based on a River Class locomotive purchased from the Highland Railway in 1915, it had been developed to include two outside cylinders mounted horizontally, 5ft 6in driving wheels and a boiler pressure of 180lb/ sq.in, giving a tractive effort of 28,624lb. But the design had an axle weight of 20 tons, which would have restricted its use south of the border, and its cylinders would have been outside the loading gauge. So Hughes and Billington decided to use this basic concept, modified to make it more suited to run throughout the network and enhance its performance.

Ernest Cox, then a draughtsman at Horwich, was tasked with developing these ideas and in late 1924 produced a number of options, containing variations on the same theme. By dint of persuasion and amendment, where politic to do so, Hughes eventually gained Anderson's agreement to proceed and this allowed a full set of production drawings to be completed.

Whilst this was happening, the company's Locomotive and Electrical Committee approved the construction of 100 2-6-0 engines. Eventually this number would be increased to 245, with production split between Horwich (70 engines) and Crewe (175 engines). Construction didn't begin until 1926, whilst Fowler considered changing the design to include standard Derby components, and continued on until 1932. So oversight of this programme and managing any modifications that arose became a key part of Tom's work. But as he later recalled:

'It gave me a good grounding in the design of bigger engines than those I'd dealt with at Stoke and introduced me to the first of the new 'standard' engines. Although performing well overall it still needed

improvement though and this gave me food for thought.'

Undoubtedly, he would have assessed these engines very closely, as he was wont to do, and he began to sketch out, as early as 1928, an alternative design, with a different boiler and valve gear. In fact, five were modified in 1931 when Lentz valve gear, built under license by the North British Locomotive Company, was fitted as an experiment.

Hugo Lentz, a South African who moved with his widowed mother to Germany when still only 6, became a talented and prodigious engineer, who would, in the course of his life, produce 2,000 or so patents, many relating to steam engines. His valve gear, which had oscillating and rotary cams which activated poppet valves, received wide attention throughout the railway world and the LMS were keen to assess its benefits. Comparative testing was carried out between 1932 and 1933, but proved inconclusive. Ever conscious of the need for analysis and re-assessment, Tom actively

involved himself in these trials and retained copies of the reports, annotated with his handwritten comments, which carefully supplemented the 'official' detail gathered during the tests. It is interesting to note that the Lentz system did not feature in any other LMS design, despite its advocates. One assumes that in the Stanier regime, he and Tom saw little need for such a deviation again.

His next project became something of a favourite with him, possibly because it was the first time he managed a design task, in its entirety, from beginning to end with the LMS. The task began shortly after Tom took his place at Horwich almost as if the scheme was set to test the newcomer. However, no record survives to describes the thought processes that preceded this decision and why Fowler, supported by Chambers, delegated the assignment to their new Chief Draughtsman. It may simply be that they were trying to balance the workload between their Drawing Offices. But they would have been aware that for

most of his time at Stoke Works new production of locomotives was dominated by tank engines, so Tom would have a level of expertise in the field. Either way, it was a task he would relish and happily recall for the rest of his life.

The project was initiated when a requirement for a 'dock shunting engine' capable of moving heavy loads in confined spaces, where track curvature was very sharp, was identified. Tom's solution was a locomotive bearing a strong resemblance to the 3F 0-6-0 *Jinty*, but with a completely different base. There were two outside cylinders, with a very low profile, connected to overhead slide valves operated by Walschaerts valve gear. The wheels were 3ft 11in diameter, with a trailing axle having sliding 'Cartazzi' boxes. With ball joints on the coupling rods, this configuration allowed the engine to negotiate curves as low as 2½ chains in diameter. The plans for ten of these locomotives passed muster and construction was undertaken at Derby and completed in 1929, with five engines being distributed to

John Billington, on Hughes' instructions, designed this new 2-6-0 engine, but it fell to Tom to complete the work and then design a new model.

The LMS saw a need for a mixed traffic 2-6-4T and 125 were designed and built at Derby by 1934. Tom's knowledge of tank engines was well used in designing the cylinders and valve gear.

Harold Hartley.

various locations in the North East and the other five to Scotland.

Locomotives often attract nicknames and it seems that these dock tank engines were known at Horwich, at least, as 'Coleman's Babies'. If this was the case, then they were a class of which he could justifiably be proud. Wherever they went, their performance was excellent and they lasted almost until the end of steam locomotion on British railways. Sadly, none of the ten survived into preservation.

As these locomotives entered service and Tom's influence began to grow, the LMS's senior team was about to undergo a radical change, partly because of the sudden death of Robert Reid, the 44-year-old Vice President of Finance and Services. Improvement had been slow in coming and Stamp felt he could no longer allow the drift to continue. He always looked around for ways of enhancing performance and felt this could only be achieved by bringing in 'fresh blood', untainted by associations with the company's past history and promote younger, more open minded LMS men. In the years since he became President and Chairman some names had come to the fore, amongst them Sir Harold Hartley, an eminent scientist and scholar, and Ernest Lemon, a railway man of long standing, who was the LMS's Divisional Carriage and Wagon Superintendent, based at Derby, and a Production Engineer of great skill. During 1930, ten months after Reid's death, Hartley was recruited as Vice President and Director of Scientific Research, in which capacity he had responsibility for the CME's Department. Also during that year, William Wood, an accountant who had been recruited by the LMS in 1924, was promoted to replace Reid as Vice President. With these two changes, Stamp's immediate executive team moved in a different direction and Follows, whilst retaining one of the two other Vice President's seats, found himself faced with less compliant, more questioning colleagues.

Hartley, in particular, realised quite early in his tenure that the CME's Department was barely grasping the problems that beset locomotive development. It was a view shared by both Stamp and Reid, though not directly voiced. He and they undoubtedly saw Fowler's apparent inability to counter Anderson's iron grip on engine policy as being the primary cause of the painfully slow progress over the previous five years. Hartley was an astute observer and analyst, more than capable of cutting through any argument or prevarication to reach to the core of a problem and make changes. He was also brave and ruthless, as his wartime career in the Army, as Head of Chemical Warfare and his gallantry awards, would confirm. So Fowler was removed from the post and, in a letter to Stamp, dated 7 August 1930, Hartley made plain how this difficult move was achieved:

'I have had another talk to Fowler about the future of his Department, and he made things very easy for me by saying that he realised that I was in a difficult position and that he was ready to go whenever I said he must, although he would like to keep some active connection for two or three years to come for various reasons.

'He told me of his suggestions to you last year viz. Anderson CME, Beames, Motive Power Supt, Symes, Crewe. I told him that this seemed to me makeshift, and that I must have a younger CME, when the time came for a change, who could look forward to at least ten year's activity. He then suggested Stanier of the GWR (who I believe is a brilliant designer), but added that the only younger man in the LMS who was capable of doing the job was Lemon, if we thought of combining CME and C&W again … By this time I mentioned the possibility of his acting for a time as consulting M.E. and I felt that he would really welcome relief from Executive responsibility.

'I have thought it over carefully and Lemon seems to have just the qualities we need. He is a genius at organisation and he has the necessary

decision and firmness … In view of the position of the Company we ought not to delay tackling our problems, and I am holding up several as I am anxious not to queer the pitch for the new man. We might be making plans during the Autumn and change over at Christmas, leaving Fowler to look after design and development while Lemon is reorganising and fusing the two Departments.

'From one or two hints he has dropped I fancy Follows would back Anderson as CME. This doesn't affect my position, but I think you should know.'

And so a master tactician and a manager of exceptional talent began to unravel the many problems besetting the LMS, as the new decade began. But he did not simply exercise his control remotely from Euston. He immersed himself in the business and regularly visited all the centres of operation to see for himself how each was run, questioning those he met and assessing their

Camden Shed - the Fowler influence takes effect with a strong line up of his new 4-6-0 engines.

The
SCHNEIDER TROPHY
Sept.
6th & 7th CONTEST 1929

THE ROYAL AERO CLUB
Official
SOUVENIR PROGRAMME

Printed & Published by
GALE & POLDEN LTD. LONDON, ALDERSHOT & PORTSMOUTH

PRICE ONE SHILLING

Following an invitation from Supermarine, Tom attended the 1929 Schneider Trophy races and kept his programme as a souvenir.

contributions and worth. He was talent spotting and looking for people who could fulfil the need to look 'forward to at least ten years of activity', and not be hidebound by the past and old allegiances.

His visits to Horwich, Crewe and Derby would have identified a number of candidates to help reach this crucial goal, Tom amongst them, as he later recalled:

'Sir Harold was certainly a new broom and came to meet his

staff singly and in groups. On one occasion in 1930 he and Sir Henry Fowler visited Horwich and stayed for two days. He questioned me about the work we were doing and sought my views on locomotive policy. It was difficult with Sir Henry there, but he encouraged me to be frank and nodded his agreement when we talked about the need for bigger engines. The earlier attempts to build a Pacific were discussed and the CME went to some pains to describe the benefits of these schemes. I agreed. Sir Harold asked me to pen a brief summary of this work, which I duly did and included some alternative proposals.

'Over the years Sir Henry was a regular visitor to Horwich and always took an interest in the work there. He was a great support. I felt it must have been a relief when he relinquished the CME post. After years of trying to develop better locomotives, his frustration at being unable to do so was palpable. He occasionally talked about the causes and his wish to have done more. His replacement by Lemon surprised many as we didn't know at that stage that William Stanier, from the GWR, would arrive a year or so later. Lemon was a good engineer but had no background in locomotive design or construction, so seemed a very odd choice at a time when the position regarding engines was fairly dismal.'

Fowler was replaced by Lemon in December 1931, who quickly set to

work. As a methodical, analytical man, he wished to establish the true extent of the problems the railway faced, vis-a-vis the condition and suitability of its engines. He was also concerned about the state of maintenance. And, of course, he had to bring together the Locomotive and Carriage/Wagon Works, as Stamp and Hartley had directed. It was true that he had limited knowledge of locomotive design and construction, but his deputy, Hewitt Beames, was proficient in this field, so would provide the necessary balance. Did Lemon know that he would only remain in this post for a year only? Probably not, though he may have suspected that Hartley was looking for a locomotive engineer from outside the LMS; a person with exceptional abilities and the drive to take reconstruction forward in a way that neither Lemon or Beames

Hewitt Beames

probably could. So it seems likely that he set to work believing that he would see the LMS through a necessary period of appraisal and only partly assumed he would implement these changes. Either way, his time as CME was crucial to the success of the programme and he achieved a great deal in a very short time, giving Stanier a head start in his 'revolution'.

He gathered around him a number of good engineers and managers, in addition to Beames. There was Sandham Symes and Tommy Hornbuckle, his brother in law, advising him on steam and diesel projects respectively, with Ernest Cox, an ever-rising star, beside them, leading, or so he asserted later, on the locomotive review:

'My job was to go out on the line, on the footplate and in the sheds to assemble facts regarding particular engine classes, and then in the office, work up proposals for modification or new design. I was teamed up with Bill Bramley, who was selected by Anderson. Together we stumped the country, visiting sheds, examining repair cards, and seeing with our own eyes the results in service. This was my first contact with motive power work, and it was a liberal education in cause and effect, with a certain element of crime detection for good measure.

'The railway now had 380 fully satisfactory modern locomotives of recent construction, Royal Scots, 2-6-4 tanks and 2 6 0 mixed traffics, these out of a total of 8,450 engines. The second

eleven, as it were, a total of 1,132 consisting of Claughtons, Hughes 4-6-0s, Prince of Wales, George Vs, 0-8-0s of both LNW and standard designs, had still to undertake a large volume of important traffic, and the passage of time did not make them any more suitable for these duties than has already been described. The large number of the purely Midland designs were all of smaller capacity, and while they leavened the mass of other regional types in low repair costs, their work was less efficient and made little contribution towards the heavier duties. Thus the activities of our new office at Euston was largely concentrated upon the above mentioned second string. When Lemon passed on to higher office, after only 12 months' tenure, proposals had already evolved as to what to do in each case.

'It was now that Beames asserted himself (over one class in particular – the 4-6-0 Prince of Wales) and he was able to persuade Lemon that all these difficulties could be overcome (if the class was simply modified) … there was something wrong somewhere with the thinking that produced this effort. Nonetheless, this is what would, undoubtedly, have been built as the leading mixed traffic class, had Stanier not come along in good time and with other ideas.'

Although Beames was a conscientious and able engineer, he seemed unable to think more broadly and looked unlikely to

Stanier arrives and the revolution begins. Although Tom was already well established, his position grew much stronger under the influence of the new CME.

take the LMS in the new direction Hartley was advocating. If we accept Cox's view that Lemon agreed with this, then the Vice President's concerns for the future were reinforced and increased the vigour with which he pursued Stanier or a person of like mind.

More recently doubt has been cast on many of Cox's statements. He does seem to have promoted his own role in these events when writing about his career. Perhaps this is true, and understandable, but from other accounts it seems that the review was not limited to him and Bramley. Tom, for example, was also closely involved in this work:

'It was a difficult time and Ernest Cox was tasked with an almost impossible job in such a short time. He needed support and there were many who could give him the benefit of their experience. For two or three weeks he, I and two of my draughtsmen sat in my office going through all the reports, maintenance records and test data we could find at Horwich, Crewe and Derby. This work tended to support the view that a lot needed to be done and quickly.'

And slowly the year evolved, with Lemon trying to establish a baseline from which to work, eager to make improvements, but facing the same restrictive views that had frustrated both Hughes and Fowler before him. With this in mind, it dawned on Hartley that Lemon's undoubted skills would be better employed elsewhere and the door was open to recruit Stanier as CME. And in January 1932, he arrived and Lemon was promoted to become Vice President of the Railway Traffic Operating and Commercial group, so replaced Follows, who retired on 1 March 1932. At the same time, the four

Horwich Engine Shed.

Vice President posts were reduced by one. It is a sad indictment of the way the LMS had been managed, in nearly ten years since grouping, that so little progress had been made. Hopefully, now the executive group would have the drive and stamina to put this right. But it was Stanier who would ensure this happened on the rolling stock front, supported by a team he would gradually put together.

Whilst these changes were taking place Tom, as he always did, observed life within the LMS, collected data and thought of the future. He was a man who liked to look beyond the immediate boundaries of his life and was interested in many fields of engineering and science, something he shared with Stanier. And the race to produce the fastest, most advanced aircraft, that was taking place throughout the 1920s and '30s,

fascinated him. He remembered the young Reginald Mitchell from Stoke days and followed his work, through Supermarine's participation in the Schneider trophy, very closely.

During September 1929, the event took place off the south coast of England, opposite Portsmouth Harbour. Tom received an invitation to attend from Supermarine and spent an enjoyable three days there watching the racing, recording times and taking photographs as one of Mitchell's S6 aeroplanes came first. Two years later, shortly after Tom's father had died, he was again sent an invitation by Supermarine and saw Flight Lieutenant Bootham, of the High Speed Flight, win with an average speed of 340.08mph in the new S.6B (S-1595). There is no record of him and Mitchell meeting then, but it is evocative of their past lives in Stoke's engineering world, and the fact that he received an invitation, that this may have been so. Tom kept the programmes, newspaper cuttings and photographs, plus a celebratory biscuit tin, to remember these events. The link between the two would take another, unexpected, turn later in the decade, by which time Tom's star had risen to its height and Mitchell's greatest achievement, the Spitfire, had taken to the air, as his life was slowly ebbing away.

For the moment though Tom's thoughts would have returned very quickly to his railway world, intrigued by the hopes and possibilities William Stanier's arrival might create.

Chapter 4

FREE TO THINK, FREE TO BUILD

I n 1962, the eminent biochemist and Nobel Prize winner Albert von Szent-Gyorgyi wrote, 'discovery consists of seeing what everybody has seen and thinking what no one else has thought'. In exploring this idea, I was struck by its relevance to engineering during the 1930s, which was often hidebound by blinkered vision and traditionalist thinking. Locomotive design on the LMS, up to 1932, was dominated by people who could see, but were unable to translate the seemingly obvious into effective designs. The 'King's new suit of clothes' truly personifies their collective state of mind. And yet it could have been so different if they had thought more broadly and with greater imagination. But some people are immoveable no matter what the consequences and eventually fail because they are unable to truly explore their science and think freely. The LMS suffered the invidious effects of a dire regime for too long and even after William Stanier became CME it still tried to impose its restrictive will upon design.

Anderson was an ambitious man who, it seems, wished to become the LMS's CME. Fowler, as Hartley related in his correspondence, rather surprisingly advocated his cause. Bearing in mind Anderson's attempts to stifle Hughes, then the

new CME's wish to think more broadly about the locomotives the company really needed, this was remarkably generous of Sir Henry. Whether warned by others, or perceiving the danger himself, Stanier politely and firmly defused Anderson's attempts to dictate locomotive policy. Ernest Lemon was less diplomatic and, growing ever more tired of Anderson's continuing interference, brought his career to an end. Most accounts suggest he retired, whereas Lemon reported

that he was summarily 'relieved of his duties with immediate effect on 31 October 1932, as it was desirable his successor should take office concurrently with pending changes'. Retirement may have been the diplomatic outcome, but dismissal was the reality.

When someone is brought in from another, alien, company, even the most outward looking employees can feel uneasy. Will their new leader understand the problems they have faced, will a 'new broom' sweep away the good

A scene that captures the state of locomotive development on the LMS in the years before Stanier took over. A small engine policy abounds.

Crewe Apprentices
re-union attended by Fred Lemon, Riddles, Beames and many other notables including Nigel Gresley. Tom and Fred's sons, who were both apprentices at Crewe, were also in the group.

with the bad and bring in a new team? The consequences of change can be unsettling and in Stanier they had acquired someone who wouldn't baulk at restructuring an organisation when required, but was also astute enough to get the best from those he inherited and only seek amendment when someone had been fully tested. His experiences with the GWR had taught him to be circumspect and ruthless only when absolutely necessary. And with so many pressing demands placed on him by Stamp and Hartley, he had little time to make radical changes anyway.

One thing is certain though; from the beginning of his reign Stanier made sure that he would determine how the need for motive power was assessed and met,

and not Anderson's department. But the battle lines had not been entirely removed and Anderson's replacement, the 46-year-old David Urie, was an unflinching, tenacious and difficult man who Lemon was not always able to control. A strong sense of diplomacy was not one of Urie's strong points and a common soubriquet attached to him was 'Irish Blackguard', though he was of Scottish descent. There is little doubt that he tried to dictate locomotive policy like his predecessor, and Lemon may have been a fellow conspirator in this, but Stanier was much tougher and more resilient than either of them. He was also a much better leader and thinker as the next few years would prove.

At Horwich Tom watched these developments with great interest:

'Events moved quickly, but so did the rumours. Eventually a circular appeared announcing Stanier's appointment. There weren't strong feelings about this either way, because Lemon hadn't made much of an impression on our work and so wouldn't be missed. Sir Henry Fowler, on the other hand, had been greatly respected and was still much missed, although many had profound reservations about his locomotive work. He visited shortly after Stanier took up post and spent a considerable time talking about the future. He made it very plain that the new CME was the best man for the job.

'I forget the date, but Stanier toured each Works early in his tenure and spent a week at Horwich, part of it with Sir Henry in attendance. I spoke at length to them both outlining the work we were doing. The conversation soon turned to wider issues and Stanier described his plans for the future and the review he was undertaking. It was based on Lemon's earlier work, but took it to a deeper level. Sir Henry had told me to put my views forward in a positive way and this certainly sparked a reaction. As later events showed, Stanier was assessing the men under his command and marking down those who might be useful in the future.'

Eric Langridge, a draughtsman at Derby, and an able, but not totally unbiased, chronicler of these events, reflects a slightly different view of

Stanier's arrival, in his book *Under 10 CMEs*:

'The news of Stanier's appointment came as a bombshell to the Derby locomotive drawing office staff. How many men would he bring in, and so on, were the questions.

'When Stanier made his first visit to Derby, he came round with Beames, hobbling as usual with his sticks, and Chambers. Some drawings of the 0-4-2T were still on the boards. Of course, Chambers was on tenterhooks and Stanier on the defensive. The only remark made within my hearing was, "Can't you get a long travel gear on it?", which, as it was a slide valve job, did not strike me as very deep thinking. Stanier had a very pleasant manner, a soft West Country "burr" and a keen look that could be determined if required. Later I came to the conclusion that he was no designer as such, but then, how many CMEs were?'

The two reactions to the same event are revealing. 'Derby' thinking had dominated during the first eight years of the LMS's existence and now Stanier posed a threat to their position, and Langridge displays the uncertainty this created. Tom at Horwich was, by comparison, open to new ideas and clearly developed a rapport with Stanier from the first. And it was a relationship that would go from strength to strength and one wonders why this was so? Was it the attraction of opposites or a realisation that much

The **ascerbic** and difficult David Urie.

common ground existed? There were differences, of course. Each represented the talents and skills of the two schools of engineering – design and production – and to this end, Langridge's slightly caustic observation of CMEs' skills may not have been not far from the mark, whilst Tom was described by colleagues as an instinctive designer. But the skills they shared were many and varied. They both knew their business, they were open to new ideas, had a scientific curiosity that went well beyond the railway world and were prepared to look, assess and try a broad range of solutions in seeking the best outcomes. They were both realists though, and knew only too well the boundaries of what was possible and acceptable in their industry.

In personality, there were similarities too. Both were honest and honourable men. By nature,

they tended to be quiet and reserved, yet this disguised immense determination and, at times, sheer bloody mindedness. The saying 'an iron fist inside a velvet glove' was used to describe Tom and this probably applies to Stanier too, yet in both cases they were diplomats and had genuinely friendly and warm personalities. They both understood human nature and accepted and compensated, whenever possible, for the limitations of those around them. If they had to exercise their authority it was done with the minimum of fuss, but also

Tom again attends the Schneider Trophy event, remembered here in his souvenir copy of the programme. Inside he kept copious notes of all he saw, coupled with technical analysis of each aeroplane taking part.

The LMS at Camden, the cleaners hard at work. This shed became one of Tom's regular haunts over the years, helped by a growing friendship with Alfred Ewer, the Superintendent.

with a degree of compassion and sympathy, particularly if someone had tried their best. If anything, Tom cultivated a slightly gruff exterior to ward off the unwary or the foolish, but in a full bodied, often uncompromising industrial world this was no bad thing. The gentle and meek rarely inherit the earth and these two engineers would soon need all the strength, skill and drive they could muster to carry through a design and construction programme without equal in Britain. It certainly wasn't a time for sissies and neither man would be found wanting in the challenging years ahead.

Ernest Cox described how Stanier gradually built up his team from those he had inherited. However, at one time he did try to recruit Sam Ell from Swindon to boost the design team under his control, fearing that they might be unable or unwilling to meet his pressing objectives:

'With the new chief came changes in the team … The small HQ office at Euston was strengthened by the appointment of two mechanical inspectors, Read and Duncan, who were the eyes and ears of the department out in the sheds, and who took over the work previously done by Bramley and myself. From the first, I became involved in the preliminary technical scheming of the series of new locomotive designs, which were then sent to the production drawing offices. Before long a small drawing office was set up under my charge in Ampthill Square, in order to amplify what was passed down the line.

'Symes remained as Locomotive Assistant (to the CME) for 18 months and thereafter was promoted to Chief Stores Superintendent. He was followed by Robert Riddles, a Crewe man, whose interest in that centre was mainly concentrated upon the maintenance and workshop side (where he had made a name for himself by assisting in the modernisation of these facilities) … Riddles represented a new generation from the ancient Cheshire seat of tradition. He wasted no time in pining over the departed glories of "Princes" and "Claughtons" and entered with zest into all that Stanier was undertaking in locomotive design.

'In the same period Beames, finding himself less and less part of the new era, gracefully retired … Coleman made a big impression on Stanier and transferred him to Crewe in 1933, but he still retained ownership of Horwich, now only a kind of outstation. Grover, former Chief Draughtsman at Crewe, was found other work. Herbert Chambers continued in charge at Derby with the same team as before. The new designs were apportioned between Coleman and Chambers, and although they were intended to be completely standardised, it has always been possible to identify small differences in detail between a Crewe and a Derby designed product of this era.'

When recalling these events years later, Cox seems to have compressed the changes of personnel into a much shorter time period, suggesting they were quick and easy. Some may well have been, but the reality was that the drag of

history and the pressing need to initiate the locomotive programme ensured the process was managed more slowly and carefully. Although he had impressed the CME, Tom's promotion was not activated until a scoping paper, outlining Stanier's proposals, had been submitted to the LMS Board. But before this could happen it had to pass through the hands of the Mechanical and Electrical Engineering Committee for close scrutiny and endorsement. By the end of the year, his paper had passed muster and the first phase of the programme entered the 1933 construction schedule. The central focus of this plan was the conversion

of twenty-five Claughton Class 4-6-0 locomotives and ten 4-6-0 Prince of Wales, but the most significant part of programme was the construction of three new Pacifics, five 2-8-0 freights, forty mixed traffic 2-6-0s and forty-five 2-6-4 passenger tank engines. A small beginning, with only ninety-three Stanier designed locomotives, but essential in proving his plans and theories correct. And it was the acceptance of this programme that allowed Stanier to authorise Coleman's transfer to Crewe, with Chambers remaining in overall charge at Derby, so creating a balance between the two establishments and the two men.

Tom, it seems, was particularly interested in the ten 4-6-4Ts built at Horwich just before he arrived there and often photographed them, as he did here.

Herbert Chambers was a Derby man without a doubt. He was born in the city during 1885 and died there. He served his apprenticeship with the Midland Railway, joining the Drawing Office after a period on the shop floor. Ambition led him to join Beyer, Peacock of Manchester as a draughtsman in 1911 where he remained for two years before the pull of Derby hastened his return. He specialised in experimental work for the next decade, then became Chief Draughtsman in 1923, when the LMS was formed. Four years later, in 1927, he was promoted to the post of Technical Assistant to the CME and the company's Chief Draughtsman. Both roles were very demanding and stressful, becoming even more so when Stanier arrived.

Chambers was, by all accounts, a good engineer who had flourished under Hughes and Fowler, and seemed able to look beyond the Derby 'view' when required to do so. Ernest Cox recalled his 'warm and attractive personality' and a 'hard worker who did not spare himself any more than his staff when there was a deadline to be met', whilst Tom found him:

'Very approachable and dedicated. We met many times over the years before Sir William arrived and I never found him blinkered or narrow in his outlook. It's true that he was brought up in the Midland's tradition, but he had a wider view and took an interest in all new developments. Sir Henry and he were not always in agreement and Herbert was often frustrated by the way locomotive development was handled in the late 1920s. I think he found Stanier's arrival unsettling, as many did. Better the devil you know, I expect.

'At one stage he offered me the post as his deputy at Derby. After much consideration I turned it down. I was already Chief at Horwich and so it seemed to be a backward step. My family were also settled in Lancashire and I didn't wish to move them at that stage.'

Stanier's view of Chambers is unrecorded. He did not write an autobiography or record his thoughts or memories of people in any other way. However, when Henry Bulleid was writing his book *Masters of Steam* in the early 1960s, he interviewed Stanier at great length. The result of this could easily be seen as being the CME's recollections and words, translated into the third person:

'The Chief Draughtsman was Herbert Chambers, an excellent and experienced designer, noted for his heroic and successful effort in co-ordinating, against time, the design work between Derby Loco Drawing Office and the North British Locomotive Company on the Royal Scot, but a dyed in the wool Midland man. He argued with Stanier about all those innovations which he could not readily accept … A good Chief and a good Assistant both know that a nice balance between querying orders and blindly following them is essential, but Stanier and Chambers were unable to find this balance with Chambers as Chief Draughtsman.'

Unamed Fowler Patriot No 5518 at Camden. Photo from Tom's collection.

If this was so, it is strange that Stanier didn't move Chambers to another post very quickly. Instead he left his assistant in situ for three years, which suggests that their relationship wasn't intolerable or unproductive. He was even ready to trust his most important project to Chambers; the design of the first Pacifics. More remarkably, in some ways, Chambers also led on producing Stanier's experimental turbine engine, in conjunction with Henry Guy of Metropolitan Vickers. The truth is that Chambers was an effective manager and designer, good enough for the work in hand, and it may have been that no better candidate was immediately available. Tom Coleman was a possibility, but a largely untried one, in which case he had to be tested before being promoted. Eric Langridge, from his vantage point at Derby, observed these events, adding a number of wry, if not wholly appropriate or perceptive comments:

'Stanier had a 2-6-0 on the list of designs; as Derby locomotive drawing office were busy, the design could go elsewhere; Martin at Crewe was not a very impressive man and they had lost their leading draughtsman, so he gave it to Horwich. They could increase their staff, an easy matter with the slump on and with good ex-contract men "walking the streets". So Coleman took on G G.R.Nicholson, L. Barraclough and two others, and thus was off to a good start.

'Coleman, tucked away at the end of a branch line, disinclined to have anything to do with Derby, making the most of Stanier's visits to Horwich, having the right confident approach to him, with fast-working contract shop men, soon made a show. They put the cylinders horizontal, not bothering about gauge clearance on curves; mounted a flowerpot safety valve casing and made the chimney height a little lower than the cab. The only drawback was that the engine had to be tried over all routes before being accepted by the civil engineer. She was also considerably heavier than the old "Crab" … Maybe Coleman thought the flowerpot the best-shaped casing for the line of this engine, he may have been trying to impress the new boss or it may have been one of his jokes; of course it was soon replaced by non-standard rounded casing above the top feed much taller than those fitted to any other Stanier locomotive … Coleman was in a hurry to make an impression and get his locomotive out first, having no love for Derby, and would not worry Stanier with lots of queries, and his new contract men were also keen to show that they could deliver the goods quickly.

'Across at Horwich, Coleman appeared to grow in favour. To follow his 2-6-0 engine and tender, on which he was complimented by Stanier, he was given the 2-cylinder 4-6-0 which became the Black Five … His scheme was chosen, and before all the drawings had been completed an order had been placed with Vulcan Foundry … Coleman was obviously on the way up, and a lack of discipline on the part of Martin at Crewe enabled Stanier to transfer him and his ex-contract men to Crewe, and let Martin finish his time "off the map" at Horwich.'

Langridge's recollections, which were written long after his retirement, are often peppered with acerbic observations. He does appear to have been overly sensitive to the perceived

The hard labour involved in steam locomotive preparation. It was this sort of scene that convinced Tom that other forms of propulsion were long overdue.

Herbert Chambers, Stanier's first Chief Draughtsman. Conscientious but hard pressed. He must take credit for much that his CME achieved.

intrigues and manoeuvrings of those around him as they appeared to seek advancement of career or ideas. Some would call this an honest assessment, whilst others could see his version of events lacking sufficient professional detachment to be of real value. So his memories and views have been treated with a degree of caution – the outline is probably correct, but the detail may lack true objectivity. There may also be a degree of personal antipathy coming through in his accounts. He and Tom Coleman, it seems, did not always enjoy a happy relationship and Langridge gives every impression of struggling with authority.

Tom's transfer to Crewe came as the workload created by Stanier's plans came to fruition and may have been in danger of swamping the Drawing Offices under his control. The extent of this work also began to change the Midlands led dynamics that had been a key

part of life in the LMS for so long. Under Tom's energetic and creative leadership the Crewe Drawing Office was revitalised:

'They had become used to being sidelined and needed to be alerted and involved in all the changes taking place. There were many good men there, but they had become too reserved and lacked initiative. Derby still directed work, but the tasks were so abundant that Herbert Chambers could not keep all design in the Drawing Office there.

'Sir William called Chambers and I down to Euston in mid-1933 and told me that I was moving to Crewe forthwith, but still control Horwich. I would be taking the 2-6-0 work with me, with the new 4-6-0 mixed traffic engine and the 2-8-0 freight engine being added. He also made it clear that I would be involved in the 4-6-2 programme, because they were being built at Crewe, although Derby would carry on with design work. Stanier hinted that this was necessary as I might be more involved later as the number of engines increased. Chambers seemed unconcerned about this, probably because of all the other tasks he faced.

'I was welcomed at Crewe and my family joined me locally shortly afterwards. I had known many of them for a long time and in Fred Lemon (the Works Superintendent) I found a good friend.'

Frederick Arnold Lemon would play a leading and often forgotten

role in Stanier's revolution. Although a Somerset man, born on 28 September 1878 in Castle Cary, by a twist of fate he didn't find employment with the GWR at Swindon, but joined the London and North Western Railway, for three years, as an apprentice at Crewe in 1896, then became a private pupil of Francis Webb, the eminent railway engineer, for a year. Posts in Running Sheds all over the region followed, including Birkenhead, Bangor, Camden, Colwick, Newry and Dundalk, before a return to Crewe where he became the Assistant Works Manager in 1916, and was closely involved in war production. When the conflict ended he led in restoring the workshops to their pre-war state and here he remained for the rest of his career, rising to become Superintendent. To demonstrate his status one needs only to look at his application for membership of the Institution of Mechanical Engineers which is countersigned by Sir Henry Fowler and Nigel Gresley in 1928. In a summary of current work, he reported that, 'I am responsible to the Mechanical Engineer for 8000 men and output of Shops in Loco Works; carried out re-organisation of Works in accordance with Mech Engr's plans.' Here was a man of some substance and authority who would become much more to Tom than a friend – an ally of great strength and resourcefulness. And in the not too distant future their families would be joined by marriage, cementing an enduring and constructive link.

Having inherited the Horwich 2-6-0 programme, Tom must have

been pleased when the requirement to design forty more engines of the same type was assigned to him in 1932. Stanier had impressed on his Chief Draughtsmen the need for urgency, but also to embrace the changes he was proposing. His small design team at Euston outlined his ideas in simple diagrams, but these were, by repute, barely sufficient for the task, leaving the Drawing Offices plenty of leeway in finding solutions. Being the first of Stanier's engines to reach the drawing board had a significance only too apparent to Tom Coleman and his team set to with great vigour to justify the trust placed in them.

Diagram No EU13 was completed at Euston in April 1932 and included a Great Western type taper boiler, a requirement for low superheat, two outside, horizontal cylinders, Walschaerts valve gear, Swindon type axleboxes, steam sanding gear and a side window cab. To complement this schedule a number of ex-GWR drawings were sent to Horwich to help guide their work. No papers exist to record the reaction of Tom or his team to this 'help', but raised eyebrows may have been their response, the wholesale application of GWR ideas having been a concern to many in the months that followed Stanier's arrival!

In fact, the new CME was much more perceptive than they realised. They weren't to know it yet, but he had an open mind capable of appreciating and absorbing ideas or developments no matter from where they came. As Ernest Cox later recalled, 'we quickly realised that he was no doctrinaire'. But for most, this was a slow dawning awareness and, initially, some attempted to second guess his

Fred Lemon very early in his career.

thoughts and appeal to his GWR heritage, Tom amongst them.

The diagram from Euston included a dome shaped safety valve casing on top, but, under Tom's guiding hand, this was translated into a GWR style cap, possibly to assure Stanier that they had looked more broadly for a solution. If so, their efforts proved of limited value, because the CME ordered its removal and insisted on the original solution. Eric Langridge hinted that the swap may have been Tom having a small joke, but he would have had to be very certain of his new CME to do this. Common sense suggests that at this stage in their relationship such behaviour could easily have been misconstrued and damaging to his reputation. In time, the design would be modified when it was pointed out to Stanier that his idea for the safety valve and its housing, on top of a larger boiler, created a gauging problem. As a result, the engines were fitted with flatter covers. Later, when

he had grown to trust Tom more completely, the CME would allow him great freedom of action. This was a hard earned autonomy that few others would achieve.

As Cox observed:

'Stanier did not immediately or blindly graft Swindon practice as a whole on to his charge. His other outstanding characteristic was that when he found he had made a mistake, and being human he was no less prone than other mortals, he would never seek to cover up bad engineering by worse, but could change direction quickly and completely, without wasting a moment of further time on what had proved unsatisfactory. In keeping with this trait he was not a man of many words. He gave his instructions in brief terms; when the resulting teams were put before him, he was apt to accept or reject with a minimum of comment.'

Black Five number 5151, built by Armstrong Whitworth in 1935 with a domeless boiler, eases away leaving a dense cloud of smoke caught by the bridge.

Tom's arrival at Crewe coincided with the start of the 2-6-0s' construction and he was able to see for himself how they developed, overseeing modifications which inevitably arise when something new is being developed. In 1934, he also became involved in comparison trials between the new engines and the Hughes designed 2-6-0. Throughout his career, Tom had always gathered information about design and performance, even during the Schneider Trophy air races and a trip to the Hendon Air Display in 1929. He knew that a wide variety of data was essential in developing good design and as he grew in seniority, he pursued this material with greater zest. But he also knew the limitations of 'on the road' trials with a dynamometer car attached:

For his part, Tom had learnt a valuable lesson that increased his understanding of the CME and his way of working. Mutual trust and respect were growing rapidly, not surprisingly, because they were men of similar disposition and outlook and a lesson learnt now would pay dividends later for both of them. One thing is certain though, Stanier had found a highly skilled and loyal ally, who would serve him well.

Of greater significance to the 2-6-0's success was the gauging problem the company's Chief Civil Engineer believed would be created by its cylinders. He was convinced that they would foul trackside structures in many places. Stanier and Tom Coleman believed otherwise and tested this view by fitting lead strips, at platform level, to three of Hughes' Mogul engines to replicate and mirror the greater width. These engines then visited all the locations where the CCE felt a problem existed and most were found to have adequate clearance. Remedial action was taken in places where the gap was too small and so the problem was satisfactorily resolved.

Construction of the forty new engines began at Crewe in October 1933 and continued on until July the following year. Even at this early stage of Stanier's reign, they had a look that all his tender engines would share to some degree – tapered boilers matched to open and roomy cabs, giving a balanced and elegant design. But the tender, being a typical product of the Fowler regime, did not quite match. In time, new higher sided vehicles appeared and this would suit his engines better, except in the case of the 2-6-0 which retained the original tenders until scrapped in the 1960s.

'They told us much, but there was a lot which they didn't, because of the many variables that came into play – the unpredictability of running conditions being the main one. A facility with a rolling road would have told us much more. In the late 1930s I visited Swindon, encouraged by the CME, and saw their static test facility, which had been in operation since Churchward's time, and was given copies of drawings by Collett himself. Stanier and Gresley were strong supporters of such a facility for the LMS and LNER and by then had begun to convince the powers that be that one should be built. We got out some basic drawings to support their arguments, but the war came before work could be complete.'

When the two designs of 2-6-0 were compared it was found that their performances were practically identical, with the Stanier engine having one small advantage in that 'the weight of steam required per unit of work done is slightly less'. It was also noted that 'the riding of engine 13284 (the Stanier) was considerably better than engine 2885, the latter engine exhibiting a strong fore and aft motion at speeds above 43 mph'.

Much was learnt during the development of the 2-6-0 in practical as well as process terms. It also began to prove the growing strength of the Stanier/Coleman working partnership, soon to enter a new phase. Meanwhile, in the workshops at Crewe, the first two Pacifics were taking shape in 1933, an event that Tom could not ignore being so close to the production line. There appear to be no surviving records to hint at a more direct involvement in the project, but he was intrigued by the design and kept copious notes of these gradually emerging giants, riding on the footplate on several occasions. He also took the opportunity to ride behind 6200 *Princess Royal* on a Press run from Euston to Crewe and back in early August, during which the engine failed. Once again, he kept notes, wryly commenting on 'the merriment of the journalists [presumably enjoying the LMS's hospitality a little too much] and 6200's good performance until it caught fire and embarrassed Lemon somewhat'.

The 1934 locomotive design and construction programme was dominated by two key projects - a

new 4-6-0 express locomotive and a Class 5 4-6-0 mixed traffic engine. The first of these would become known as the Jubilees and result in 191 being built by 1936, whilst 842 of the latter would appear, in varying forms, between 1934 and 1951. The Black Fives, as they were called by railwaymen and public alike, were destined to be one of the most numerous engines ever to run on British rails. When steam locomotion came to an end in 1968, this class were still going strong and would have gone on for many more years if allowed to do so. Few could have foreseen all this when the requirement landed on Tom's desk in the early 1930s. Whilst Derby led on designing the Pacifics and then the Jubilees, Crewe took on the less glamorous, but probably more productive projects.

Any railway company needs a good mixed traffic locomotive to undertake a wide variety of duties

across its network in an effective and economical way – from express work, to freight, to branch line duties and so on. The LMS had struggled to develop such an engine and one of the company's most pressing needs was to design and build a class capable of undertaking these varying roles. In many ways, the search for these engines was akin to the pursuit of a Holy Grail, so important was the need. The Horwich 2-6-0s had been one attempt to do this, followed by Stanier's updated 2-6-0. The LNW's Prince of Wales Class 4-6-0 had been another, but had suffered from serious problems, including a very high number of fractured frames. Hewitt Beames had proposed a modified design when Mechanical Engineer at Crewe and later as Ernest Lemon's deputy. The result was a proposal for ten, superheated conversions in the 1933 programme, but before work began the requirement was reviewed and changed. Fowler's

The early months of Stanier's reign were dominated by the development of three types of engine - 4-6-0s, a 2-6-0 and, as portrayed here, the Pacfics.

hand, would produce something entirely different and in so doing begin to stamp his authority on the way design on the LMS was directed:

'I had seen for myself the Halls in operation during holidays in the West Country. They were efficient machines, but we could do better and, of course, our needs were different.

The variety of duties and conditions on the LMS demanded more. Sir William by this time had made it clear that an adherence to GWR ideas wasn't essential, though we could learn much from their experiences, which was true. So we were allowed to think for ourselves and he managed us at Crewe with a very light touch indeed.'

The detailed designs that appeared were so well thought out that axle loading, height and width would have allowed the engines to operate over 70 per cent of the network without the need to modify bridges or track side structures. The plans also revealed a very distinctive shape, where sound ergonomic principles had been incorporated to maximise output with minimum effort and hardship to operators. Put simply, in Tom's design, ease of usage and maintenance were given high priority, pushing back the boundaries of what was possible on steam locomotives to the limit.

The engine would have outside Walschaerts valve gear over which Stanier, it seems, needed little persuasion, although some expected him to prefer a Swindon

Whilst the LNER were turning out their new A4s, the LMS responded with the Jubilee Class, producing this highly polished example for publicity purposes in 1935.

three-cylinder, 4-6-0 Patriot Class had proved satisfactory on fast express and fitted freight work and the Chief Operating Manager recommended that an additional fifteen be built in place of the ten converted Prince of Wales. These, plus five new 2-8-0 class engines, would slip into the 1934 programme. As things turned out, the 2-8-0s were translated into the first five Jubilees and the remaining ten became Stanier's new 4-6-0 mixed traffic engine.

The broad specification for this design was outlined in diagram EU 44, which was issued to Tom, when still at Horwich, to begin design work. Initially a three-cylinder engine was considered the best solution but its weight could have restricted route availability, so a two-cylinder version was inserted into the diagram instead. Tom's promotion to Chief Draughtsman followed shortly afterwards and this work, and some of his staff, transferred to Crewe.

Ernest Cox believed that this new design bore a strong resemblance to the GWR's highly successful Hall Class mixed traffic engines that had begun appearing in the late 1920s. If so, Tom, under Stanier's guiding

The changing scene captured at Camden as Stanier engines begin to make their presence felt.

solution. The domeless low degree superheat tapered boiler chosen for the task created a working pressure of 225lb, and a tractive effort, at 85 per cent working pressure, of 25,455lb. At this stage, Stanier's views on superheating, influenced by his experience on the GWR, held sway and a low degree was thought adequate for the task at hand. It was a debate that was just beginning, sponsored in part by concerns over the performance of the first two Princess Royal Class Pacifics just entering service.

Stanier would, in time, give grudging acceptance to the need for a higher degree of superheat, but for the moment this was not forthcoming. And the first few Black Fives tended to support his view, performing excellently even though working with a low degree superheated steam, unlike the Jubilees, which struggled.

Tom was one of those who realised that working conditions on the LMS were unlike those on the GWR and needed a different approach when it came

to superheating. But it was an issue that had to be tackled with a great diplomacy if suitable modifications were to be made. The principle of applying a low degree heat was well established at Swindon. It meant that fewer tubes were needed in the superheater, creating more space for upward circulation of water at the firebox tubeplate. On the LMS this was more difficult to achieve – driving conditions could be harsher, the quality of coal more variable and Stanier's new locomotives had larger grate areas and this required a different firing technique. The end result was that heat was being lost, without renewal, at too great a rate, so removing any benefits the superheater might bestow. As the quality of coal improved and the firemen learnt new techniques the performance improved, but much more was achievable and this meant adding more elements to the superheater. The Princess Royals were built with sixteen and the Jubilees and Black Fives with fourteen apiece. In time, these were increased to 32, 24 and 28 respectively, but it took a long process of testing to demonstrate the advantages. Even as late as 1936, Stanier restricted six of the Princesses to 24 element superheaters, which they kept for

some years until, in the natural course of events, boiler changes became due.

Tom later wrote that:

'The superheater question is one that Ernest Cox and I pursued for some time. Sir William was generally amenable to new ideas and other options, but didn't give up easily on the level of superheating and the number of elements best suited to each type of engine. The slower freight locomotives could operate with a low degree of superheat, but the express engines, particularly on the harder sections of the West Coast Main Line, benefitted greatly from more. So both arguments could be

applied with equal strength. The comparison trials that took place during 1933, '34 and '35 with the Princess Royals proved the case for long distance, high speed services, but the CME never entirely accepted our arguments for the other classes.

'Even as late as the 1930s the thermodynamics of steam engines were not always fully understood. At evening classes early in the century this science was explained to me very clearly and John Hookham, at Stoke Works, supplemented my knowledge of the subject. In the years that followed I kept up with all the advances and tried to keep a clear understanding of the principle that 'when mechanical energy is produced from heat, a definite quantity of heat goes out of existence for every unit of work done' and how this effect might be countered to boost economy and performance.

'Allen and Bursley's book *Heat Engines* (both renowned Professors of Mechanical Engineering in the United States) set out, in 1910, how thermodynamics should be applied in steam engines and the benefits of superheating. Their research concluded that 'when superheated from 100 to 200 F there is a saving of 1% for every 12 degrees of superheat. Engines of the piston-valve, or poppet-valve, type may utilise much higher degrees of superheat with corresponding increase in economy. In these cases, steam having a temperature of 500 F to 600 F may be used to advantage.

As Tom's career blossomed so his interest in cars grew, particularly sports models. Here Tom and Harriet enjoy a day out in his 1930 Lagonda whilst serving at Horwich.

Jubilee 5562 *Alberta*, built by North British in 1934, was an engine Tom rode on several times in 1936 to gauge the performance of the class.

Where steam turbines are installed present practice tends toward much higher pressures and superheat ... until recently the limiting temperature of the steam has been 750 F.

'What we discovered in practice was that the economies achieved had to be balanced against the deteriorating effect higher temperatures had on the pipes and fittings and the extra maintenance this required. So a balance had to be struck and this was affected by the role of each type of engine.

'It was probably the development of 'Stanier's Baby' (the turbine Pacific) which helped bring these discussions to an end. It needed a higher level of superheat and a 32 element superheater achieved this, improving its performance considerably. This, plus the trials with the Princess Royals, finally convinced the CME about the

whole question and to trust us to come to the right conclusions. He always took an active role in all design work, but he learnt by experience that he could delegate much more to his designers at Crewe, then Derby.'

In 1933, the resolution of these arguments was still in the future and the initial batches of these mixed traffic engines, and the Jubilees, went with Stanier's favoured option of a low degree of superheat. But the number to

Gresley's converted W1 engine 'Hush Hush`, now a conventional 4-6-4, was another engine that captured Tom's attention. A photo from his collection.

be constructed increased. With Tom's work well advanced, and the capabilities of this class becoming clearer, it was decided to implement a scrap and build policy more emphatically. A Board meeting on 26 October 1933 gave voice to this requirement:

'The Chairman referred to the memo dated October 1933 giving particulars of the estimated stock of locomotives at 31 December 1934 and recommending that 121 locomotives be replaced by 100 (new) engines, fifty of which would be 'Improved Claughton' type (Jubilees) and fifty the improved 'Prince of Wales' (Class 5) type. This would result in an 18% saving on coal consumption and 25% saving in cost of repair, per mile. It was agreed that the Locomotive Trade be asked to submit alternative tenders for each type in lots of twenty-five and fifty locomotives.'

Within a month, tenders had been invited and bids submitted. The Jubilees were outsourced to the North British Locomotive Company in two batches split over 1935 and '36, and all fifty Black Fives went in a single order to the Vulcan Foundry for delivery in 1934 and '35. Capacity within the LMS's workshops was thought to be insufficient to allow greater in-house construction, but this decision was reviewed and sixty-nine Jubilees and twenty Black Fives were assigned to Crewe in 1934 and '35, with ten of the former going to Derby. It seems that Fred Lemon had put his considerable weight behind a case for building these new, more modern engines in their own workshops, now geared up to production line techniques, following a major review of working methods.

In sub-contracting these tasks, it was important that the development work undertaken by Tom on the Black Fives and his team be fully understood by their opposite numbers at Vulcan's Works at Newton-le-Willows, near St Helens in Lancashire. To help them in this process, Tom visited regularly to talk through the requirement, a programme made easier because he knew many of the team there, having dealt with them on various issues when at Stoke and Horwich. In July 1934, to accompany the detailed specification sent to Vulcan Foundry, Tom prepared a general description of these engines in a document that would, in time, be issued widely to many parties, including footplate crew, maintenance and shed staff and the railway press. Usually this work would have been delegated, but Tom decided to write it and kept the draft as a souvenir. It was the first major project he had managed in its entirety and any paternal interest would have been difficult to conceal. And this theme could be traced through the few papers he decided to keep denoting key events in his career as a design engineer - the Endon Dip, the NSR's 4-cylinder 0-6-0 tank engine, the 2F Dock tank and now the Black Five.

With both these new types of 4-6-0s rolling off the production lines, the need to test and evaluate them became paramount, as it did for the other classes beginning to make their appearance. Tom, who had always been in the forefront of collecting and analysing data, now found himself getting closely involved in a large, expansive appraisal programme greater than anything that had gone before. Essentially this work was sponsored by a need to ensure the company's huge investment in new engines was providing efficient and effective solutions. But the tests would also compare the performances of comparable

Tom's interest in the A4s didn't slacken throughout his career and features heavily in his papers, as this photo from his albums confirms.

types and examine the individual elements of a design, such as the degree of superheat needed.

In October 1934, Herbert Chambers wrote to Tom informally asking him to conduct a series of assessments of the new Class 5X. In Chambers' mind, there was a growing concern over the steaming qualities of the first few engines being built at Crewe, but one wonders why he asked somebody as senior and as busy as Tom to undertake this work and not someone from his office in Derby. Perhaps it was simply a case of needing a person of his great skills and independence to sort out a growing problem or, alternatively he was urged to do so by his CME. Either way, the initial series of tests took place between 30 November and 4 December, with the fifth and final set being completed in January 1935. Engine number 5556 was used throughout.

Tom kept his hand-written notes of each run, plus Stanier and Chamber's comments. It is interesting to note the level of trust both men placed in his assessments and the extent of his analytical skills, even in this extracurricular task:

'For the purpose of general observation I rode on Engine No.5556 between London and Birmingham on four separate journeys. The engine has run about 28,000 miles since being built and is fitted with a 5' blast pipe cap. The engine was as originally designed, except that a continuous blow-down valve has been fitted and is in operation. Dalton Main coal was supplied throughout and

the engine was well handled in every respect by the driver and fireman.

'With regard to the trains taken; it will be seen that trains No 1 and 2 were considerably under the load which these engines are scheduled to take, while the load on the down train (No 3) approximates to this load. In this case, however, arrangements were made by the Operating Manager for an assisting engine to be provided at Euston. The down train No 4, therefore, represented the heaviest load and afforded the most complete test of the four runs. In the case of all four trains the normal sectional running times were adhered to, and these were practically kept in each case.

'As regards the handling of the engine, the regulator was fully opened when working on the up gradients, being reduced in amount on the falling grades. The water level in the boiler was, in general, well maintained on each run. Except on the occasion when the engine was assisted, the front damper was mainly employed for the supply of air, being kept about half open. On trip No 4 I had the back damper used in conjunction with the front portion of the run. The attached tables will indicate the condition as regards boiler pressure and position of the valve gear, which were observed. It will be seen that on no occasion was the full boiler pressure maintained.

'The pressures observed on the lightly loaded trains Nos 1 and 2 are in general higher than the others, as the operation

of the injector is not quite so continuous as is the case of the heavy trains. Actually the most consistent steaming was that on the down train No 4, as although the engine was running considerably below boiler pressure yet the pressure was maintained against the action of the injector at this point.

'When the engine was being operated with a cut-off of 15% the effect of the engine exhaust on the fire was insufficient. The quantity of smokebox ash on trains 1 and 2 on arrival at London was relatively small, and the amount accumulated at the end of the return run of Nos 3 and 4 was not excessive, having regard to the train. I am carrying on with the investigation of the steaming of these engines.'

Over the next few weeks, the tests continued and some minor modifications were made to the engine and method of firing. The horizontal deflector was detached from the smokebox and then refitted for later trials, a build-up of sediment was removed from the exhaust steam injector, a modified blast pipe fitted to the smokebox, 'the front damper was used for the supply of air to the underside of the grate, being open from 1/3 to ½ throughout' and so on. Despite these changes Tom was unable to report any improvement, in the summary of his final assessment:

'The steaming of the engine on the two runs (21st December with loads of 310 and 384 tons respectively) was not

The Black Fives begin to dominate and become an everyday presence across the whole LMS network.

satisfactory at any point. There was no defect in the engine except that there was a rather considerable steam leakage from the lubricator connections to the piston valve liner of the inside cylinder. This leakage, while being a source of loss, could not, I think, account for the poor steaming of the engine, and I formed the impression from my trips on the 19th December as well as on the above trips, that the smokebox conditions were less satisfactory in effect than the conditions which I had previously observed and given in my Reports B and C.'

By January 1935, the first batch of new Black Fives had arrived from

Vulcan Foundry and were well established in service. By May they would be joined by twenty built at Crewe. They didn't suffer from the very poor steaming qualities that afflicted the Jubilees, but, equally, they could still be improved and so were swept up in the superheating debate. It was estimated that the Jubilees used 20 per cent more coal than the Patriot and Royal Scot classes. By comparison, the Black Fives appeared to hold up well in comparative trials held in September 1934. Until, that is, the figures were deemed to have been affected by erroneous readings recorded in the dynamometer car. So the exercise was repeated a month later, and again in October, and the new Class 5 was found to

consume more coal and water than expected, though far less than the Jubilees.

Armed with this information, plus Tom's assessments of the Jubilees' steaming qualities, the debate turned to improving the superheating qualities of both classes. Approval to upgrade the type 3A boilers on the Jubilees and 3Bs on the Black Fives, by increasing the elements from fourteen to twenty-one, was given by Stanier. The design task was allocated to each originating Drawing Office, rather than just one, and this led to slightly different solutions being adopted. Whilst Derby installed 1⅛in elements and 2½in tubes, Tom concluded that 1¼in elements and 2in tubes would be better – fitting 138 tubes into the barrel, rather than the 160 originally installed. In the original 3Bs, superheater elements were fitted in two rows, but the revised system placed them in three. By April 1935, five engines had been fitted with these boilers allowing comparative trials to take place between the 16th and the 25th of that month using engines 5067 and 5079. Report number 55, which was published on 31 May, was unequivocal in its findings:

'From Table 9 a clear reduction in coal and water consumption is shown by the 3 Row Element in Engine 5079 when compared with the 2 Row Engine 5067. On the combined average of the passenger and freight workings, the reduction amounted to 18.6% in coal and 20.6% in water per drawbar horsepower hour. It will be noted that the results are consistent if the

Black Five 5434, built by Armstrong Whitworth, living up to its reputation of being a 'maid of all work`.

passenger and freight workings are considered separately.'

Even if maintenance costs were thought to be greater when using a higher level of superheat, the savings on coal and water would, it's assumed, outweigh this concern. So the methodical testing of the Princess Class, then the Jubilees and now the Black Fives had slowly revealed the benefits of changes to Stanier's original concept. And this is an approach that underscored all of Tom's work – methodically collect data, a measured scientific analysis unsullied by pre-conceived views or beliefs, a consideration of

all options, suggest improvements where necessary and justify with facts, then test and re-test until a theory is proven. He was, in truth, a scientist, as was Stanier, and he was a man with tremendous drive and stamina, whose spreading influence was soon to be recognised.

There is no doubt that Herbert Chambers had had to shoulder a terrible burden as Chief Draughtsman and Technical Advisor to Stanier. Although a tremendous support to his CME, he probably wasn't his natural ally. His role was to turn outline proposals into reality and advise his leader accordingly. It is clear that he felt passionately

about many issues and tried to draw the CME along particular routes. So there were differences and this led to disagreements. But it says much for Chambers that he still managed to deliver a huge locomotive programme for Stanier, a task that might have defeated many other men. However, in the early months of 1935 the cracks were becoming only too obvious. It may have been that Chambers was exhausted by the herculean task that had devolved upon him, was made edgier because of it and was now exhausted. And so it seems likely that concerns for his health and wellbeing led Stanier to 'move him on' and

Crewe Drawing Office.

over the changes about to be made. When I spoke to the CME, in due course, I found that he had strongly supported my promotion. He continued to support me until his death.

'Although much had been done and most Stanier designs were well advanced, many problems abounded and a whole host of challenges still existed. So it was unlikely that the pace would slacken in the foreseeable future.

'The Drawing Office at Derby were less enthusiastic about my arrival, having become set in their ways for too long.'

Tom's brief expanded considerably with promotion to Chief Draughtsman. It had, under Chambers, been extended to cover carriages and wagons as well as locomotives, so was in a pivotal position for all the changes Stamp, Hartley, Stanier, Lemon and Urie could conceive. And he had tasted, from the side lines, the problems this could create, as recounted by Eric Langridge when debates about the Jubilee Class surfaced:

'Apart from the rumours and the long face of Chambers, the first sign of trouble the draughtsmen saw were hurried requests for tube comparisons between the parallel and taper boilers … It seems all and sundry, including Coleman, were asked 'what shall we do?' … Rumour had it that there was a high level inquiry at which Urie, besides complaining about the bad steaming, cited all the vast number of things that had to

appoint someone newer and fresher to the post. If this is the case, Chambers' death two years later, at the early age of 52, suggests that Stanier's concerns were well founded.

In reality, Chambers would be 'moved upstairs' to take on a more direct role at Euston in supporting Stanier as his Technical Assistant there. Meanwhile Tom would replace him at Derby on 18 March 1935 and later recalled his thoughts when this happened:

'Herbert Chambers was a man of the greatest skill and determination. He didn't get the credit he deserved when at Derby and most forgot

that he was there during the big standardisation and construction programme. He may have had a Midland bias, but he always kept a fairly open mind and was prepared to consider other options, though not always accept them. He became a good friend and took pains to ensure I received support when at Horwich, Crewe, then Derby. He was a kindly and polite man who had a strong sense of duty which he expected those around him to emulate. Before Sir William let it be known that I would be moving to Derby, Herbert came to see me and talked

Crewe Works.

be maintained: top feed trays to be withdrawn, feed pipes under fiddling cases, smokebox jumper, baffle plates, ashpan damper, etc. Some said that Stanier contemplated throwing his hand in; I doubt if we shall ever know the truth of that, but obviously he was a very shaken man. Chambers was even more so, for he had been caught between both sides … No doubt if there had been a strong reliable lead anywhere things would soon have settled, but Stanier's forces were scattered. He was away up at Euston with a small staff and inspectors.

An unfriendly Motive Power Department was across the road. Chambers could hardly see his point of view. Coleman seemed more understanding … but the situation looked grim.'

Such was the state of affairs when he took office and revealingly Langridge succinctly summed up why he thought Tom would make a good replacement for Chambers:

'Coleman was more inclined to rely on flair and experience, and was thus in some ways closer to Stanier's outlook … Having played League Football in his

younger days and more used to shop floor methods, would have done a bit of gate crashing.'

Before taking up his new appointment, Tom had been tackling two other projects, in addition to the Black Fives and helping Chambers sort out the Jubilee's firing problems. The first of these would prove to be one of the most successful designs on which he worked – in numbers as well as effectiveness in peace and war. Whilst the second began when the joint LMS and Superheater Company's high pressure locomotive experiment, built in 1929 and named *Fury*, came to an end and offered the potential for research and rebuilding. Each project, in their own way, revealed aspects of Tom's methods as a designer.

In Stanier's 1933 locomotive programme, a requirement to build five new 2-8-0 engines had been identified, but the plan was modified and construction was deferred until 1935, when twelve were authorised. This development probably reflected Stanier's experience of 2-8-0s on the GWR, but it was also a type that had found favour during the First World War when the Ministry of Munitions purchased 521, 273 of which were subsequently bought by the LNWR in the early 1920s.

Gresley on the Great Northern had also experimented with the design, as had the Great Central Railway. One of the LMS's constituent companies, the Somerset and Dorset Joint Railway, had also constructed eleven engines, in two batches – the first in 1914, the second eleven years later, when Fowler was CME. So experience of the type was well established, but now it would be developed by Tom Coleman and his team at Crewe, with an ever more powerful 8F classification.

If importance is judged by the items collected by an individual during their lifetime, then this class of locomotive was of

great worth to Tom. During construction, and later in service, he paid particular attention to all aspects of their performance and preserved documents, drawings and photographs in great quantity. It seems that all he espoused as a designer came together in these unglamorous freight engines. But why should this be? They were not his first or even his most significant project; a right surely claimed by the magnificent Coronation Class. 852 were built to various specifications, across various workshops and contractors, but quantity, whilst denoting success, does not explain his fascination with the type. Sadly, he didn't record his thoughts on the subject, beyond some very broad comments, or leave any other sign, so all is conjecture except for an assumption drawn from the quantity of the papers he collected and left behind him:

'My first involvement with the 8F came in 1933 when still at Horwich. We did some preparatory work, but put it to one side giving priority to the Class 5 and so the requirement to build five was deferred. Urie was troubled by this decision and urged that work should go ahead as soon as possible. He was concerned that there was a lack of good, reliable freight engines as traffic requirements began to pick up. The idea was that the two designs would share many common features – the boiler, three cylinders, Walschaerts valve gear and so on.

'Both projects moved with me to Crewe. Little did we know at

Crewe Erecting Shop. A photo from Tom's collection that captures the many elements of loco production and maintenance that fascinated him.

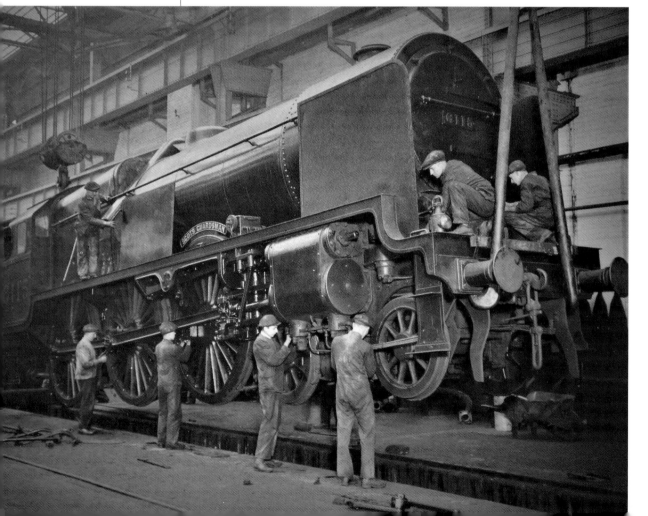

the time that so many of each would be built. It surprised me that work on the 8F carried on until the post-war years and I supported construction by the LNER, the Southern Railway, the GWR and contractors, some of them on behalf of the War Department.'

Although initially not given the priority attached to Stanier's other locomotives, it was a class eagerly anticipated by the company's Traffic Department as committee meeting minutes from July 1932 bear witness:

'As a result of experience gained with the No 7 0-8-0 standard freight tender engine, it is considered that material advantage in reliability and haulage capacity would be obtained by the introduction of a standard locomotive of the 2-8-0 type instead of the present 0-8-0 and with this object in view, only fifteen of the twenty 0-8-0s authorised in the 1932 programme will be built, the remaining five to be included as 2-8-0s in the 1933 programme.'

The delay was, it seems, simply a matter of design capacity, but the 1934 programme did include a requirement for two 2-8-0s, down from the five expected and these to be regarded as experimental, in the same way as the first two Princess Royals. As things turned out these two were combined with ten more added in the 1935 construction programme. Undoubtedly, the problems being experienced with the Princess Royals and Jubilees

played a part in these production delays, but it did give Tom a chance to consider the proposal in slower time. It also allowed him to take the broad outline prepared by Stanier's Euston team, which resembled the GWR's Class 28XX 2-8-0s, and turn it into something with a very distinctive LMS look and design.

Initially, both the 8F and mixed traffic Class 5 were to have three cylinders, but it quickly became apparent that this would increase their weight considerably and so restrict their route availability, so both were built with two cylinders. Boiler compatibility was also an aim with both classes

receiving type 3B units. But Tom discovered that the weight distribution over each wheel configuration required different solutions. On the 8F this meant moving the firebox forward and to accommodate this change the boiler barrel had to be shortened by a foot. The modified 8F boiler was designated the type 3C. From the outset, these units were fitted with twenty-one element, three row superheaters, so benefitting from Tom's work in trying to correct the steaming problems of other new classes.

Construction commenced in June 1935, shortly after Tom transferred to Derby, and by

The second batch of Princess Royals make their appearance under Tom's guiding hand and with greater superheat.

October that year the first twelve locomotives were in service. It was a very small beginning for a project that would continue to expand exponentially and absorb the new Chief Draughtsman for the next ten years. So it is small wonder that his collection of papers should contain so many items and reflect the extent of the effort he expended in making the class such a success.

When it came to *Fury*, by 1934 a project largely disowned and discredited by the powers that be, Tom and his team had a discarded toy to play with. And

they proceeded to take the Royal Scot based locomotive and give it a new lease of life, and in doing so highlighted how Fowler's Scots and Patriots might also be improved. In fact, Tom had been interested in this experimental locomotive from its design stage. He was intrigued by innovation and took the opportunity to study the engine at close quarters, taking photographs and acquiring a number of drawings from Derby and the Superheater Company in the process:

'With Sir Henry's agreement I was able to see for myself how

the engine was progressing when under construction and rode on the footplate on two occasions, neither particularly successful. It did seem to me to be an idea with limited potential and unlikely to improve on anything we had. Gresley was trying something similar with a 4-6-4 compound locomotive, with a high pressure water tube boiler. In both cases the work didn't result in any more production and both gradually slipped out of service, even though the CME allowed trials to continue

6202 Turbomotive begins her long period of testing. Tom took a particular interest in this experimental engine for the remainder of her career.

into the early part of 1934. "*Fury*" was kept in store at Derby pending a decision to scrap or rebuild and I believe approval for conversion was given in July of that year by the Locomotive and Electrical Engineering Committee, after the CME had spent a month considering our plans.

'The CME believed that the Royal Scots were capable of improvement and wanted to see them rebuilt. With 'Fury' likely to be scrapped it seemed an ideal opportunity to strip away all the experimental apparatus and see what was possible.

'In my last few months at Crewe we progressed this work and in March 1935 the engine entered the works for conversion to take place.'

Tom was correct in his recollection that the go ahead for *Fury* had been given in July as the minutes of that committee confirm:

'It was therefore recommended that the engine be converted to a "Royal Scot" type, the alterations including provision of a new boiler of the taper barrel type, which it is proposed to fit to the "Royal Scot" class as a whole, as and when present boilers fall due for renewal.'

'As and when' would take some years to come to fruition and *Fury* would be converted many years in advance of the rest of the class. But for the moment, Tom had pressed ahead with redesign, apparently autonomously, if Eric Langridge is correct:

'The next scoop for Coleman was the rebuilding of *Fury* with

The 8F makes its appearance. A work horse, maybe, but a thoroughbred nonetheless. Arguably Tom Coleman's greatest achievement.

a new design of inside and outside cylinders, and a new design of taper boiler. The boiler, done by Nicholson, one of Coleman's importees, more nearly resembled a Swindon product than any so far designed by LMS men, perhaps to show Stanier how co-operative Crewe Drawing Office were; the cylinders were more original in design and were done by Willcocks, a clever Horwich-trained man. As originally turned out, the steam pipe casings outside the smokebox sloped backwards, and as the smokebox front was so far forward, the effect of the boiler having overshot the frame was created … Derby Locomotive Drawing Office knew nothing of this job until it appeared; Chambers could hardly have been consulted about the details.'

It does seem as if Tom initiated this work himself, aware that Stanier had such a project in mind, and developed it to a point where he could present his findings to the CME for approval. If so, it demonstrates the level of trust Stanier had in his management and design skills and suggests that the two men had developed a very deep understanding of each other. With so many problems to be negotiated and a hostile Operating Department, guided by Urie's uncompromising hands, it is little wonder that Stanier valued and trusted Tom so much. Now, as Chief Draughtsman, he could support his CME more directly and guide locomotive construction more effectively, correcting many mistakes and taking design to a higher, unforgettable level.

The Black Five programme saw nearly 500 in service by 1938.

Chapter 5

COLEMAN'S CORONATION

At 50, Tom had reached the pinnacle of his career and occupied a position of enormous responsibility and potential. It takes someone of great talent, political acumen, prescient insight, a mind open to new possibilities, the sharpest analytical skills and an ability to lead often conflicting groups to succeed when so much is riding on their performance. Tom was just such a person and was ideally suited to the challenging tasks before him. The young man who had so ably led on the sporting field, then translated these leadership skills to the engineering world, now had the opportunity to demonstrate his prowess in the most dynamic of worlds. He would not be found wanting.

But the tasks that awaited him would have been daunting to even the strongest person. Planning for ten more Princess Royals was advancing and construction was programmed for completion by the end of October 1935. Their two reciprocating sisters still required modification and the third, Turbomotive, was nearing completion and faced a testing future, watched carefully by the LMS Board eager to see a return on their investment. And Stanier was looking to extend the class still further as the earlier locomotives gradually proved themselves and the demand for their services grew. The Jubilees were still creating their own problems, and were still in production, the Royal Scots were demonstrating design weaknesses that had to be corrected. To this end *Fury*'s conversion at Crewe would play an active part. And then there were the other new build programmes still in their infancy – the Black Fives, the 8Fs, the 3P 2-6-2T and 4P 2-6-4T tank engines. In addition to this were the many tasks being undertaken in the carriage and wagon works over which Tom now had domain. Chambers had done much to progress all these tasks and many more, but a huge bank of work still remained, much of it of the highest priority.

To help achieve this, Tom had a substantial team under his control and the ability to recruit more if necessary. But first, he had to absorb a group at Derby long used to different practices. There were some who were likely to resist his overtures, especially as they may have felt that he had set up a rival organisation at Crewe, which had undermined their position. Eric Langridge was probably not alone in finding Tom's promotion difficult to accept. His later comments were peppered with such enunciations as 'Coleman [was] disinclined to have anything to do with Derby', he 'was offered the post [as Chambers' deputy at Derby], but declined…' and 'Chambers could hardly have been consulted [by Coleman] about the details', all of which suggests a degree of antipathy.

Tom would also have to deal more closely with the company's Research and Development

Tom becomes the company's Chief Loco and Carriage Draughtsman, based at Derby.

Department, based at Derby, which also came under Harold Hartley's control. Chambers did not always have the closest relationships with this group, seeing it as competition not collaborators. Thomas Herbert, its Cambridge University educated, Euston based head, enjoyed a close friendship with Chambers, having worked with him at Derby in the early 1920s, but this did little to bridge the gap that existed between the two teams. This was a problem made public, in a diplomatic way, several times by Hartley before Tom took over and it is likely that the message was repeated in the weeks that followed.

The LMS's famous clock tower and offices still stand and have a new life as part of Derby College. Here Tom worked from 1935 until 1949.

And Stanier and Tom Coleman tackled another issue that had begun to tax them both – the relationship between the draughtsmen and the workshops. They had both become concerned about an information gap which meant that drawing office staff at Derby often had insufficient knowledge of manufacturing techniques and processes. The CME's Conference in February 1936 reported the progress made on this initiative:

'Arrangements had now been made for Draughtsmen to go round the Works and this had resulted in a better understanding between those responsible for the designs and those actually carrying out the work.

'As an instance of the progress which had been made, such details as bogie centres, pony truck centres, etc, which in the past it was considered necessary should be steel castings, were by now being fabricated with very satisfactory results.'

Tom had always managed to establish good working relationships with all Departments at Stoke, Horwich and Crewe. Experience had taught him how beneficial this could be, but particularly at Crewe where he and Fred Lemon enjoyed the closest rapport. This undoubtedly smoothed the passage of work there, especially when under the extreme pressure exerted by the LMS's ambitious locomotive programme. It seems strange that Derby had cultivated a more

remote arrangement, but it wasn't unknown in large industries where a divide can easily grow up between white and blue collar workers. And now a simple, but effective measure had been adopted at Derby. A new broom may not be always be welcome yet it may see something familiarity has hidden or disguised.

A number of other staff changes took place when Tom took office, as Langridge recalled:

'Nicholson moved up to be chief draughtsman, Crewe locomotive drawing office. Sanford remained chief draughtsman, Loco, Derby. One or two men came too; Barraclough who, from his attitude, soon expected to become leading hand. However, although Jock Henderson now lost his authority, a complete outsider appeared on the scene to take the post of leading hand. Durnford was the new man; he had apparently lost his job in the Argentine and had come home. Stanier took compassion on him for reasons we do not know but could guess. Armin, who had been Jock's No 1, nominally at least, was naturally disappointed.'

Dudley Sanford, who remained in post at Derby supporting Tom, was a product of Cambridge University, where he gained a BA(Hons) in Mechanical Services, before becoming a pupil in the Midlands Locomotive Department at Derby in 1912. He then saw service with the Royal Engineers for five years before returning to the Midland to complete his professional training

The Loco Drawing Office at Derby.

as a draughtsman. For some years, he was involved in experimental work and in 1927 was promoted by Fowler to be his Senior Technical Draughtsman, then to Chief Locomotive Draughtsman at Derby, by Stanier, in 1934. Roland Bond, in his book *A Lifetime with Locomotives*, recalled that Sanford:

'Had a truly scientific, yet intensely practical, approach to all engineering problems. He was an accomplished mathematician, and had the unusual facility for making mathematics understandable to others less gifted than himself.'

Eric Langridge added a little more to this brief description:

'When a meeting included Dr Andrews with his light voice and Tony Benn with a like delivery and Sanford with his deep bass, one could be sure of some good humoured repartee. Sanford must have had one of the finest brains in the business at the time. He had a very practical outlook, however, and the gift – not common amongst test engineers – of explaining in clear terms complicated processes for the benefit of lesser mortals … He devised the injector-controlled continuous blowdown valve, also the guides that were lowered in front of the tender water pick-up scoop. He used physicists' results to compile his boiler tube resistance theory and A/S ratios and so compiled a list of possible comparative superheat ratios and temperatures … He was a modest, likeable character.'

Sanford's skills in the test and evaluation area were well established by this time, less so his locomotive design credentials. But with other draughtsmen

Tom Herbert, Head of the LMS's Research Department.

The LMS's great and good gather at Horwich in 1936 to celebrate George Shawcross' retirement- Stanier,Riddles, Coleman, Fred Lemon,Ivatt and Chambers amongst them.

well advanced in this field, Sanford's analytical evaluations of performance provided an essential balance to the team.

Whilst the new regime was settling down, Ernest Cox, who had transferred from Euston to Derby, as Assistant Works Superintendent, was slowly moving into Coleman's sphere of activity. This relationship clearly helped build up a stronger partnership between the two groups. With a design background and having been an assistant to Stanier during the development phase of his locomotive programme, this is not surprising. A year later, and at Tom's request, Stanier decided to move Cox into the Chief Draughtsman's area of responsibility:

'I was again summoned into Stanier's presence and in a minimum of words, and without commentary on my past performance, was commanded to transfer forthwith to the Derby Drawing Office where as Development Assistant I was to set up a new section for forward thinking on design matters ... I can only say thank goodness the change was made, for my true flair and happiness has always lain with Design.

'I now passed under the control of T.F. Coleman ... his blunt and craggy manner made short work of the remaining independence of Derby, Crewe

and Horwich, and thenceforth design knew its master, who wielded undisputed sway in the former temples of disharmony.'

Cox neatly summed up the effect the Chief Draughtsman had on locomotive design when considering his work on the Black Fives and 8Fs:

'At Crewe, Coleman, to whom the production design was entrusted, at once imposed his own individuality upon the projects and re-assembled them in a manner which produced much more balanced designs, adjusting the boiler heights and bringing the centre of gravity forward. These two designs were notable in another facet in that both went straight into traffic without teething problems or initial modifications. The mixed traffic engine, in particular, was so good in basic conception, that it proved worthy of steady development over the next 15 years.'

Cox greatly admired Coleman and in describing how the relationship between Stanier's HQ team and the Chief Draughtsman worked – one would initiate new designs and the other work them up into drawings – he hit upon the secret of Tom's success:

'With so powerful a personality in charge of the Drawing Office things were unlikely to remain as simple as that, and this juncture allows me to pay tribute to one of the

great locomotive designers of the steam age. Coleman had in his own field an inborn flair for effective and even brilliant engineering. Without anything much by way of academic achievement, and abhorring public speaking and all communal activities

such as Institution affairs, he nevertheless, by some hidden instinct, was able to hit the target of practical and effective design in nearly everything he undertook.

'He reached his greatest heights in partnership with Stanier who knew what he

As design work on the new Pacifics proceeded, hundreds of Black Fives were in service with many more to come. Here an Armstrong Whitworth loco streaks by.

Ernest Cox(L) and the Cambridge graduate Dudley Sanford(R) during the 1926 General Strike. Both men would rise to become leading lights in the LMS.

wanted but was not always able to visualise it in precise terms. Coleman was able to interpret an initial idea and exploit it in a highly individual manner, and Stanier's biggest successes all owed a great deal to Coleman.'

As an engineer of some standing himself, Cox's assessment carries great weight, but he was mistaken in a number of ways. He hints that Tom's design skills were intuitive, even mystical by nature and his academic background was too slight to support such advanced skills. And when saying that Tom simply interpreted Stanier's initiatives, which ultimately were often produced by Cox in his role as design assistant to the CME at Euston, he is being a little disingenuous. In truth Tom's training had, by the standards of the age, been of the highest quality, supplemented by eagerly attended external engineering courses. He was no amateur and his educational background was equal to, and may even have exceeded, many of his contemporaries, including Stanier and Cox. He also possessed very keen analytical skills and carefully studied all aspects of his trade, collected immense amounts of data which he absorbed and considered at length. To some he appeared to produce good ideas with apparent ease; this may be so, but like an iceberg much was hidden below the surface; ease of output should not be mistaken for ease of input. In reality, his approach was scientific and displayed an academic curiosity usually found in the great research centres around the world.

My father, who was a design engineer of some note, often saw individuals of exceptional ability limited in their development by the constraints of their own areas of expertise. By the time Stanier and Coleman were in their working prime, steam locomotive design had virtually reached its limit; most possibilities were exhausted just waiting for a new form of motive power to take over. Tom was possibly constrained in the way my father described and his prodigious efforts to expand and improve his creations may have been a sign of this happening. We shall never know, but a suspicion remains that wherever he may have gone he would have excelled, pushing back the limits of what was possible. In this he was similar to Reginald Mitchell, who was lucky enough to work in a field of infinite, unexplored possibilities, only to be constrained by illness and an early death.

Cox, and several others, commented on Tom's 'artistic eye' and here we do enter the realms of something that might be intuitive or even mystical in its nature. But is it simply a question of beauty being in the eye of the beholder or something deeper to perceive in the nature of aesthetics and engineering? It is probably true to say that steam locomotives have a naturally appealing shape and function. They impress immediately, leaving an indelible mark in the mind of the beholder, even those uninterested in railways. And perhaps it is a mixture of looks, power and nostalgia that is the key to this question? Whatever the answer each locomotive he and Stanier produced had a grace of line that is hard to define and even harder to understand. One wonders if they were simply delivering an engineering response to a series of design questions and this dictated shape – function over form and not vice versa. Whatever the reason, or the cause, their locomotives were some of the most eye catching ever built and, as some hard-bitten engineers often assert, they 'looked right'.

Even though Tom did not join either of the two professional institutions open to mechanical engineers, as most of his contemporaries did, he was not ignorant of the research each recorded. He kept many papers that they produced and he avidly consumed them as well as the contents of many science books and periodicals. To this he added specific trade journals, such as the *Gazette*, the *Engineer* and the *Locomotive*, and items produced by manufacturers, including Metropolitan Vickers, Brush, Ljungstroms and many more. Whenever possible he also sought out other specialists to discuss their work and how this might impact on his own research. Henry Guy of Metrovick, who, with Stanier, created Turbomotive, became just one of these regular points of contact. And this he supplemented by developing a close relationship with Thomas Herbert and one of his deputies, Frederick Johansen, in the LMS's own Research Department. Over the next few years these contacts would play an important role in the package of work set by Stanier and the Board.

Now in its third year, the scrap and build programme was at its peak. Seventeen new engines appeared in 1933, then 164 in '34 and 358 in '35. From this high point, numbers slowly declined until 1939, but in the four years before war came, 635 more locomotives rolled off the production line. So, in total, Tom would oversee the design needs of nearly a thousand engines whilst at Derby, but gave no indication of being daunted by this huge task:

'I had a good team around me and support from Sir William who probably absorbed much criticism of the locomotives and the rate of construction. Once we had sorted out the superheater question, through trials and modifications, many of the problems eased, so we could concentrate on other designs. The turbine engine made its appearance shortly after my arrival at Derby and its construction proved something of a distraction. It was an interesting idea and worth developing, but it consumed a lot of Drawing Office and Workshop time that could have been better spent on other work. Although only a small number of Princess Royals were being built at this stage, they were given high priority. During their construction Hartley, Lemon and Stanier constantly monitored progress and it was a great relief when they were completed and turned over to Urie to play with. They were good engines, but with faults that needed correcting. In due course, we redesigned them.'

Tom placed great emphasis on locomotive testing and over the next four years sponsored 29 full trials, some of which

Frederick Johansen, left, gets to grips with Gresley's W1 'Hush Hush' in the NPL's Teddington Wind Tunnel.

The wind tunnel built at Derby. Simple in concept, but greatly increased the understanding of aerodynamics. Frederick Johansen can be seen in the background.

he participated in, riding on the footplate or in the dynamometer car. At no stage in his career did he lose the habit of data collection and kept his own notes of the trials taking place. The range and depth of these exercises were intriguing. Most set out to establish the benefits of new engines over old or ways of enhancing the performance of those early Stanier designs produced by Chambers at Derby. During 1935 alone, taper and parallel boilered locomotives were compared twice, different levels of superheater elements were assessed four times, a Princess was run against a Royal Scot and a Black Five underwent test running against a Jubilee, both of which had been modified with twenty-one superheater elements spread over three rows. 1936 saw more of the same. Turbomotive was added to the programme, being compared to a standard

Tom's sketch of a locomotive with a Huet streamlined front end.

reciprocating Princess, plus a Class 7F 0-8-0, running with flangeless and standard tyres on intermediate driving wheels. Only the coming of war would curtail these activities, but even then, Tom undertook a series of informal trials when able to do so.

From the first, Tom focussed on the Pacifics being designed and built at Crewe. He was under pressure to do so, but, it seems, he was naturally attracted to these engines anyway. With work on other classes well underway, or awaiting test results to suggest another way forward, he could quite justifiably take a more active interest in the Princess programme and how it might be developed.

In 1934 and '35 he took the opportunity to travel behind LNER Pacifics on several occasions. From Robert Thom, Gresley's assistant at Doncaster, he received details of

these engines and was made aware that their new A4 was on the stocks. When the first four locomotives appeared in late 1935 he visited Kings Cross to see them in action, as he recalled later:

'They were remarkable engines and through Robert Thom, who had become a friend of Fred Lemon and myself, I was able to view them at close quarters. In this I was greatly encouraged by Frederick Johansen, who had played a part in their design.

'They were basically of traditional design, but engineered to their limits. There was no doubting that they were fine, good looking locomotives. Their streamlining was a novelty, but had grown from work undertaken at the National Physical Laboratory by Johansen on other Gresley designs and Fowler's Royal Scots. It gave the A4s a unique look, though the valances over the cylinders and driving wheels were cumbersome and too square in shape to my mind. I believe they were removed in the war to make maintenance easier. Johansen thought this reduced the aerodynamic airflow around the engine making them less efficient at speed.

'I had one footplate ride on *Silver Fox* early in 1936 and, about the same time, two journeys on the new Silver Jubilee sets, keeping notes on the newly designed locomotives and carriages which made up this service. I also took a number of photos with my Leica II camera. I don't think the

Two more rough sketches by Tom showing how the Huet concept might be adapted to the Coronation Class. The upper picture is slightly reminiscent of Virgin's West Coast Pendolino design.

A4 affected our designs in any way, except that streamlining was considered for a time. Some thought it was a passing fancy driven by publicity departments, but it was more than that. There were benefits to be gained from external, as well as internal, streamlining, which were, to my mind, not fully developed.'

Johansen found himself in a unique position whilst a research scientist with the NPL at Teddington. As an early proponent and expert in aerodynamics, his research into the subject came to the attention of designers in many fields, including aviation and the railways. Some of his work was seminal in this field and led to him working alongside some of the leading designers of the age in Britain and overseas. He advised them on the effects of wind resistance. Amongst them he could list Reginald Mitchell, his deputy Joseph Smith and Sydney Camm of Hawkers, plus Gresley of course – and now the main thrust of his activities centred on the LMS.

Johansen was the only son of a part Swedish, part Dutch master mariner. Born in Goole, Yorkshire, in 1897, his family moved to Devon when he was five. At school he showed great promise, but his life was deeply affected by his father's death, at sea, in 1907. He and his widowed mother returned to her family home in Yorkshire shortly afterwards. Although left without an income, she did inherit a substantial amount from her late husband, so could support herself and her son in some comfort. She didn't re-marry and young Frederick finished his education at Kings School in Pontefract.

In 1918, he began a civil and mechanical engineering diploma at Kings College, London, completing this, and a BSc, by 1920. In this he gained 1st Class honours and would later study for an MSc and PhD. After a temporary appointment with Scott and Middleton, he joined the Yorkshire Electric Power Company and a year later became a graduate member of the Institution of Mechanical Engineers. As a rising star he came to the attention of Sir Thomas Stanton, Superintendent of Engineering at the National Physical Laboratory, who recruited him as a research scientist in the embryonic field of aeronautical engineering during 1922. Stanton, who was one of the first experts in the field of aerodynamics and the use of wind tunnels, had a profound effect on Johansen, who benefitted greatly from his tutelage and guidance.

In the years that followed, his knowledge of aviation science quickly grew and he became involved in a number of design projects for various companies, but also the RAF. Between 1927 and '31, he spent a considerable amount of time studying Reginald Mitchell's highly successful designs for the Schneider Trophy. Each type was tested in the NPL's wind tunnel and the shape was gradually refined to make them more aerodynamically effective, as well as correct problems with performance – eradicating 'flutter', improving the effectiveness of control surfaces at high speed, establishing stalling criteria and

so on. Through this he became intimately involved with Mitchell's design team and gained the trust, and friendship it seems, of the great man himself and his deputy, Joseph Smith, who, after Mitchell's death, would lead design work on every mark of Spitfire produced. The link with Johansen would last for many years.

It is interesting to note how the tests and assessments carried out by Johansen and others at Teddington allowed Mitchell to enhance the performance of their early high speed aircraft. The wing was lowered and the cockpit moved forward to improve line and visibility. The unbraced cantilever design of the S4 was replaced by streamline wire bracing between floats, fuselage and wings, which reduced drag and weight. Flat surfaced copper wing radiators were installed and the fuselage

and floats were greatly modified to allow the aircraft to cut through air resistance more cleanly. Propeller efficiency was also improved, partly by shape and partly by the installation of a higher geared engine. All this work was captured by Johansen in a series of drawings he kept and a number of wind tunnel models constructed, tested and photographed at Teddington.

On the advice of Professor Ernest Wilson, of Kings College, and William Duncan at the NPL, an aviation specialist with a particular interest in scale effects, Gresley cultivated the young scientist. He then began presenting Johansen with a series of projects involving the air resistance of locomotives and how the effects might be minimised. The first project concerned the external design of his 4-6-4 locomotive, with its high pressure water tubed boiler, followed by the P2 2-8-2 engines, in several forms, and finally the A4s. In each case he came up with attractive streamlining solutions that achieved good results during tests in NPL's Duplex supersonic wind tunnel. Form and function were seemingly in balance, though a true assessment of performance awaited more detailed analysis when the locomotives entered service.

As a scientist, Johansen knew only too well the benefits of publishing the results of his work in learned papers or in scientific books. By the mid-1930s, he had a solid bank of work to his credit. Amongst his achievements was a book entitled *The Basics of Aeronautics*, produced by the Royal Aeronautical Society, and items relating to such things as the effects of fluid motion, aerodynamics and

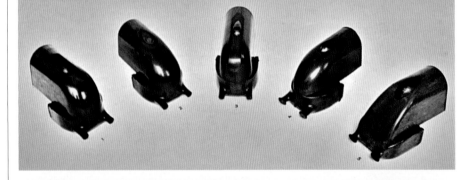

Possible front end designs developed as part of the Princess Coronation programme by Johansen and Coleman.

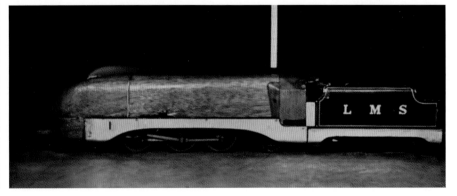

Many shapes were tried but Tom's solution was deemed the most effective.

Tom's view of the streamlined Coronations - colours and shape. The scheme seems to pay tribute to R.J. Mitchell who also died in 1937 and whose aircraft so impressed Tom.

Mitchell's classic seaplane design, with a shape and colour scheme reminiscent of the Coronations; hardly surprising with Tom and Frederick Johansen's input and connections.

the air resistance of trains. The last of these was presented to the Institution of Mechanical Engineers in 1936, though much of his research in this field dated back to the previous decade.

When Harold Hartley was recruited by the LMS in 1930, as a Vice President and Director of Research, he set up the Advisory Committee on Scientific Research. This group commissioned work, internally or externally, believed to be of great value to the LMS. Thomas Herbert became the committee's secretary, whilst Johansen undertook work for the company as an external consultant with the NPL. This arrangement carried on until 1932 when he was recruited by Hartley as an Engineering Research Officer, based part time at Euston and Teddington, where he could continue to make use of their

wind tunnel. In a most unusual move, he continued working as an advisor to the LNER, the LMS's main competitor, Supermarine and Hawkers. One wonders whether this might have been a condition negotiated by Johansen when his employment contract was under discussion. Either way, he would continue with his consultancy work for some years, even though there may have been a conflict of interest at times. However, Hartley was keen to build up an air service within the LMS and this might also explain why he wished to employ Johansen, the aviation specialist, then allow him to continue with this diverse workload.

In 1932, Hartley, with Stamp's approval, decided to develop his in-house scientific group still further and set up his own, much bigger, Research Department, with Herbert as its head. This new organisation

began work in January 1933 and, two years later, a new Physics group was added, containing individual engineering and metallurgy sections, with Johansen in charge. To this end, he was based part time in Derby and Euston, so still allowing him to gain ready access to the NPL's facilities. But, as things turned out, Hartley and Herbert kept him busy, allowing him less scope to undertake other work, though he did participate in the trials of Camm's Hurricane in 1934 and Mitchell's Spitfire. But to balance this reducing commitment to aviation a small concession was made. His proposal for a scaled down Duplex wind tunnel at Derby was approved in late 1935, and construction completed six months later.

With Johansen now in place, and a fully equipped laboratory available, some of the work he was doing

R. J. Mitchell in the mid-1930s at the height of his powers in a career that closely mirrored his fellow Kerr, Stuart apprentice.

for the LNER and others could be focussed on the LMS, with particular emphasis on locomotive design. It didn't take long for him to make his presence felt, sponsored in this by Hartley. Stanier's reaction to these developments is unrecorded, but years later the Vice President wrote:

'Although Stanier was not altogether happy in his relations with the Research Department, they did help him in various ways, particularly in the metallurgical problems associated with metal fatigue of tyres, axles and laminated springs and corrosion fatigue of boilers. Their studies of combustion led to improved firing, little and often as it was

called, that gave savings of from 5 to 10%. Cinematograph records showed the relationship of steady riding to the coning of tyres and also the coupled wheels to lift slightly from the rails at high rotational speeds. Measurement in a wind tunnel showed the saving in wind resistance given by streamlining at high speeds.'

As these words were written by Hartley following Stanier's death in 1965, they were probably toned down considerably for publication. If this is the case, they may well reflect a significant difference of opinion over the role of the scientific group in the 1930s. But it wasn't a view shared by Tom, as he described later:

'There was some hostility between the Drawing Office at Derby and the Research Department under Thomas Herbert. It was almost as if there was a clash of two professions, one gradually superseding the other as education improved. But there was a role for both and I for one took advantage of their scientific skills. They had a lot on their plate, though, and as their list of tasks increased so they could get less involved in locomotive and carriage design. I for one was glad to have them working alongside me and called upon their services on many occasions. Johansen became a close associate and friend, helped by our shared interests in engineering, aviation and photography. As he was still involved in work at the National Physical Laboratory, I went with him on

three occasions to Teddington, when we were planning the Coronations. This allowed me to view the Spitfire development work being carried out there and meet Mitchell again, then obviously very ill, as well as Joseph Smith who held a position very similar to myself at Supermarine.'

With Tom as Chief Draughtsman, commanding a more focussed design team, Herbert and Johansen leading in the Research Department, and Fred Lemon managing a modern and effective production line at Crewe, the LMS had achieved a level of dynamism that Hartley and Stanier could exploit if they wished to. And in the years that followed, this creative energy would drive many projects to completion and add a new one which would prove to be the company and Stanier's masterpiece.

With the appearance of the next ten Princess Royal locomotives in 1935, modified to absorb the lessons learnt from the first two engines, the LMS could continue developing its West Coast Main Line services more effectively. It was long overdue, but even now they barely scratched the surface of the LNER's lead in high performance, long distance locomotives, in number or type. But once the Princesses had proved themselves during 1936, Stanier could turn his mind to increasing their number still further. If Chambers had still been in charge at Derby, he would probably have added more of the same. But Tom was cut from a different cloth and, if allowed to, would use his undoubted talents to produce something truly exceptional.

The first Coronation slowly emerges at Crewe.

Locomotive building was a hard and exhausting business. Here re-heated metal for the flanged firebox is hammered into shape.

Sandham Symes, an engineer of note, who became the LMS's Chief Stores Supt and Stanier's stand in on occasions.

In some ways, he and Johansen were the product of different worlds. One from the realms of academia and research, the other from an equally skilled environment, but one developed closer to an industrial coal face. Despite this, they seem to have recognised each other's skills and developed an understanding of the way their two departments could work together. If Stanier found fault in this, perhaps sensing interference, he could trust such a strong leader as Tom to achieve a good working balance. As a man of few words, it seems likely that he gave his Chief Draughtsman little in the way of instructions in this matter, having confidence in his engineering and leadership skills and objectivity to get things completed successfully. Just as well, because Stanier was soon to depart the scene on two prolonged visits to India, with Sandham Symes substituting for him in 1936/37 and

Charles Fairburn during his second absence during 1938.

For many years it had been an ambition of Josiah Stamp and his Board to run high speed, long distance services equal to those working on the LNER's east coast route. A slow gestation and a number of false starts had made this seem a distant possibility. But the Princess Royals seemed to offer a chance of success, though their development had been painfully slow. As the end of 1936 approached, with twelve class members now available, it was decided to undertake a non-stop run from London to Glasgow and back the following day, to demonstrate that such a service was possible within a 6 to 6½ hour schedule.

To achieve this, some upgrading of track and lineside structures had taken place, though much more was needed. In addition, a number of other scheduled services had been altered to clear the path for the express, but the success of the trial was largely dependent on the capabilities of 6201 *Princess Elizabeth* and her crew. Despite a few hitches, which could have proved disastrous, the two runs were completed successfully and the engine's record breaking performance grabbed the headlines. But for Stanier and Coleman the long-term prospects of a regular service such as this, especially when a 400 ton plus load was added, needed more Pacifics, probably of greater strength and durability than the early Princesses, capable locomotives though they were.

Tom recalled that:

'During the latter part of 1935 I worked on improvements to the Princesses to try and eradicate a number of problems we had encountered and improve their performance. The position of the cylinders, the motion and the boiler being three concerns. We got out a plan that would have shortened the wheelbase, replaced the four separate sets of motion with inclined inside cylinders driven

A pair of connecting rods for the first batch of Coronations are 'fluted' in a milling machine.

A set of main driving wheels are lowered into its tyre.

by rocking levers from the outside valve gear and added a bigger boiler. But this work was overtaken by events, though the plans were kept updated just in case it was decided to modify the first 12 engines plus the turbine locomotive.

'At a meeting in my office at Derby in March '36, Sir William and I discussed what we should do next, with five more Pacifics due to be approved for 1937. We had some spare capacity in the Loco Drawing Offices, now that schemes for most new engines had been completed, and it seemed an ideal opportunity to take the Pacific development a step further forward. He wasn't convinced that some of my proposals were necessary or required, but he wanted to consider them at a later date.

'He was under pressure from Hartley to streamline all the Pacifics, but wasn't convinced of the benefits of doing so, though he kept an open mind on the subject. Consequently, he allowed me to begin work with Johansen and my Chief Draughtsmen, both Loco and Carriage, on designing an improved Princess and carriages to go with it. In the meantime, Johansen had been running wind tunnel tests on scale models of air smoothed Princess Royals and Turbomotive. These models were based on drawings we had prepared in 1935 to see what benefits might be gained from streamlining. As it turned out the work didn't get beyond the model stage, Stanier ostensibly asserting that we had so few in service that we didn't

have the capacity to release them for modification. But the test results weren't wasted and we took them into account when we looked at the next group of engines to be built.

'By this time our understanding of air resistance was improving and there seemed much to be gained if we persevered in building high speed trains capable of cutting through the air more cleanly … I believe some thought streamlining was just a publicity exercise, with little practical value. I didn't agree because the science was in a very early stage of development and so we still had much to learn and understand. With other forms of locomotion being developed it was likely that the idea might be better suited to them than steam engines … Personally

I liked the streamlined Princess Coronations.'

Lemon, at the Executive Committee meeting on 2 November 1936, when setting out his plans for the trials with 6201 later in the month, stated that:

'The train should be streamlined and be worked by an engine of the 'Princess' class, and, with a load of about 250 tons, substantial time savings should be secured over the rising gradients, thus avoiding uncomfortable speeds elsewhere.'

A week later he confirmed the arrangements for the tests and simply refers to a train 'drawn by a Princess Royal class engine and the weight limited to 202 tons'. One wonders whether he expected to

A Coronation's crank axled wheels being balanced.

see 6201 in streamlined form on the 16/17 November or was he simply describing his aspiration for a future service? Stanier and Lemon didn't always enjoy an easy relationship, particularly with the troublesome Urie at work, and one wonders whether the Vice President was given to believe that a streamliner would be available by then. If so, he would be disappointed.

So by the time the November trials had been completed, design of the next group of engines was well advanced. But the inclusion of the extra five locomotives in the 1937 building programme seem almost to have been an afterthought, if the minutes of the Mechanical and Electrical Committees are to be believed. They are covered in a postscript to the main item, which

authorised 100 new locomotives for that year. This late entry suggests that the requirement was far from clear, with others, perhaps, arguing that more Pacifics were unnecessary. In the absence of any written confirmation of this there is only conjecture, but it does seem to be a possibility.

If there is one characteristic that underpins the development of the Princesses from 1935 onwards, it is lack of transparency over what was happening at any stage. Usually with any process there is a clearly defined pathway, but this programme seemed to lack clarity or shape. Perhaps this was due to the many influences being brought to bear on the project, each demanding some addition – streamlining being an obvious example. Whatever

the reason, work on developing the class seemed to move forward in a seemingly unplanned, uncoordinated way. But behind all this apparent disorder, Tom's influence and jurisdiction were at work. He couldn't initiate new projects himself or commit funds without approval, so had to manage by stealth and guile if the ideas he thought most effective were ever to be developed. And behind all this was a CME of few words, who at times seemed loath to give anything but very broad instructions to his Chief Draughtsman, backed up by his small team at Euston whose outline plans were at best sketchy and open to re-interpretation. So by slow degrees, and some sleight of hand, Tom took the Princess Royals and gradually sublimated them into

Brass fittings being mounted on back head.

6220 emerges, her wheels and casing soon to be fitted.

the Princess Coronations. It was a process that Eric Langridge observed from the side lines, as recorded in a letter years later:

'All this time Gresley was forging ahead with the LNER 'Silver Jubilee' trains … all the LMS could do [in response] was to renumber a new 5X, as if it were the first of a new class, decorate it with 'silver' beadings, and call it *Silver Jubilee*. By the end of 1935 we only had thirteen 4-6-2s.

'Coleman asked Barraclough to see if he could get a larger boiler on the next lot of 4-6-2s [although at this stage they hadn't been ordered]. We started ordering up material and marking up drawings for what we expected was engines Nos 6213 to 6217. After the November tests with 6201, Coleman came out asking for a diagram of a 4-6-2 with 6' 9' wheels and as big a diameter boiler as we could get in the loading gauge.

'It was then that E402 was issued; Coleman and one of his senior men at Derby [though presumed to be Nicholson at Crewe] had been working for some time on various schemes for a "bigger and better design" than the Princess. You might well ask why? From a designer's point of view, I can only reply that that there is always an urge to improve. The true designer wants to be kept busy. Like any other artist they improve with practice. To achieve change, broadly the old requirements of having the right men in the right position at the right time apply.

'Apart from the detail troubles that could be put right fairly easily, to the discriminating eye the Princess design did not seem to be using material to best advantage. There were the four valve gears and the spread out wheelbase, while the boiler seemed to be a long drawn affair. From the technical press one could see what was happening elsewhere and felt that one could do as well, or better than others.

'In achievement little could be finer than the demonstration runs with No 6201 … Yet the thought that the design could be improved persisted and Coleman convinced the "powers that be" to do so … He asked me to get rid of the inside motion of the Princess design. Sanford with his quick brain at once pointed out that if we connected a rocker to an extended outside valve spindle, and drove the rear end of the inside one from the other end of the rocker, the effect of expansion of spindles would cancel out.

'I suppose my addiction to what had gone before made me think of Drummond's 4-cylinder 4-6-0s where he advanced from the staggered pitching of the outside and inside cylinders to his 4-cylinder in line arrangement and valve gear. By doing so he got rid of the racking forces which loosened cylinders and stretchers [a problem that afflicted the Princesses]. Also, the arrangement of the L&YR class 8 appealed to me as the thing where a rocking lever was driven by a short link having pin

joints, one to the outside valve spindle extension and one to the rocker. The Chief Draughtsman, from his earlier position at Horwich, was familiar with this arrangement, so I got out a scheme on these lines.

'Coleman seemed more keen on his big boiler than on the motion schemes, but said he would show them to Stanier; he did not think that Stanier would want to change the former cylinder layout. So I was agreeably surprised when on his return he said "He has gone for your layout, get on and cancel the material sheets, we are going to number these engines 6220-24". This was a few days before Stanier's departure for India. How nearly we went ahead with more Princess Royals is reflected by the fact that drawings were actually being marked up and material being ordered for engines 6213 to 6217, when the last minute effort by Coleman at Euston succeeded in getting the decision reversed, obtaining the agreement to the new cylinder and boiler layouts … Stanier had also said that five locomotives must be ready for the 1937 6½ hour London and Glasgow service. In this chancy way history is made.'

I think chance had very little to do with it. Tom had simply demonstrated some of his unique talents – to see the future clearly and guide his fellow workers to an effective solution. Better still, few realised that they had been managed this way, with some later claiming a bigger role in this process than the facts

The loco is lowered onto her leading truck.

Her streamlined casing slowly takes shape like a massive jigsaw puzzle.

justify. 'Success has many fathers, failure dies an orphan', seems an appropriate maxim. But with Stanier leaving on a five month visit to India, having issued his instructions, the door was left open for Tom to develop these ideas still further. And with streamlining on the menu and the Research Department fully involved at Derby with the Chief Draughtsman he was unlikely to get some 'back seat driving' by Hartley, Symes or any of Stanier's advisors at Euston.

Stanier's absence resulted from an invitation by the Indian Government to undertake an enquiry into the running of the State-owned railway which had just reported a £7.5 million annual deficit. He

and Sir Ralph Wedgewood were asked to recommend measures they thought would improve the railway's finances. With journey times to and from India and the audit, they were away from home from early November until the end of March 1937. But a second visit to India proved necessary, shortly after Stanier's return, when a serious accident on the East Indian Railway, in July, killed 119 and injured another 180. A judicial enquiry blamed the accident on the locomotive and recommended the appointment of an International Committee to consider all elements of the accident and recommend improvements. Stanier and Ernest Cox were selected as members, but their active involvement in India

didn't begin until the summer of 1938, ending in November when the report was finally drafted.

In demonstrating how little Hartley involved himself in the design work undertaken by Tom, in developing the Princess Coronations, it is revealing to read the section of the obituary he wrote for Stanier on the subject. Bearing in mind the significance of the class in railway history, his comments make these efforts seem almost paltry:

'Experience with the prototype Pacifics resulted in an improved design with increased superheat in the Princess class in 1935. Still further improvements in grate area and in superheat were made in the design of the Duchess class in which Stanier had streamlined all the steam

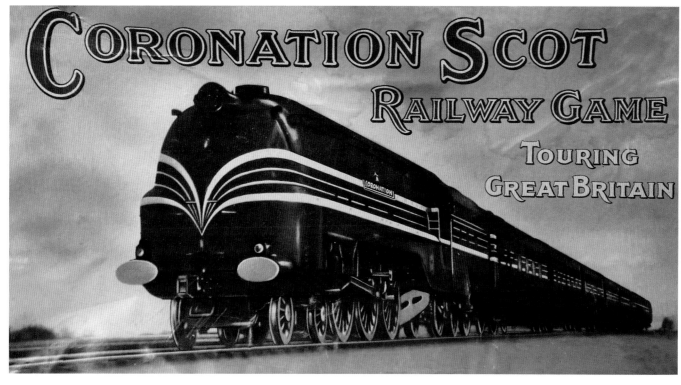

In advance of the new Coronation Class being introduced a game was rushed out to help gather publicity - here in its original 1937 box.

passages and increased the valve area to give a very free running engine of great power and steady riding thanks to Stanier's re-design of the front bogie.'

Such a muted narrative tells us much about Hartley and Stanier's relationship, and by association, his attitude towards his Chief Draughtsman and designer. The obituary is peppered with subdued praise, even academic snobbery, which suggests there may have been professional rivalry or professional jealousy. Hartley, though distinguished by his brilliant academic career, plus his work on developing poison gases for use in the First World War, must have realised that Stanier and Tom Coleman had achieved great advances in railway technology and design and created something of

great significance. He was a good leader and gave them opportunities to develop their ideas, but his involvement in their work seems to have been minimal. This may have been frustrating to a scientist of such great standing – creative people are, generally, happiest when creating and exploring. And he could do neither at this stage in his life. This may be an over simplification of course and does little justice to such an eminent scientist, but he is probably damned by his own words. But it is interesting to note that Hartley's name is now largely forgotten, whilst Stanier's is still widely revered. Meanwhile, Tom's contribution has been hidden from view because that is what he wanted, driven by an inborne wish for anonymity.

Throughout this period, work on developing a suitable air smooth

casing continued, with Johansen and Tom taking the lead. Having helped design the A4, Johansen may have been tempted to create a similar looking locomotive for the LMS, but this wasn't to be, although one model tested did bear a strong resemblance to the LNER locomotive. However, the shape that gradually evolved, and was tested in Derby's wind tunnel, seemed to bear the hallmarks of experimental work in the United States and Germany, which Johansen had visited to view developments there, encouraged by Hartley. But as clever people do, he looked more widely than the body shell itself and included such things as wheel discs, designed and built by the Scullin Steel Works of St Louis, in his research.

In late 1936, he also looked closely at a deflector system

Being painted and lined out and soon to be launched.

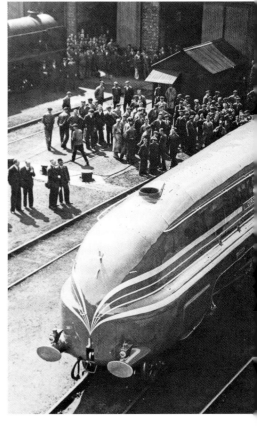

Roll out at Crewe attended by the staff who had built her. In a small group to the left Fred Lemon and Tom watch proceedings.

designed by Andre Huet and then corresponded with the inventor. He passed these details on to the Chief Draughtsman suggesting some models be built for testing purposes. But having committed the LMS to a specific streamlined shape for the new Pacifics already, Tom noted the request, but held back action until Stanier returned. By this time, Johansen had undertaken more research and developed a brief paper on the subject which he sent to the Chief Draughtsman. Discussion with Stanier followed and in late June Tom replied:

'I have been asked by Mr Stanier to get in touch with you so that I can let him know in due course whether there is any justification for carrying out tests on model locomotives and carriages with the Huet deflector plates. He also

requests an estimate of the cost of carrying out such tests.'

Johansen provided details but no further action appears to have been taken, though Tom did produce a rough sketch of the system applied to a French Pacific. He wrote later that 'the scheme had merit, would have been cheaper to fit and probably been as effective as the solution reached'. It is hard to say whether traditionalists would have accepted this wonderfully curved shape more readily than the system fitted, which some later referred to as an upturned bath, proving that beauty is in the eye of the beholder.

In deciding upon the shape of the streamlined casing, one of the main issues concerned the nose. There were a number of proposals, one of them designed by Tom. He also produced drawings showing a colour scheme for the engines – in

blue with white or silver stripes that curved around the nose to converge at a single point. He kept a copy of his hand-coloured proposals and was pleasantly surprised when his design and suggestions were accepted, after wind tunnel tests had been completed:

'The colour scheme was seen by Lemon and Hartley who raised no objections or suggested alternatives. When seeing Mitchell's S6 perform in the Schneider Trophy races of 1929 and '31, I was struck by its blue and silver colour scheme. He died about the time the first

Princess Coronations were being built and it seemed to be a small nod to his great work. Engines that came out later were painted red, which many preferred, but I thought blue to be better.'

In May 1939, the Research Department produced a paper summarising the results of streamlining trials with the Princess Royals and Coronations between 1935 and '37 in both forms – dressed and undressed. Why it took so long to be published is unclear, but it concluded that the most important reductions in air resistance were achieved by:

'Rounding the front end of the engine and making the external surface of the whole locomotive smooth, continuous and free from irregularities and projecting fittings.

'Shrouding the wheels and motion by side valances. It is noteworthy that, if the wheels are wholly or, as is the case in the Coronations, partly unshrouded, a considerable reduction of air resistance in side winds can be obtained by disc wheels instead of spoked wheels.

'Raking back the front of the cab at its junction with the boiler casing.

'Covering the tender to the general contour of the train and extending its roof and walls to the rear so as to enclose the gap between the tender and first coach. In this case the reduction associated mainly with the prevention of frontal pressure on the end of each coach.'

With Stanier working overseas for many months, and unavailable for consultation or to approve drawings, the design team had only a short period to complete their work and order materials, if the workshops at Crewe were to be given a sufficient time to complete construction and testing. And Tom didn't want to run the same risks that had attended the appearance of the first two Princesses in 1933, when they were pressed into service largely untried. Few in the know could forget 6200's left hand driving box catching fire on a press run to Crewe and back. Better to seek publicity with a known quantity than risk public embarrassment with an unnecessary gamble. Even the trial run to Glasgow and back in November 1936 had been fraught with problems and potential pitfalls. So a more measured approach was needed, with any effort to rush things through too quickly being carefully managed. Undoubtedly, there was pressure applied by Hartley and Lemon particularly, sponsored in part by the need to gather much needed publicity, but the dangers inherent in this were only too apparent.

Inevitably, drawings had to be passed by Tom to the workshops at Crewe in advance of Stanier's return. Any other course was impossible if the scheduled completion dates of June and early July 1937 were to be met. In this situation, retrospective approval of the final design by the CME was unavoidable. Stanier doesn't seem to have been overly concerned by this and appears to have added his signature without seeking any alterations. One suspects that he and Tom had such a close understanding

of each other that such a course of action contained few risks.

Roland Bond, Assistant Works Superintendent at Crewe, later recalled how smoothly the construction programme ran:

'It seemed from the drawings I saw on their way to the Shops, that there were not likely to be any unduly difficult production problems. The steel and copper throat plates were just about as large as the presses could accommodate, but we had already learned a lot about deep flanging when building

Publicity was essential to this unveiling and the engine received widespread attention in the press and ran to a cover shot on the LMS's in-house magazine.

the latest version of the Princess Royal boilers. Time was short and we were certainly going to be very busy in the Pattern Shop, Foundry and Millwrights, producing a complete set of new boiler flanging blocks, to say nothing of new cylinders, wheel centres and general iron and steel castings.

'Nothing was allowed to stand in the way of turning the new engines out to time. Late evening visits to the Shops to see how things were progressing on the night shift were part and parcel of our daily routine and sustained the drive to meet the promised dates. The engines went together beautifully in the Erecting Shop.'

But behind all this effort lay the guiding hand of Frederick Lemon, whose management of the workshops at Crewe was of the highest order. He and Tom had become good friends in 1933 and it was a relationship soon to be cemented by the marriage of Fred's son, George, to Tom's daughter, Marion. Undoubtedly, this bond played an important part in the development and construction of locomotives. With the Chief Draughtsman and the Works

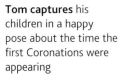

Tom captures his children in a happy pose about the time the first Coronations were appearing

A cartoon that clearly tickled Tom's sense of humour and which he kept amongst his papers. It's punchline reads – *'Don't touch Bertram, you might break something!'*

Superintendent so close, any other outcome would have been unlikely. It is also a link unexplored or analysed by their contemporaries who later wrote memoirs, or historians. Perhaps their strong sense of privacy and strong management styles kept the curious at bay. But for whatever reason the relationship flourished and must have smoothed the passage of work quite considerably and the Princess Coronations clearly benefitted from this.

Like Tom, Fred Lemon was a tough but astute and fair man with the keenest sense of the way the workshops should be run, as Roland Bond recalled:

'I knew my new chief, F.A. Lemon, both personally and by reputation. He had received me some five years earlier with kindness and an old world courtesy which was typical of him. He had a reputation for irascibility, caused no doubt by his deafness from which he suffered. He had a sharp tongue, and certainly did not mince his words in dressing down anyone who displeased him. More than once in the years ahead, senior foremen, less tough than some of their colleagues, were to come into my office, white faced, and shaking with fury or emotion, to receive comfort at my hands. Lemon never used a fountain pen. He signed his letters with an old fashioned, sharp pointed nib. There was a story, probably true, that one morning when he had been more than usually irked by someone's stupidity, Lemon stuck his nib through the paper he was signing. He threw the pen away in disgust, exclaiming to Richard Darroch, one of his assistants, a most gentle and cultured man, "Even the pens have gone to hell!"'

In June 1937, when the first engines rolled off the production line at Crewe, Stanier felt moved to write to Tom and Fred expressing his deep appreciation of the work they had undertaken. He wrote to the Works Superintendent:

'Dear Lemon
'I think that with the results of yesterday's trial, and with the results that we have obtained up to the present with the four engines which are now out of the works, that I should write to you of my appreciation of the work that has been done at Crewe under your direction in the construction of the locomotives.

'I have in my short time with the LMS made a great many demands on both the designers and the Works, but none have been so great as that which I have asked to be done in the building of the latest Coronation engines.

'The short time available for their building has meant, I know, long hours of work, not only for your men, but for you and your staff, and to the men and to you and your foremen. I am very grateful.

'The results that we have so far obtained prove that the workmanship has been of the very best, and I am sure that in no part of the world have any locomotives been turned out with a greater degree of accuracy in measurement.

'I should like you to convey to all those concerned on your staff, and to the men, my very great appreciation and thanks for what they have done, and for maintaining the prestige of our Department in this great railway.
Yours very sincerely
W.A. Stanier.'

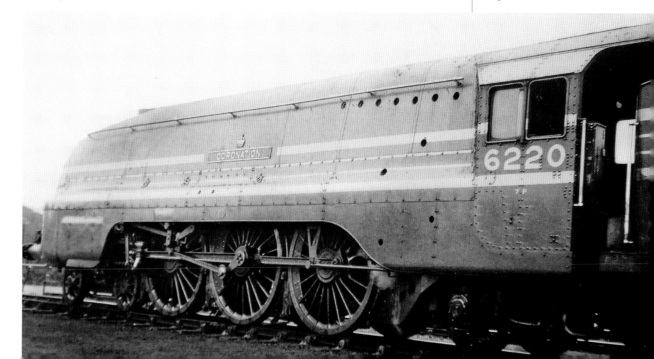

A study in balance and elegance.

The Coronations begin to ply their trade. 6222 passing through Tebay Troughs.

His sense of relief is almost palpable. Being out of commission in India at such a crucial time must have been difficult, but the team he had led so ably didn't fail him, and that, ultimately, is the measure of a good leader. Even when he was absent they worked effectively, shouldered responsibility and delivered a new class of locomotive under the most extreme pressure.

Yet when recalling these achievements much later, Tom was quite phlegmatic and understated when expressing his thoughts:

'We were pleased to get the locomotives constructed on time, but in some ways it was a distraction from our main business. Both Princess Classes were magnificent, but were never likely to earn the company as much as the freight services. Publicity was vital and the coverage they received was important, but from my point of view, it was more important to move onto the next job and there was plenty left to do.'

They had had a brief moment to enjoy their success, but great endeavour quickly fades and all glory is fleeting. The future would soon call for a re-marshalling of effort and a new set of pressured targets to meet.

Chapter 6

NO PASSING GLORY

When the first few Princess Coronations were gradually put together on the Crewe production line, their creation was attended by a co-ordinated PR campaign. The LMS embraced the need to publicise work wholeheartedly after a slow start, by comparison to their main competitors that is, who had moved ahead in leaps and bounds. And new technical developments were one area they sought to exploit, particularly on film.

In some ways, this was a very modern concept because it moved advertising well beyond the holiday posters that adorned billboards and re-appeared in press adverts. Some of the LMS work was simply to be used in-house to show their own workers the major advances that were being made; developing an esprit de corps was an essential part of Stamp's business planning. But it could also be used in a wider way to exploit new mediums, particularly the cinema through such things as Pathé News and short films that linked the main pictures. The press were also avid devourers of anything glamorous or new and the railways in the 1930s were selling new high-speed trains designed for an elite, but also something the less well-off could aspire to. And the

central core of this news gathering were the railway magazines then selling in huge numbers and feeding an ever-growing interest in the Big Four. Whether streamlining, as some thought, played any part in this burgeoning interest is difficult to assess, but what is certain is that locomotives had developed an unrivalled and discerning following.

The development of the Royal Scot Class had shown the way for the LMS, but by the time the Princess Coronations arrived, the formula was being exploited to the full in a most professional way. Throughout construction, journalists seem to have been given free access to locomotives under construction, were provided with specifications and were able to take photographs. It was a process that seemed to fly in the face of commercial and scientific confidentiality and some, Tom amongst them, felt that the company and its employees might have been better served by being more circumspect. At one stage, when he felt that Eric Langridge had spoken to a journalist too openly, Tom dropped him a short written rebuke for doing so and an instruction to be more careful in future. As his draughtsman kept the letter, it suggests that the comments may have stung him and caused some resentment. But Tom was a forthright man when necessary

and felt it better to let everyone know where they stood, rather than let something fester or lead to more serious problems.

If possible, the company sought out members of the press who had a specialist interest in the rolling stock and infrastructure. First amongst these was the *Railway Gazette*, a periodical that mapped all developments on the railway, but had a strong focus on locomotives. And with Stanier in the chair, presumably sponsored by Stamp and Hartley, the magazine began producing assessments of each engine class as they appeared.

In 1933, a detailed article was published describing the first two Princess Royals, followed two years later by Turbomotive. In due course, they were produced as stand-alone booklets sold across the counters of news outlets at stations. In 1937, the Coronation Class, and their rake of carriages, received the same treatment with sixteen pages of detailed notes, photographs, plus a series of key drawings on a single, large fold out page, all wrapped in a pleasant red card cover, and priced at three shillings. It sold in substantial numbers and provided the reading public with a guide which kept little back and created a great deal of interest. More would follow over the years including a *Sectioned Perspective*

Driver Tom Clark inspects 6220 before her record run on 29 June 1937.

6220 in full flight and in pristine condition.

of (the Coronations) Locomotive Front End. Meanwhile the press published all sorts of articles and hoped to gain access to the footplate so that they might record the drama of a hot, fast run.

The LMS's PR Department, under the guiding hand of the very talented publicist George Loftus-Allen, pursued the promotion of the company's new assets with great vigour through film and two of these were of particular significance. The first described the work of the Scientific Research team, ending with the Princess Coronation's wind tunnel tests managed by Frederick Johansen at Derby. Though meant for internal consumption only, it soon found a wider audience, especially when the first engine made its spectacular appearance on the rails. The second film was pure publicity for the new locomotives from construction to operation, ending with spectacular

footage of 6220 at full speed shot from an accompanying aeroplane. It is a piece of film that still stuns today, even though we have become inured to spectacular sights made immediately accessible by the internet and news broadcasts. So it is small wonder that in 1937 the impact of this new locomotive, and Gresley's A4, was felt so intensely.

When the first engine rolled out of the workshops on 26 May, glistening in her new blue livery, attended by managers, workers and the press, the cameras caught these images. Tom, who was never one to seek publicity or the limelight, was there, standing in the background, his tall, slightly stooped frame easily recognisable near Fred Lemon in one shot. Sadly, he didn't record his thoughts or feelings about this event, so one can only guess what he felt as the product of his efforts and leadership slowly rolled into view, then came to a standstill as the 'world' looked on.

Amongst his papers Tom left a copy of the *Railway Gazette* booklet, with a number of pencilled comments, question marks and a few of his own photographs added. Though not noted for cant or rhetoric, it is interesting to follow the sections he has underlined and guess why these may have been of particular interest to him:

'The locomotive, which by courtesy of Mr W.A. Stanier, CME of the London Midland and Scottish Railway, we illustrate and describe herewith, is the first of five new engines now being built at the company's works at Crewe. The engine, No 6220, bears the name *Coronation*; it has just been completed and will be followed in due course by others in the series, which will be named as follows:-
'6221 – *Queen Elizabeth*,
6222 – *Queen Mary*,

6223 – *Princess Alice,*
6224 – *Princess Alexandra.*

'The latest locomotives represent a development of the earlier engines of the Princess Royal type, but in addition to being provided with streamlining, the boiler is of considerably greater capacity, whilst certain improvements have been made to the frames and valve motion. The tender is also of increased capacity, and is fitted with a steam operated coal pusher to bring the coal forward to the fireman's shovel when the supply is getting low…. The form of streamlining adopted was finally decided after very careful experiments with models in the LMSR Research Department's wind tunnel at Derby, where tests were carried out to represent both headwinds and winds crossing the track at various angles.

One of Tom's action photographs showing a Coronation at high speed.

Stanier congratulates the crew in bringing 6220 safely home. If Stanier ever felt his position in the company was insecure, this event made him for life.

'In the course of our recent visits to the Crewe works during the building of the first engine, <u>one of the most interesting features seen was the manner in which the bulbous front end</u> of the boiler streamlining was achieved. It was built up on a specially prepared wooden jig or framework, <u>ensuring accuracy and the proper fitting together of the casing when mounted on the engine.</u> We later witnessed the fittings of the streamlined portions of the engine itself.

Publicity was always sought and here the LMS managed to get a complete front page of the now long departed *Daily Sketch*.

'It is interesting to compare particulars of the earlier 4-6-2 locomotives, Nos 6203-6212, with those of the new series, so that the differences between them can be readily noted:

	6203-6212	6220-6221
Cylinders (4), dia x stroke	16 ¼ in x 28 in	16 ½ in x 28 in
Valve gear	4 sets of Walschaert	2 sets of Walschaert
Valve Travel	7 ½ in	7 1/32 in
Coupled Wheels	6ft 6in	6ft 9in
Boiler		
Working Pressure	250lbs per sq in	250lbs per sq in
Firebox heating surface	217 sq ft	230 sq ft
Tube heating surface	2,097 sq ft	2,577 sq ft
Total	2,314 sq ft	2,807 sq ft
Superheater	653 sq ft	856 sq ft
Combined heating surface	2,967 sq ft	3,663 sq ft
Grate Area	45 sq ft	50 sq ft
Tractive effort at 85% boiler pressure	40,300lbs	40,000lbs.

Tom caught on camera in the crowd that welcomed 6220 back to London. It was rare to find this retiring Chief Draughtsman at any public event.

Tom then left various comments against each element of design described in the booklet – boiler, firebox, frames, cylinders, motion, axles, wheels and springing – and paid particular attention to any part of the engine's description that focussed on the footplate crew. Safety, comfort and ease of usage were as important to him as performance, though in steam locomotives very hard to attain, the basic concept being one of hard labour in trying conditions. But the Stanier designs were noted for the sound ergonomic principles they sought to develop and Tom clearly was pleased that their work was given some credit.

He then focussed on the editorial comments, lifted straight from the May '37 edition of the magazine:

'The attractiveness of the 6½ hour timing between Euston and Glasgow will be increased by the fact that the journey will be made in new and very comfortably appointed trains hauled by streamline locomotives specially built for the service…..<u>The style of painting adopted, namely Coronation blue</u> [to which Tom has added 'not Coronation blue'] <u>with silver striping, gives a most striking outward appearance to the new locomotive and trains, and the use of chromium plated fittings and new pattern electric lighting and upholstery designs in the coaches, combine to effect a tour ensemble upon which it would be very difficult to improve.</u>

'The streamline locomotives are of the 4-6-2 type, <u>and in their general assembly follow the</u>

<u>lines of Mr Stanier's 'Princess Royal' class</u> [against which Tom has written in pencil 'no they don't']; there are several features in the design, apart from the streamlining, <u>that rank them as an improved edition of that very excellent class</u> [to which Tom has added, 'they are new, not improved engines'].'

With so much attention being paid to 6220 it was easy to overlook the work of Tom's Carriage Drawing Office, and it seems that he may, made every effort to ensure they received due credit for their work. In the booklet, this element of the design was given some prominence and was described in some detail. One wonders whether Tom may even have prepared it himself for publication, because each paragraph has been ticked off as though he was checking that all points he had made had been included:

'The first of the new Coronation Scot trains to be introduced has just been completed at the LMSR works at Wolverton. Three trains are being prepared. <u>The total seating capacity of each train is 232 passengers – 82 first class and 150 third class – and the total weight of the train is 297 tons.</u> The general construction of the coaches follows LMSR standard practice, the body sides, ends, and roof being covered with steel panels finishing flush with the windows. <u>The exterior painting is carried out in blue, with four bands of silver running the full length of the train between the windows on the carriages and continuing at the same level on the engine to</u>

<u>finish with a V' shaped point on the front of the smokebox streamlining.</u> The car numbers and lettering are in silver plain block characters, and the exterior fittings, such as doors and commode handles are finished in chromium plate. The cars are carried on steel underframes with specially selected bogies.

'All the vehicles, with the exception of the kitchen <u>are equipped with pressure heating and ventilation on the Thermo Reg system</u>, the hot and cold systems being isolated in order to ensure the maximum range of nozzle temperature control. <u>The air is delivered through nozzles situated above the windows in the vestibule cars, and above the windows and corridor doors in the corridor cars. The nozzles can be adjusted by the passengers to give any desired temperature.</u> In addition, the usual steam heaters are provided under the seats in every saloon or compartment. Double sliding lights, which can be adjusted to serve either as an extractor or ventilator, are fitted above every window.

'The three third class vestibule cars in each train are finished flush with horizontal inlaid bands similar to the first class cars, but each is finished in different timbers as follows:-

English weathered sycamore, and English Burry sycamore.

English curly oak butt, and English brown oak with tiger stripe.

Canadian silver elm.

'<u>The last named veneer was cut from the piles recovered from Waterloo Bridge; the piles</u>

June 1938 and 6225, turned out in red with gold lining, gets underway from Euston with a large party of guests from the Institution of Locomotive Engineers.

had been under water from the time the bridge was erected in 1817 until it was demolished in 1936. The corridor third class brakes are finished in South American peroba, with contrasting inlaid horizontal bands of walnut. The metal fittings are finished satin matt chrome in the first class cars and oxidised Venetian bronze in the third class cars, and the ceilings throughout the trains are covered in cream Rexine.'

It seems that Tom was very interested in all the train's design features and not solely the locomotive. In fact, his eye for detail and wide knowledge

of materials was most unusual, perhaps reflecting much broader creative gifts. He certainly seems to have involved himself in the fine detail of the work his drawing office teams produced and left little to chance. But this had been a chief characteristic of his work from the beginning – he had always been painstaking in his approach, especially when facing such close public scrutiny. In this, he was different from Ernest Lemon, who seemed to be imbued with a degree of recklessness when it came to launching new locomotives or services, if the trials he sponsored with the Princess Royal locomotives were anything to go by.

The launch day had started when Stanier welcomed the press for lunch at the Crewe Arms Hotel, just outside the main line station, before handing them over to Fred Lemon who escorted them around the works. Tom accompanied the party, having spent the morning looking over the other four engines then in different stages of production:

'I always visited Crewe at least once a week by train to discuss progress with the Works Superintendent and the draughtsmen there. Before 6220 appeared these visits became much more frequent and on one occasion Sir William and I undertook a very close inspection with Fred Lemon in attendance. I understood that when 6200 first appeared in 1933 the CME had expressed his concerns about the state of the engine, particularly the poor condition of the castings. Fred Lemon didn't intend repeating

this mistake and the locomotive had been well prepared.

'The inspection took several hours and included climbing into the firebox so that one of the fitters could show us his handiwork. First he climbed in through the firebox door, followed by Sir William and then me. It was a bit cramped, but the fire hadn't been lit so we weren't bothered by the heat. Getting out afterwards was a little more difficult and raised a few wry smiles and laughter in which the CME joined.

'By this stage Fred Lemon's hearing was very poor and conversations were louder because of it and couldn't be confidential for that reason, but as Sir William was praising not criticising this didn't matter.'

Once the launch had been completed, and much good publicity gathered, the serious business of testing the locomotive could begin, in preparation for a specially arranged press outing on 29 June. Initially, she was limited to short runs by herself, but at the end of May, as confidence in her performance grew, she successfully completed a fully loaded running in turn from Crewe to Shrewsbury and back. Three or so weeks later, 6220 transferred to Camden Shed where footplate crew and maintenance staff began the process of familiarisation, taking her out on the main line on several occasions, as Alfred Ewer, the District Locomotive Superintendent, recalled:

'6220 arrived at Camden to great fanfare and was inspected

More publicity, this time of a more scientific nature.

A new Coronation Class locomotive arrives at Euston. Its name and number are not clear.

by all and sundry, from Board Members to cleaners. We had become used to the Princess Royals and Turbomotive, all of which received their share of attention, but the Coronations were more impressive than anything we had seen up

to then, helped by their streamlined casing. We all knew that the LNER with their A4s were well ahead and so were proud of our own version, which looked bigger and more powerful than our rivals. It definitely lifted our spirits,

especially when she gained her record later that month.

'Tom Coleman, who I had got to know quite well by then, was a regular visitor to Camden and was interested in all we were doing to get her ready. On the morning of the 29th June he and Fred Lemon were there as 6220 was prepared, and went with her as she backed down to Euston to pick up her train. I don't know if they accompanied her on the run north, but I expect they did. In the weeks that followed Tom was often with us checking how 6220 and the other four of the class were performing.'

History does not record if Tom was a passenger on the 29th, though Fred Lemon most definitely was. Robert Riddles, Stanier's Principal Assistant, recalled later, when describing the run from Euston

Tom on the track of his engines, this time caught with his head down at the front of the small crowd looking through the viewfinder of his Agfa camera.

to Crewe and back, how close the whole enterprise came to disaster:

'On June 29th 1937 at 9.50 am we set out from Euston with the new Coronation Scot train on its Press demonstration run. Again I was fortunate enough to be on the footplate, and with my diagrams laying down the postulated speeds, all was set to make an attempt on the world's maximum speed record at Whitmore, where after a rise, we entered on a falling gradient down to Crewe, 10 ½ miles away. We had decided not to pick up water from the trough at Whitmore, and so avoid reducing speed. The exhaust was humming with a continuous roar like that of an aeroplane engine.

'The white mileposts flashed past and the speedometer needle shot up through the 90s into the 100s to 110, 111, 112, 113, 114 miles per hour; but beyond it – No! Basford Hall sidings 1½ miles away now; spectators from Crewe coming into view at the lineside, and the train still hurtling along at 114 mph. On went the brakes; off the regulator; but on we sailed with flames streaming from the tortured brake blocks. To my horror the signal was set for Platform No 3 at Crewe, which has a reverse curve with a 20 mph speed restriction. We were doing 60 to 70 mph when we spotted the platform signal;

down to 52 mph through the curve, the engine riding like the great lady she is: there wasn't a thing we could do about it but hold on and let her take it. And take it she did; with the crockery smashing in the dining car: past a sea of pallid faces on the platform; till we ground to a dead stand – safe and sound and still on the rails. We had set up a new world's speed record for the steam locomotive!'

After the experience of the Princess PR run in 1933 and now 6220 in 1937, it seems that these sort of duties were set up to tempt fate rather than sell a new locomotive or train. And one wonders who decided that this journey should contain a world record speed attempt. Unnecessary risk is rarely the product of a rational mind. As Ernest Lemon had been pushing hard to set up high speed, long distance services, and controlled the running department, it is possible that it was his search for headlines that drove the attempt. If so, the result could have backfired badly and one assumes the press were more docile then than they are now or the near miss would have made front pages and led to resignations. But the LMS did seem to have a cavalier attitude to safety at times and their poor accident record had few equals.

At lunch in the Crewe Arms Hotel, which Ernest Lemon hosted, the railway correspondent and historian O.S.Nock reported that:

'Lemon presided and very wittily and successfully made light of the precipitate entry into Crewe, which one correspondent afterwards wrote "strewed the floor of the dining car with a mosaic of broken crockery". In the course of his speech, however, he was handed a slip of paper; it was the result of a scrutiny of the speed recorder chart taken off the locomotive. Up to that point he had quoted the 112½ mph agreed among the four of us, but as he read the paper a broad smile spread over his face, and he said, "I have not been bribed, but I can now tell you that the maximum speed was 114 mph". It is, I am afraid, no exaggeration to say that those of us who had been taking so detailed an account of the running regarded this claim with some scepticism. We would all have readily agreed that a peak of 113 mph could have occurred although it had eluded four independent stopwatches; but 114 took some stomaching, particularly as by this the British railway speed record was snatched by one mile per hour from the LNER. We had, however, little time to reflect on the ethics of the situation.'

Stanier, who was also on board, left no record of his thoughts about this journey to Crewe. But he worked in close co-operation with Henry Bulleid, when writing his book *Master Builders of Steam*, and so the description it contains may be said to have been authorised:

'Frederick Lemon, sitting opposite Stanier, put his legs on the seat as a precaution

against what he thought was an inevitable derailment. When Stanier stepped down on the platform at Crewe after the breathless arrival, he found among the waiting officials Charles Byron [the LMS's Chief Operating Manager], who rather testily said "How foolish to come in so fast". "How foolish to turn a high speed test train into a reverse curve merely to bring it alongside a platform", retorted Stanier briskly – and thinking, but not saying, that they would probably have been derailed but for the de Glehn bogie.'

During the return run to London that afternoon, Nock recorded that, 'we were treated to a grand exhibition of sustained high speed on the way home' in the

expert hands of Tom Clark, the locomotive's soon to retire veteran driver from Crewe. During the last few years of his career, special duties often fell to him and he became a very familiar presence on the footplate of the Princess Royals from 1933 onwards and the Coronations in their first two years of service. He had taken the controls of 6201 during her record breaking trip to Glasgow and back in November 1936, and now he handled 6220 with equal aplomb. On his return from Glasgow, Charles Byrom said of the driver's performance:

'He has given us a wonderful example of scientific engine driving. He has shown us that it is high speed up the banks which counts and not the reckless running down them which any man can do.'

Loco and location not recorded, but a photo that sums up all that is attractive about a steam locomotive in flight.

Very soon the Coronations became an everyday part of business, barely attracting a glance.

It is a comment that applied equally to the descent to Crewe in June 1937 and probably underlines the rebuke he gave Stanier when he stepped down from the train at Crewe. Driver Clark was a phlegmatic character and seemed to take the whole affair in his stride and made no mention of the near miss or who had encouraged him to take such a risk.

In the aftermath of all the shenanigans that took place at Crewe, Tom, as a good scientist and engineer, looked beyond the headlines and 'speed record' to analyse exactly how 6220 had performed. If anything, he found the return trip more interesting, because the crew and the train's passengers were calmer after the morning's

exploits, so normal, more balanced running was more likely on the 158 mile run. In a short timekeeping summary, he noted that the outward journey had been covered in 129 mins and 46 seconds, against a scheduled time of 135 minutes, with an average speed of 73 mph. But the return was completed with a saving of 16 minutes, at an average speed of 79.7 mph.

He would also have been pleased to read other assessments of her performance. Smooth running, reserves of power, superb riding qualities, free from rolling, little or no vibration or axle knocks, no tendency to kick on curves, runs economically and easily at high speed being just some of

the comments made by engineers and footplate crew alike. A full testing regime lay ahead, in which a more scientific way of collecting information would be implemented, but for the moment the first five of the class were made ready for the inaugural runs of the Coronation Scot. And until the service had proved to be a success, all five engines would be based at Camden Shed. Here, the experienced hands of Alfred Ewer would manage them until 1939, when they would be shared amongst other sheds, greater numbers having been constructed in the meantime.

The inaugural run to Glasgow of the streamlined Coronation Scot service took place on 5 July, and was attended by a large crowd at Euston of interested bystanders and the Press. Although 6220 had been on display at the terminus on 24 June, and had become a regular sight in the area since then, this first revenue-earning trip caught the imagination, some hoping that a record attempt would again be attempted. But with speed, reliability and comfort being the cornerstones of the LMS's publicity campaign there would be no repeat. The Press and railway employees may be thrown around, but not the fee-paying public it seems.

With the service up and running, Tom and his team could turn their attention to the many other projects awaiting their attention. Amongst them was a requirement for ten more Pacifics in 1938. Whilst planning the first five Coronations, a decision to streamline them was far from clear. It seems there was a difference of opinion and the debate over the value of air smoothing must have been a

central issue. Stanier, or so the story goes, wasn't a great fan and favoured the locomotives in a more traditional form. But other more senior managers, including Hartley, preferred to experiment with a more aerodynamic shape. Tom sat between both camps, happy to pursue either option.

Whether apocryphal or not, a tale has been told of him producing, through his draughtsman Arthur Edlestone, 'unfrocked drawings of a Coronation shortly after the streamlined scheme had appeared, with the name 'Lady Godiva' added. Popular myth has it that this helped persuade the Board to approve construction of a conventional group of engines. On balance, the story appears a little trite and fanciful to be entirely true. Hard headed business men and engineers are unlikely to be swayed by such a juvenile act. And Tom, who believed in the conventions of management and the persuasive power of well-constructed arguments, would have found such an approach naïve and counterproductive. However, as a good manager and designer he would have addressed the question early in development and considered all options. He would also have been aware of Stanier's thoughts on the subject and, as he

was prone to do, prepare drawings with alternative solutions. It is probably here that the 1938 building programme had its roots and produced five with streamlining and five without.

Between 22 and 25 November 1937, the first series of tests using a new Princess Coronation took place. 6220 was chosen, having run 29,788 miles since being built, and the Euston to Glasgow route was selected. The object of the exercise was quite straightforward, and didn't include a comparison with any other locomotive over the same route:

'The test was carried out to investigate the general efficiency of the Class 7 4-6-2 Streamlined Engine when working on its usual service.'

Without comparison, the tests were limited in their scope and findings, so the summary lacks true meaning, although they suggest that 6220 performed well:

'Conclusions – From the results obtained during this test it will be seen that the operation of the service was performed by the engine with a high degree of efficiency and that the performance was satisfactory from every point of view.

A press shot kept by Laurie Earl, a top link Camden driver. This spot was used quite often and the staged race with horses was very effective.

Very soon with five new locomotives to play with, the LMS launched the Coronation Scot service with extensive publicity.

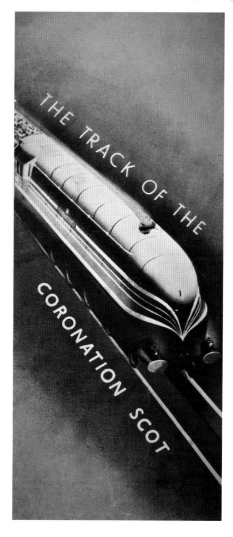

Taking the schedule and the actual load throughout the test, while a high average power development is called for, the engine had a margin of power available if required.

'A detailed examination and analysis of the Dynamometer Chart has been carried out and from this calculations have been made. From these figures the following data has been deduced. Making allowance for the steam required for carriage warming, for exhaust steam utilised by the injector which forms part of the effective feed, and for radiation loss, the weight of steam per IHP hour was approximately 14.5 lbs.

The weight of coal required per IHP hour was 1.622 lbs.

'Taking the calorific value of the Grimethorpe coal as high as 14,500 BTUs per BTUs per lb, the absolute efficiency of the engine was 10.82%. The heat obtained per lb of coal was 10,990 BTUs which taking the calorific value of the coal as given above, indicates a boiler efficiency of 75.8%.'

Tom's copy of this report – Number 47 in the LMS sequence – contains a number of pencilled comments and some facts and figures taken from earlier Princess Royal tests. He doesn't appear to have drawn any conclusions from this, but

evidently found the new locomotive superior in many respects to the first 12 Pacifics, a summary he later recalled:

'It occurred to me that we should undertake comparability trials, but 6220's performance was such that this proved unnecessary.

Cleaning steam locomotives was always time consuming, none more so than when it was a high profile engine.

A Panel for this and panels for that.

It outperformed the Princess Royals in all ways, a fact which was underlined by reports coming back from footplate crew. I concluded that a better comparison would be between streamlined and non-streamlined Coronations, when the two types became available.

'Sir William rode in the Dynamometer Car on two of these test runs and took a great interest in the results. A Metrovick-Dodds Cathode Ray Indicator was also installed as a trial. The instrument was placed in the leading end of the car and was connected to pressure elements in the indicating plug holes of the left outside and inside cylinder covers. There was a constant search to increase the technical aspects of testing and this indicator showed great promise, though the findings from these tests were not included in the main report.

'Stanier was noted as keen to improve the way engines were tested and is recorded on paper as strongly supporting the building of a test centre with a rolling road. He and Gresley, and most engineers I discussed the idea with, believed that Dynamometer Car trials had their place, but were too often affected by the variable conditions met during each run. A test centre was, most conceded, the most effective way of achieving more stable, scientific results. Eventually the powers that be approved construction, but the war meant that work was postponed for the duration.'

With the new long-distance service and the first Coronations proving successful, more were recommended by the CME and the Chief Operating Manager for construction as the minutes of the October meeting of the Mechanical and Electrical Engineering Committee revealed:

'With a view to meeting the increased demands for engine power likely to arise in 1938, ten additional Class 7 4-6-2 express locomotives (Coronation type) be provided at a total approximate outlay of £138,000, the expenditure to be dealt with in conjunction with the 1938 Rolling Stock Building Programme.'

Board approval followed, yet so confident of success were they that material was ordered in advance of this being given. 6225 to 6229 would be streamlined but painted red, with gold stripes, whilst 6230 to 6234 would be built without the casing, ostensibly to provide a comparison between the two types. If, as many believe, Stanier was a strong advocate of this alternative design and wished to disprove the streamlining concept, this was undoubtedly the best way of proceeding. Robert Riddles would later quote Stanier as saying, 'They can have their bloody streamliners if they want them, but we will also build them five proper ones', when discussions about the 1938 programme were at their height. If this is true, he was expressing an unexpected depth of feeling on a subject which perhaps it didn't demand. Tom took a slightly different view when recalling his CME's reactions:

'Many disliked the look created by streamlining on the Coronations, Sir William included, although he did remark on the good looks of the Gresley A4s. So I don't think he was against the idea of streamlining as such. The biggest benefits to having a non-streamlined version were the

An interesting comparison of designs and shapes at Camden.

The non-streamlined version appears. A new front end and the beginning of the iconic Coronation Class look.

6225 to 6229 made their appearances between May and September 1938, being given the names of Duchesses – Gloucester, Norfolk, Devonshire, Rutland and Hamilton respectively. Whilst 6230 to 6234 came out of the workshops between June and August the same year, without smoke deflectors and painted red, also with the names of Duchesses – Buccleuch, Atholl, Montrose, Sutherland and Abercorn. No explanation for the change of colour scheme from blue to red has survived, but crimson lake was a shade of paint with strong LMS links so may have sponsored the change. Equally, the LNER had begun painting their A4s garter blue and this colour was strongly associated, in the public eye, with *Mallard*'s record run during July 1938. Asserting a company brand made a change to red necessary if unfortunate comparisons were not to be drawn. Either way the colour scheme that Tom had sponsored was dropped, but remained on four of the first group of engines until 1944, with 6221 alone being repainted red, in November 1940 following a heavy general repair.

Comparison trials took place between August and October 1938 and were based on coal consumption in that period. When a Loose Minute was issued on 25 October, rather than a full report, it seemed to suggest that streamlined engines used less coal, with a saving figure of slightly more than 2 per cent declared. It is now perceived that the CME and his team found these findings wanting. The story now widely accepted is that suspicions were aroused that the results may

weight saved and easier access for fitters at the sheds when servicing the locomotives. The engines were approximately 3 tons lighter when the air smoothed casing was removed and it was expected that this reduction would outweigh any benefits that streamlining achieved in performance at high speed. But only trials would

prove this and the Research Department began a series of tests by themselves in 1938 once the five non-streamlined engines had worn in. But without the CME Department's participation or the use of a dynamometer car, which was questioned at the time, the trials were incomplete and didn't assess all relevant aspects of performance.'

have been manipulated to favour streamlining and had not taken into account the variations of duties and loads assessed in the trials.

So many years after these events it is difficult to draw any conclusions, but the simple truth seems to be that the trials were poorly thought out and conducted, and were not broad enough to test the two types of engine on proven scientific principles. Did this reflect a desire by the Research Department or the CME to prove a point or was it simply a sign of the relationship problems Hartley described in his obituary for Stanier? Tom, it seems, stood on the side lines during this debate, seeing strengths in both designs and expressing no opinion either way except to assert the need for more detailed tests that would fairly assess the streamline and non-streamline concepts. However, amongst the papers he left is a copy of a 25 October Loose Minute. He has underlined a number of paragraphs that suggest that the author knew the limitations of these exercises and their findings and hints at correspondence with the Chief Operating Manager and Ernest Lemon before publication so that some balance may be brought to the analysis:

'The method of test employed during the 8 week trials, ended on 1st October, is open to serious objection on the score of accuracy. It has been ascertained that the weight of coal, on which the consumption figures are based, were taken from the jigger recorders on the coaling plants. These records are said to be

Duchess of Atholl caught between turns.

Duchess of Sutherland freshly turned out at Shrewsbury and ready for service.

frequently in error to very considerable extents and are adjusted over a period to bring them into agreement with the total weighed wagon loads supplied to the coaling plant hopper. The coal supplies to either of the two small groups of locomotives over a period of 8 weeks may therefore be expected to be uncertain within a much wider limit than the coal saving due to streamlining which it is desired to measure.

'The following comments refer to the figures furnished by the Chief Operating Manager and the Chief Accountant:

1. The streamlined engines covered decidedly less mileage than the other group. In particular streamlined locomotive No. 6225 appears to have made only 3 or 4 trips during the 4-weekly period. The coal consumption actually refers to 5 non-streamlined locomotives, though only 4 were supposed to be on the trial.
2. Comparisons of coal consumption figures for different locomotives of the same group on the same job, and the same locomotives on different jobs (here Tom has placed a large question mark) reveal far greater disparities than the difference due to streamlining. The latter is a little over 2% of the overall consumption.'

Whilst Tom underlined these comments, the minute does go on to cover other limiting factors inherent in the way these trials were conducted before reaching very broad conclusions:

'In order to obtain an accurate result it seems essential to:

1. Weigh accurately the coal consumed between terminals.
2. Employ the same number of locomotives in each group.
3. Extend the trials over a long period and keep the results of each locomotive under continuous supervision to ensure that inconsistencies are detected, and to note disparities of performance for the same locomotive on different occasions and for different locomotives in the same group.
4. Note any differences of technique among the crew of the locomotive under trial.
5. Take particulars of weather conditions, actual timing and other factors.'

The basic theme is that the tests were flawed, so neither Stanier or his team could take exception to the contents of this Loose Minute, which underlined system weaknesses and how these might be overcome. So time and money were wasted in trying to prove that streamlining reduced coal consumption. No doubt someone with Tom's experience would see this as an opportunity missed and could point to the way he had gradually introduced the concept of superheating as a better way of doing business. The comparability trials were not repeated and if any were scheduled, the coming of war a year later changed all priorities. If more trials had gone ahead what might they

have proved? Probably very little except that both types were excellent locomotives and there was very little to choose between them.

Although these tests proved of little or no value, a broader, more measured trials programme, relating to the Coronations, was underway. The Research Department were looking into such issues as improving the return airflow in the streamlined tenders and enhancing working conditions on the footplate, in addition to the main streamlining experiments. Johansen was also closely involved in analysing the performance of the Coronation Scot carriages after concerns had been expressed over their riding qualities and the durability of their wheels.

In the short period leading up to the war, there was also a variety of other locomotive tests going on. Stanier's experimental Turbomotive featured in one set. Its potential was still being explored, but it was gradually slipping into relative obscurity as predicted benefits failed to materialised and the Coronation Class grabbed the headlines and became more numerous. Work on the Jubilees continued in the hope of improving their performance, whilst tests on Fowler's rebuilt *Fury*, now 6170 *British Legion*, were proving that adopting 'Stanier's' principles would greatly enhance the Royal Scots.

At the same time, there were more general assessments taking place of such things as engines fitted with different boiler feed arrangements and resistance to flow of steam through cylinder parts. Tom also had close involvement in producing manuals that defined the rules for *The Design of Connecting Rods and Coupling Rods* and instructions for the *Balancing of Locomotives*. And this work highlighted another aspect of his working principles – to ensure that his staff had clear instructions on many basic issues concerning design and engineering. He believed in careful preparation. For some this would seem unnecessary, but experience had taught him to take little for granted or at face value. Professionalism, not just gifted amateurism, was the cornerstone of everything he did and believed in.

In early 1937, two strangers slipped into the test programme almost unnoticed – a pair of 0-6-0 diesel electric shunting locomotives, one built by English Electric and the other by Armstrong Whitworth. Despite the supremacy of steam on British railways, caused in part by the domination of this well-established technology, but also the easy availability and price of coal, other forms of locomotion were gradually being investigated. Advances were being made in diesel and electric designs, but the price of experimentation is always high and progress slow. Tom had been exposed to some of this development work with the NSR when their single 0-4-0 battery powered locomotive had been built in 1917. And his papers include a number of items and articles describing other schemes being considered by designers around the world.

So it seems that he wasn't hidebound by a strict adherence to steam, but was prepared to look more broadly and scientifically for better solutions. Undoubtedly, steam locomotives would have

dominated his thinking, but this was inevitable whilst his employers saw them as the most cost effective option. This would change in the post-war years and when it did, Tom would adapt to the revolution, though the time available for him to stamp his authority on this new technology would be limited by his age.

But even in 1937 as the Coronations, 8Fs and Black Fives dominated the LMS, some were thinking in term of dieselisation and electrification of the West Coast Main Line. In May of that year, Ernest Taylor wrote a paper entitled *Estimated Cost of Operating High Speed Diesel Trains between London and Glasgow,* in response to a memorandum from Charles Byrom.

A personal copy was sent to Tom, presumably because he had been involved in these deliberations.

Taylor wrote:

'You agreed that it was essential, in order to meet Mr Lemon's requirements, that the costs in regard to diesel high speed trains should be on the same basis as, and comparable with, the costs for the high speed steam trains and you requested me to get in touch with Mr Stanier with a view to adjusting the diesel train costs on these lines. He has expressed the following views:-

a. That having regard to the fact that the time for the

The LMS's diesel programme was more successful and exploited partnerships with other companies.

A family day in Tom's Jaguar SS1 Airline Coupe.

Tom's children enjoying a day out before war is declared.

Additional cost of Power Equipment - £1000.
Comparison of Costs
Steam Train/Diesel Train
First cost of trains including power unit £59,000/£92,000 operating service in both directions.
First cost of spare rolling stock to cover 40,000/46,000 both directions.
Total first cost of rolling stock 99,000/138,000.'

service has been extended from 6 to 6 ½ hours with resultant reduction in the average speed from 67mph to 62mph, he is of the opinion that the difference between the proposed service and the ordinary express is scarcely sufficient to justify diesel operation being considered.

b. That if a comparison between steam and diesel working is required, the only modifications to the diesel train costs previously supplied would be as follows:-

Weight increased from 250 to 300 tons.
Cost of additional passenger accommodation - £5000.

Even without a diesel capable of pulling such a load at such a speed, it is interesting that minds were turning to the possibility of diesel traction and one wonders how clearly they understood what was entailed. The potential of these engines had been explored for many decades before the LMS considered it as a possibility for their main line. And as happens with so many scientific developments of the twentieth century, eyes often turned to the USA for guidance in exploiting potential. In early 1934, the Union Pacific, with the Pullman Car and Manufacturing Company, developed an articulated diesel set called *City of Salina*, but described by one journalist as a 'monster airplane fuselage on wheels'. This passenger train was fully streamlined and wind tunnel tested, could cruise at 90 mph and reach a top speed of 110 mph. Meanwhile the Budd Company built a high speed, long distance articulated passenger diesel set for the Chicago, Burlington and Quincy Railroad, known as the Zephyr.

These services proved hugely successful and it was probably this concept that caught Ernest Lemon's attention during a month long

Two **USA** mid -1930s diesel multiple unit designs that impressed visitors from the LMS. The Union Pacific '*City of Salina*' and the Budd Company '*Zephyr*`.

visit to the USA in May 1936, with his fellow Vice President, William Wood, and Harold Hartley on two separate trips in 1936 and 1938. Their reaction to Taylor's paper isn't recorded, but having invested so heavily in the highly successful Coronation Class and other passenger engines, the LMS were unlikely to speculate too greatly on this new system. However, a full construction programme of diesel shunting engines was initiated instead. Their role was much easier to justify on cost benefit grounds and by 1938 they had become a common presence on the LMS.

There was one exception to this though, progressed with Harold Hartley and Ernest Lemon's backing. The LMS, having supported some experimentation with diesel passenger railcars by English Electric, Leyland Motors, the Michelin Company and Armstrong Siddeley earlier in the decade, allowed design boundaries to be pushed back even further.

Advantages inherent in lightweight diesel units had not been fully exploited because of an inability to couple them to other units and their apparent fragility. Proposals to overcome these shortcomings were considered and a single articulated multiple unit diesel railcar was designed and built in 1938. Twenty-six sub-contractors provided parts and the unit was assembled at Derby, under the design guidance of Tom Coleman and his staff in the Loco and Carriage Drawing Offices.

It appeared in January1938, turned out in a distinctive aluminium and red livery, and was numbered 80000-2; though latterly this scheme was described as cream above bright red with a black dividing line and a silver painted roof. The first test run from Derby to Burton took place on 16 February and this was followed by more runs of increasing duration and complexity throughout the summer until it was felt that the design was good enough to cope with a

full schedule. During these tests, problems connected to braking, cooling, springing and other teething problems arose, but its performance showed some promise and speeds up to 80 mph were recorded.

A more regular service began on 5 September when the unit began running 462 miles a day between Bletchley, Cambridge and Oxford. In early January, the unit was withdrawn from traffic for maintenance and in March

A Zephyr advert sent to Tom by a colleague in the States.

re-appeared at Bedford to run a regular passenger service between London St Pancras and Nottingham. Time keeping, performance and reliability were good and the potential for more development seemed likely and may well have gone ahead if the war had not intervened. During the early months of the conflict, senior managers looked carefully at the rolling stock under their control and, rightly or wrongly, decided to withdraw any item deemed experimental or requiring special treatment. 80000-2 and Turbomotive were two such items and were mothballed. For the turbine engine, there would be a reprieve, but not for the diesel unit, which was gradually cannibalised to support other projects. Tom was a keen supporter of the unit, riding on it several times:

'It was a good design and ahead of its time. But for the war we would have built many more. I don't think it could

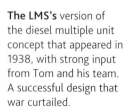

80000-2`s cab - a driver's delight after the hard graft of a steam locomotive's hot, heaving and uncomfortable footplate.

The LMS's version of the diesel multiple unit concept that appeared in 1938, with strong input from Tom and his team. A successful design that war curtailed.

have competed with the steam services on the West Coast Main Line at that time, but elsewhere it could, though diesel fuel costs were high when compared to coal and the technology still largely untried. It was a great surprise to me when the war was over that we did not build more and develop these ideas. Riddles' steam standardisation programme for BR owed more to pre-war days than the future.'

Tom, it seems, did try and engage himself in the design of diesels, which suggests that he saw their future potential. But in an internal minute dated 9 August, Stanier wrote to his Chief Draughtsman suggesting that Tom shouldn't become too involved in their development. 'Will you please note I have asked Mr Harper to look after any work in connection with these Diesels at this end.'

Of course, Stanier may have been concerned that Tom's workload was already too large and wished him to focus on other issues, particularly the development of steam projects. But it is also possible that he was unhappy with the way diesels were threatening the dominance of his own science and saw them as an irrelevant distraction. It is difficult to say which view might be correct, but, if the latter, he would not have been the first or last to struggle with change.

Meanwhile, the LMS's locomotive rebuilding programme still required considerable drawing office support. In 1937, one hundred Black Fives, forty-two 8Fs, twenty-seven 2-6-4Ts and twenty-seven 2-6-2Ts, plus the five Coronations, appeared.

This was followed by forty-seven Black Fives, two 8Fs, seventy-two 2-6-4T and 2-6-2Ts and the ten Coronations in 1939, but only thirty-four engines the following year as the programme ran down. Some may have wondered what might lay ahead, especially after such a busy six or so years of the LMS's locomotive rebuilding programme, but they could not have failed to see the threat from Hitler growing in strength from day to day. Everyone would have remembered the gradual transfer of industry onto a war footing in 1915-17 and expected the same thing to happen now. But this time the threat seemed to demand a different approach and in 1938-9, plans were laid and activated to bring industry on to a war footing much earlier. The weapons might not always be as good as the enemies and tactics on the battlefield might hark back to 1918 not forward to 1940, but a degree of realism over the use of industrial might did begin to prevail. The railways, with their massive construction potential and skills, would feature heavily in these plans and some masters of this work would be sought in many other areas of industry to advise and direct. So, at Derby and Crewe, in the workshops and drawing offices, the changes were only too apparent.

But life went on as usual and hope, that war might be avoided, prevailed. And in the last months before war was declared, construction went on as usual, as did planning for a peaceful future and the pursuit of locomotive excellence. The Pacifics, both Princess Royals and Coronations, became the focus of much of this

effort and trials work set out to establish how they might be improved or simply to measure their potential.

On 8 June 1938, No 6225 *Duchess of Gloucester* was rostered for 'Special Train' duties and ran from Euston to Glasgow with a dynamometer car attached. Its purpose was made clear in LMS Report No 77 which appeared two weeks later:

'In connection with the Summer Meeting of the Institution of

Before war was declared, the LMS sent a locomotive to the US for display. It was an event that drew publicity from many sources.

In early '39, 6234 was chosen for a series of trials to compare single and double blastpipes on performance.

Locomotive Engineers held in Glasgow and the visit of the Officials of the German State Railways, a special train was provided for the members and guests.

'The Dynamometer Car was attached to the train in order that observations could be made by the party en route, and that a complete dynamometer car test could be made. The train consisted of 7 vehicles, with a total weight of 232 tons. The engine was a standard class 7, 4-6-2 type (Streamlined) and had run 3,502 miles since new. Grimethorpe coal was used and was weighed on and off at Willesden and Polmadie sheds respectively.

'The steaming and operation of the engine was very satisfactory throughout. Owing to the light load hauled the engine was mainly worked with a partially opened regulator, a full opening being used on five sections only. The schedule of 6 hours and 35 minutes gives an average speed of the train of 55.5 mph throughout whilst the actual average speed obtained on the test was 59.2 mph.

'In consideration of the total weight of the engine and train (387 tons), and the high average speed, the results obtained, both on the Drawbar Horse Power basis and in general, indicate exceptional economy.'

Such a run was most unusual, but Stanier was a strong advocate of this Institution and had been, and would be again, their President, so wished to involve members in the work the LMS was undertaking. One wonders how the cost was justified, although suggesting it was a more formal test probably made it more palatable. Tom accompanied the run north, but did not feel suitably swayed to break the habit of a lifetime and become a member of the Institution. And his copy of the report bears evidence of the many observations he made during the trip and during the engine's preparation and 'disposal' at Polmadie, so he clearly found it useful. Once again, he kept the results with material on Princess Royal test runs and did some comparison work.

A few months later he was able to add information relating to a non-streamlined version of the Coronations. In February 1939, No 6234 *Duchess of Abercorn* underwent a series of trials with a standard blast pipe and a twin blast pipe arrangement. Report No 80 recorded that the tests were:

'To ascertain the maximum power developed by a non-streamlined express passenger locomotive when working a heavy train at special limit timings [on 12 February]. A further test was made on 26th February when the engine was fitted with the twin blast pipe arrangement. The engine tested was a standard Class 7, 4-6-2 type. A special train of 20 vehicles [including the dynamometer car], having a tare weight of 604 tons, was provided for the test, and was worked from Crewe to Glasgow and return to special limit timings, leaving Crewe at 8.10am and Glasgow at 2.45pm respectively.'

Tom was unable to accompany the train on the two trials but briefed James Sutherland, a noted expert on locomotive testing, to attend and provide him with detailed comments immediately after each run. He did as requested and his hand written notes were with Coleman in a matter of hours of the tests ending. Once again, he displayed his desire to absorb information and consider the impact it had on design, and at this stage he was considering how the Coronations might be improved still further.

Sutherland is a little-known figure now, but in the 1930s had an excellent reputation for his technical analysis, which Ernest Cox recalled in his book *Chronicles of Steam*:

'Another confirmed bachelor was "Uncle" Sutherland, badly knocked about in World War One, but of dry and searching humour which was a delight to listen to. He was the footplate expert, who rode the engine on test, and was welcomed by all the motive power people out on the line as one who could diagnose

their entire working problems with a sure and practised eye.'

Sutherland's assessments, and the final report, are full of statistics and analysis which would have joined the substantial bank of information which Tom was collecting. But the author reached only one conclusion:

'From an examination of the whole of the results, it will be evident that the high sustained powers and combustion rate required by the test schedule was secured more effectually and satisfactorily with the twin blast pipe arrangement than with the single blast pipe.'

Intriguingly, Tom has pasted a smokebox diagram taken from the

'Rhodesia Railways 5-11th Class Boiler – Order No T.9278' on the inside cover of his copy of the report without explanation, although it does show the blast pipe arrangement in some detail. How he came by the drawing or its significance is now lost in time, but it may have played a part in Tom's continual search for improvement and innovation.

As part of their continuing PR work, a journalist from the *Railway Gazette* was invited to join the train for these tests and, on 14 April, a full report appeared, a copy of which Tom cut out and kept:

'With a view to investigating the power development of which the Class 7 'Coronation' 4-6-2 type are capable, and

A very rare shot of the trials underway. The effect of fitting a double blast pipe were dramatic and greatly enhanced performance.

to obtain a variety of other technical data relative to them, a test was recently carried out on the LMSR main line between Crewe and Glasgow, when some remarkably interesting and important results were obtained.

'The route followed was the main line from Crewe to Glasgow and return, 487 miles, and the schedule running time, based on that of the 7 hour Royal Scot Euston-Glasgow service, provided for an average speed of 55 mph on the outward journey and 54.5 mph on the return. The test load was 184 tons in excess of the 'XL' limit of 420 tons now obtaining on the Royal Scot service, and it will be observed from the

gradient diagram that the route involved the ascent of Shap and Beattock when running in each direction.

'The weather conditions were fair at the commencement of the test, with a light wind, but north of Carlisle the wind increased, and on the return run from Glasgow a strong oblique wind, with sleet, had to be contended with; these conditions modified south of Carlisle. The engine was capably operated throughout by the following footplate staff:

Crewe to Carlisle: Driver G. Garrett and Fireman S. Farrington (Crewe).

Carlisle to Glasgow: Driver J. Marshall and Fireman D. Lynn (Polmadie).

Glasgow to Carlisle: Driver N. McLean and Fireman A. Smith (Polmadie).

'On the outward journey from Crewe to Glasgow the train was brought to stand, after running 5 miles, at Minshull Vernon (owing to a single line working being in operation) and it then proceeded at caution a further 3 ¾ miles, to Winsford Junction. From the latter point to Glasgow the scheduled running time was 255 minutes, with booked stops of 2 minutes each at Carlisle and Beattock. On the actual run the train stopped for 4 minutes at Crewe and the Beattock stop was cut out, but a stop of 4 minutes 35 seconds was made at Symington for water; the net running time from Winsford to Glasgow was 245 minutes, 10 minutes being gained on the overall schedule. The average running speed between Winsford and Glasgow was 57.2 mph. From Glasgow to Crewe the schedule arranged was 271 minutes, including a 2 minute stop at Carlisle, or 269 minutes running time, but owing to early arrival the stop at Carlisle was 9 ½ minutes; the total running time was 259 minutes and 35 seconds. Thus the train gained 9 minutes and 25 seconds on the up test schedule, the average speed between Glasgow and Crewe being 56.2 mph.

'The performance of the test called for a high and sustained power development, and the drawbar horsepower was almost continuously in the region of 1,800, the maximum sustained d.b.h.p being approximately 2,500.

LMSR. & LNER.
LOCOMOTIVE TESTING STATION.
RUGBY.

Stanier and Gresley had long sought a British Test Centre and work began as war threatened but wasn't completed until 1948. Here an architect's drawing captures a red Coronation in the proposed test centre.

Calculations have been made to the total power developed in the cylinders on the main gradient and it will be noted that the highest sustained cylinder power was approximately 3,350 hp. For a considerable part of the test the engine was operated with a cut-off range of 20-30%; the maximum cut off was approximately 40.

'The ascent from Beattock to Beattock Summit was one of the most outstanding engine performances of the tests, the 10 miles – graded throughout at between 1 in 69 and 1 in 88 up – being run at an average speed of 36-8 mph. More notable, however, was the climb from Glasgow to Beattock Summit in the southbound direction, an average speed of no less than 63.4 mph being sustained from Symington to Beattock Summit.

A matter of obviously great importance was the efficiency which attended the carrying out of the tests…. Although a high average rate of combustion was necessitated, the consumption shows that the economy of the engine was well maintained.'

O.S. Nock would later provide a fascinating footnote to the way this locomotive performed when he wrote, 'Not only was this exceedingly heavy train taken without assistance, but the uphill work was such as to be termed phenomenal, even by the standards set up by the Stanier Pacific engines.'

It seemed to many at this time that *Duchess of Abercorn*'s performance of strength, speed and

endurance was unlikely to ever be equalled or bettered by any other class of locomotive on British rails. True, they were too heavy and powerful for duty over a number of routes, but this wasn't their intended role. Here Black Fives, 8Fs and the many other effective classes now available would hold sway and fulfil their potential. But these trials proved that Coronations were much more than simply high-profile locomotives for use on premier services. Although thoroughbreds they could do much more. When war came, and traffic demand quickly outstripped peacetime needs, engines of this capacity, capable of pulling exceptionally heavy

loads over demanding routes, would be at a premium. And over the next few years the full impact of the LMS's huge locomotive development programme, exploited to the full by Stanier and Coleman's great design skills and determination, would bear fruit.

1938 and '39 also witnessed more tests on the Princess Royal Class. Although largely overshadowed by the Coronations, Tom had not lost sight of their potential and looked for ways of improving their performance. A series of trials took place to determine 'the effects of specially lagged elements, headers and steam pipes, on the degree of superheat obtained with this class of engine, which is fitted with 32 elements.'

Driver Fred Bishop enjoying this unusual view from a Coronation shortly before accompanying 6229 (temporarily re-numbered 6220 *Coronation*) on her trip to the USA.

6220 on display in the USA with Driver Fred Bishop and Fireman John Carswell.

Interestingly, Tom wrote a detailed report for Stanier during March 1939, who, in turn, passed it to Harold Hartley for consideration. He gave joint authorship to 'H. Chambers', who had died on 15 September 1937. And in this one act parts of Tom's character are clearly revealed. His integrity, generosity and his dislike of being feted even for work which he could justly claim as his own are only too clear. Hartley and Stanier commended the work and the Vice President added a short comment which summed up their collective view of the need for better test facilities:

'I agree that this investigation should be suspended until we have the testing plant, but I am anxious that it should not be forgotten as a possible means of increasing the efficiency of the boiler.'

Almost in anticipation of a rapidly approaching time of hardship and austerity, 1939 had one last touch of railway glamour to enjoy before all had to be sacrificed for war. In 1933, the LMS had been invited to send a new Royal Scot locomotive to the USA as part of the Century of Progress Exposition in Chicago. The visit proved to be a great success, which the company were able to exploit in PR terms. So, when the opportunity arose

to send a locomotive to the New York World's Fair, it was snapped up and on 26 January 1939, engine No 6220 *Coronation*, and a rake of Coronation Scot carriages, began their voyage across the Atlantic. In fact, *Coronation* and 6229, the red painted *Duchess of Hamilton*, changed identities for the visit, normal service only being restored when the engine, but not the carriages, returned to Britain in 1941. The declaration of war in September changed priorities for shipping and a locomotive was given low precedence in deciding what could be transported. The engine and her carriages were placed in store until their future could be decided, although this did allow them to be shown at the 1940 World Fair.

The visit was a great success and 6220 travelled widely along west coast and mid-west routes. Tom kept a number of magazine articles describing the visit, and many photographs, and highlighted sections of one in appearing in the *Meccano* magazine:

'The train itself consists of eight vehicles made up of two-coach articulated sets and two independent vehicles. Starting from the front end, the first articulated set consists of a brake first and a first class corridor coach. The second set consists of a first class lounge car and a first class dining car. Then comes the kitchen car and a third class dining car, articulated to form one unit. The next vehicle is a first class sleeping car. Sleeping cars do not run on the 'Coronation Scot' in normal service, but this sleeper has been included in the formation to demonstrate how first class travellers by night are catered for in this country. Finally, there is a club saloon which, like the sleeping car, is an independent vehicle.

'Steel has been used to a considerable extent in the construction of these vehicles and welding has been largely employed in their assembly. Teak body pillars are bolted in position in sockets welded to the solebars and cant rails, and to these pillars are screwed the steel body panels, which are welded together in units, each extending from one door to the next, and to the cant rails. The roof panels are of steel and these too are secured in position by welding.

'The bogies are welded throughout in accordance with the latest LMS practice. The outer ends of the articulated units are provided with the standard draw and buffing gear, but the inner ends are fitted with the Gresley type of articulated coupling used on the LNER. The two independent vehicles conform with standard LMS practice in these respects.

'Exterior projections have been reduced to a minimum throughout. The body panels are flush with the windows and between the bogies sheet metal valances are fitted with 12' of the rail level. In order to preserve continuity of line the space between the adjoining ends of each pair of vehicles is closed with special rubber sheeting. This is stretched into position so that the exterior of the train presents a

uniform and practically unbroken appearance throughout its length.

'The train has certainly aroused the interest of American railway men and has already been described as distinctive in design and styling and quite different from its American counterparts.'

Perhaps not the most prosaic of descriptions but it clearly appealed to Tom, possibly because it sums up some of the design and engineering features he and his team, plus Frederick Johansen, had worked so hard to achieve. But it was the Coronation class engine that gave him the greatest satisfaction, although as war loomed it seemed unlikely that this triumph would be repeated. The challenges ahead would be of a different hue. Nevertheless, in the weeks before Germany invaded Poland, making war with Britain inevitable, Tom sat in his offices at Derby and produced a very neat drawing himself of a non-streamlined Coronation with a number of modifications. He signed this work, though he gave it no title, but 'the next generation', may have been an apt description.

Wherever she went people turned out in large numbers to see 6220, with flags draped and bunting to signify the relationship between GB and the USA.

Chapter 7

ANOTHER DAY, ANOTHER WAR

Just before war was declared, Tom and his wife visited the West Country and returned with this Heath Robinson souvenir. Perhaps a must for any designer.

t would be too simple to say that those facing war in 1939, with recent experience of the 1914/18 conflict still fresh in their minds, approached another struggle in a phlegmatic or impassive way. No one but a fool would do this. But to generations brought up in hard social circumstances or having fought in the trenches and experienced their dire consequences, the power to shock was greatly depleted by experience and loss was a common expectation. They were a tough breed, far tougher and more resilient than we are today, our lives cosseted by many health and social services in a land of plenty. By today's standards, most still lived with a harsh reality that war was unlikely to change too much, though fear of the unknown would have affected the lives of even the most experienced old soldiers.

Pre-war years had seen a rapid growth in the news media, greatly enhanced by cinemas, the radio and a ready access to many more magazines and newspapers. These reported the war in Spain, the growth of Fascism and the gradual erosion of peace across Europe in an uncensored and graphic way. In the First World War, the media was in its infancy and was controlled very tightly, but by the mid-1930s access was easier and harder to censor. Such open reporting was new and had the power to shock. It also encouraged wild speculation on what might lie ahead and few were left with any hope that the coming war would not see cities destroyed in days, poison gas used indiscriminately, followed by starvation and invasion. With hindsight, these predictions proved to be simplistic and gave too much credence to Hitler's power. But by this slightly melodramatic means, politicians, the military and society in general began to wake up to the threats they faced. Peace does breed complacency and enhances the power of self-deception. But the sight of bombs raining down on Spanish cities and Hitler's fevered, hate-filled rhetoric, followed by his gradual assimilation of countries to the east, gradually struck home. Re-armament and preparation for another global war couldn't be avoided.

Despite the long post-war recession, when much of industry had stagnated and living standards barely improved for the masses, the 1930s had seen a slow improvement and expectations of a better life grew. This was no better illustrated than on the railways, where a degree of hope was fed by a policy of regeneration and improvement. These changes may initially have touched the wealthier, but eventually these advances would have fed down through society. The high-speed services provided some glamour and fed aspirations, but it was the improved freight services that did the greatest good, making the speedy and efficient movement of consumer goods possible as markets began to grow.

For the moment, Britain's leaders were unsure in which direction to go. A wholesale move to a wartime economy, with large swathes of industry laying aside its peacetime role to concentrate on armaments and the coming battles without knowing the dangers hardly made good sense. The armed forces were significantly larger and better equipped than those available in 1914, when the danger was much closer as the German Army quickly drove through Belgium and France in the first few days of war. This time around, preparations focussed on building up the RAF's fighter and bomber strength, the development of radar and airfields, organising the Army for service in Europe with an expeditionary force large enough to help counter a German move westwards, preparing the civilian population for war with evacuation schedules and gas masks, and laying plans for industry to move onto a war footing.

At the centre of all this activity were the railways, with their singular ability to move passengers and freight in the vast quantities demanded by war, and their manufacturing and engineering strength, which could boost productivity considerably. These were things that had only been slowly utilised in the last war and now it was essential to assimilate them much earlier and to greater effect. But at the same time, the work of the railways had to continue or their essential service

might be rendered ineffective. A balance had to be struck, although it seemed unavoidable that maintenance standards would slip as capability was stretched to the limit. Locomotives were at the core of this pressing need and their capacity, strength and durability would be tested to the limit. There had been much re-equipping across the regions in the inter-war years and many of the engines now available would play an effective part in the trials ahead. But more of these were needed and here the Government had to intervene and fund new construction.

The LMS was well placed to contribute to this programme having achieved a high degree of excellence in its designs and the way it had introduced production line methods to its workshops. Amongst all the new locomotives that had appeared in the 1930s, the Stanier-Coleman 8F seemed best to sum up the type of engine required in war, as well as peace. It was a proven design that seemed to thrive on hard work, maintenance was fairly straightforward, they were economical and they were popular with footplate crew for their ease of handling. But by 1939 only 126 were available; a painfully small number by comparison to the increasing requirement placed on the network. However, in 1939 the priority for more engines of this type hadn't been fully established and for the moment the LMS continued with its normal construction and maintenance schedules.

But changes were taking place as the declaration of war was followed by a hiatus as each side watched and waited. The LMS moved its headquarters from

Euston to Watford, whilst the CME's immediate entourage in London transferred to Derby. With an eye to the skill of many of its senior managers, some of them were seconded to government departments where they could offer advice on industrial processes and systems. Josiah Stamp, with his great influence on public affairs and many contacts, clearly played a part in this programme. Ernest Lemon had been an early departure in the summer of 1938 when he became Director-General of Production at the Air Ministry, and was followed by Robert Riddles, who took up an appointment as Director of Transportation Equipment at the Ministry of Supply. Meanwhile Stamp and Harold Hartley sat on various committees, until the former was killed during a bombing

The GWR had always interested Tom and he acquired or took photos like this. Although Stanier brought a GWR influence to the LMS, some of like mind were already there.

6232 Duchess of Montrose at Crewe, 1938.

1944, this promotion was made permanent. Henry Ivatt, Stanier's Principal Locomotive Assistant, continued in this role with Fairburn. Although the new CME had overall control, it seems that he tended to focus his design skills on the new diesel schemes, relying on Ivatt to lead, with Coleman, on steam locomotive work.

It is hard to judge how Stanier's departure affected relationships between the CME and its Chief Draughtsman. Tom and Stanier had enjoyed a unique relationship. Their different skills were mutually beneficial and produced great things. Trust, after an initial period of analysis and work to the common good, had shone through and they developed an unequalled rapport. The Fairburn and Ivatt succession meant an end to this rewarding relationship and might mean the freedom Tom had enjoyed being curtailed somewhat.

It is unclear how well the three men interacted, but Eric Langridge hints at some friction, though gives little clear evidence of this in his letters or books. And whilst only acting CME, Fairburn may have felt a more determined onslaught on Tom's status to be unadvisable, though he made it clear from the beginning of his tenure that all his heads of departments would lose the degree of independence they enjoyed under Stanier. A letter he wrote to Tom in early 1943, and repeated in June 1945 when he decamped to Watford from Derby, reminded him that all matters of great or small importance should passed through the CME for approval and his signature. The second letter was very specific and made Fairburn's intentions clear:

raid in 1941. Stanier remained solely employed by the LMS until 1942 when he was seconded to the Ministry of Production as one of three full time scientific advisors.

As things turned out, his transfer to this Ministry effectively ended all Stanier's involvement in company matters. Charles Fairburn, his Deputy, was made acting CME, a role he combined with being the company's Chief Electrical Engineer. When Stanier retired in

Harriet in a photo taken by Tom. The clarity and depth of the picture not only capture Tom's skill as a photographer but also Harriet's character.

Reg photographed by Tom in 1938.

Tom and Reg shared a love of cars and Jaguars of the SS1 series in particular.

1. All requests for information from consultants, contractors, etc, to be submitted to me at Watford…. I will decide what information should be supplied. As regards information from other Railway Companies, it is the usual practice to give the information required. Any requests so received should be forwarded to me, accompanied by sufficient information to enable me to reply.

2. All letters to Vice Presidents must be sent to me for signature. Replies to letters signed by Chief Officers to be sent to me for signature.

3. All my instructions to Works and various outstations which are really matters of policy should be sent out under my personal signature. Copies of instructions of a character which are signed for me should be forwarded to me at Watford.

4. All reports to Directors' Committees must be submitted for my personal signature.

5. All letters sent for my signature should be undated.

6. Relevant correspondence should accompany all letters sent to Watford.'

Tom's reaction to the CME's instructions isn't recorded, though he may have sensed a loss of the freedom he had enjoyed under Stanier. He and Fairburn met a few days later to discuss this and other matters and Tom issued a brief instruction to his staff shortly afterwards, containing an agreed method of obtaining costing details for projects. It made no reference to the CME's request:

'Please note that in future all estimates for locomotive and carriage and wagon work will be dealt with by Nelson Street Offices (the wartime base of the CME's HQ team) and any costs or figures will be supplied by them.

'In any cases where we are asked to prepare drawings for schemes which require costing or estimate and allocation forms, the procedure will be to send over a statement to

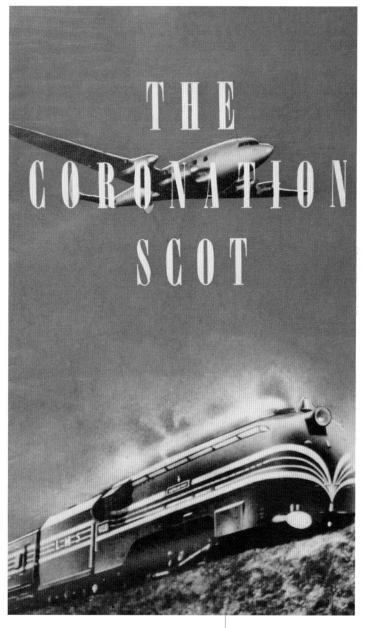

A brochure from the visit Stateside that Tom kept and had wide circulation in the early years of the war. Memories of a better world perhaps.

Nelson Street referring to the correspondence, if any, your proposals with the necessary drawings which are involved and they will do the rest even to the issuing of instructions to the Works.'

Stanier's delegation appears to have come to an end, but one wonders whether Tom followed Fairburn's instruction in spirit only. But, as an electrical engineer, Fairburn would have to leave much of the steam locomotive work to Tom, with Ivatt being his potential eyes and ears. To do otherwise would have swamped him, deliberately or otherwise, with work, which is the usual response to a perceived, overly bureaucratic process. But in Ivatt, Tom had a relationship going back to North Staffordshire Railway days which was likely to bear fruit in the new

regime and soften any possible friction with the CME.

Ernest Cox provided a very perceptive account of the way Ivatt worked; in some ways, it was very reminiscent of Tom himself:

'Ivatt was that rare type, the truly instinctive engineer who had a flair for arriving at effective action with minimum of intermediate thought processes or paper work. Son of a famous CME and occupying throughout his career the inside curve of the track as regards familiarity with the railway hierarchy, he maintained an effortless efficiency in attaining maximum results with a minimum of effort or fuss. He valued word of mouth communication from his staff, and looked coldly upon all but

the briefest and most essential of reports and memos. He was apt to blow people out of his office who came in with letters for signature after 4 pm and to chase others off the premises who felt the need to work beyond 5.30 pm. He was indeed a kindly martinet in reverse, so different from those who seemed to measure worth by the willingness to make a display of long hours, and all the time leading his staff towards his own ideal of greater effectiveness by cutting down unnecessary bother.'

With all this going on, the company had to face the loss of staff, as a considerable number continued to leave to join the services. Reserved employment status again applied to many railway workers, but the call to arms was often too strong to be ignored and this left many gaps in the ranks of those remaining, including the drawing offices. But the work undertaken by those who stayed changed enormously. New construction on the pre-war scale was unlikely, at least until wartime requirements were known, and maintenance tasks required little input by designers, whilst locomotive testing was put on hold. The production of armaments, at the railway works, was largely in the hands of specialists in these fields, particularly if it involved the hi-tech construction processes connected with aviation. There was some design work connected to machine tools and workshop layouts, but this was a fairly minor role. So there was a danger that Tom and his draughtsmen might gradually slip into obscurity.

Duchess of Hamilton in disguise as 6220 on display in the USA.

Ernest Cox caught a flavour of the time when he wrote:

'From mid-1939 into 1940, when the department had returned to Derby, there was a run down and putting into cold storage of locomotive design and development. From 1940 to almost exactly halfway through the war there was the utmost pressure to spare as many men and workshop facilities as possible for Government work, guns, tanks, aircraft, etc, coupled with the maximum make-do and mend with the existing rolling stock. From mid-1942 until the end of 1944 there was equal and opposite pressure to get Government work out of the railway workshops again. In 1944/45 there was the gradual re-awakening of interest in locomotive design and development, in anticipation of the end of the war.

'A residue of the older draughtsmen under Coleman continued quietly with various locomotive modifications which war service required. In between times they did a certain amount of doodling by way of diagrams for future locomotives.'

During the First World War, the Government imposed central control on all the railway companies to ensure that they worked together towards a common goal. It was nationalisation, in all but name, for the duration of the national emergency, with management being exercised by a central Railway Executive Committee, under the Chairmanship of Sir Alexander Butterworth, General Manager of

Evacuation gets underway with a Black Five transporting some of the vulnerable to safety.

Bletchley Rail Smash 23·10·39 View from Nº 4 Platform. Engine Nºˢ 5025 and 9169.

If a locomotive was involved in an accident Tom was eager to learn all he could about cause and effect, often visiting the site himself, eager to seek design improvements.

the North Eastern Railway. With the uncertainty that followed the Armistice, it was felt necessary to keep this regime in place until 1921.

A similar arrangement was activated in 1939, under the Chairmanship of Sir Ralph Wedgwood, from the LNER,

Another from Tom's collection. Royal Scot 6130 is lifted away after an accident at Bletchley on 23 October 1939 which killed four people.

are deemed easier to absorb than reality allows. The response of Government to the developing crisis, in the early years of the war, mirrored this dichotomy and their lack of preparedness. Today we want fighters, tomorrow tanks, then more freighters and escort vessels and so on. There seemed to be a naive belief that industry had the capacity to turn about overnight and produce the latest new product to guarantee a solid defence or the drive to victory. There was a muddle whilst the kings of industry gradually increased their influence and brought reality to Government and military planning.

These were trying times which could only be tolerated with patience and fortitude, adapting to changing needs and pressures as ably and flexibly as possible. But, on a day to day basis, life was profoundly affected by the conflict, as described by Eric Langridge:

'I well remember Owens coming down the office one bright morning and saying excitedly, "They have invaded Poland", and thinking "Great Scot! Have we got to go through all that lot again?" – not that the first war had injured me a great deal – but one thought of all the horror and wasted time and energy that war would entail. As it happened, things went on in much the same way, with the usual sketches of blackout sheets as an extra. The Local Defence Volunteers was formed and some did a turn at nights, "guarding" the C&W works area in which our office was situated. One walk round the perimeter and perhaps looked in one or

two shops, and came back to sit by the phone in the messenger's lobby in the main office entrance waiting for the air raid signal. One night Vic Stockton brought along a rifle and to while away the time we rigged up a range the length of the corridor. No doubt it was quite illegal, but no one got hurt! And a little damage was done to the walls. When the LDV got a little more organised and became the Home Guard, with parades, I opted out in favour of the Auxiliary Fire Service.

'The war also meant the closing down of the Development Office under Sanford: he went across to Nelson Street as a technical assistant; his staff went to the special drawing office there or to the Ministry of Supply. Most never came back to locomotive design again.'

The war would affect the Coleman and Lemon families more directly. Tom's daughter Marion and Fred's son George married in 1939. George, who was an engineer having served time at Crewe as a pupil, was already a commissioned officer with the Royal Engineers when hostilities commenced and would see service throughout the war, rising to the rank of Lt Colonel. Tom's son, Reginald, also a railway engineer who trained at Crewe, joined the Army and was commissioned with the Leicestershire Regiment. Both survived, but each family had to bear the absence of their sons, experiencing the extreme anxiety that only war can produce. But even in the middle of such a dire conflict, where violent and premature death is commonplace,

with representatives from each railway company, all working for the Minister of Transport. It was an arrangement that added many levels of bureaucracy in time, but did not necessarily lead to a clearer understanding of need or create greater efficiency. War by its nature is disruptive and unpredictable and there is always a danger that rapidly changing circumstances, demanding a flexible response,

life goes on. Renewal is a constant theme of nature and in the summer of 1940, with the Battle of Britain at its height, Tom and Harriet's first grandson, George, was born in Derby. Five years later, with the war entering its final phase, a brother, Michael, arrived.

With the aerial battles in Britain's skies, it was soon apparent that this would be a war fought on many fronts, where civilians were as close to the fighting as those serving in the Armed Forces. The First World war had provided a small taste of what might lie ahead. Some towns on the east coast had been shelled by the German Navy, then there was a limited bombing campaign by Zeppelins and then Gotha bombers. With hindsight, these attacks were pinpricks by comparison to the aerial attacks on Britain in the Second World War. So, for long periods many cities were targeted, some specifically for their importance to the war effort, others just to terrorise and ferment a breakdown of a will to resist. Destroying industrial centres across the Midlands had been a primary strategy in pre-war German planning and they were quickly targeted when airfields became available in France and Belgium from which they could launch attacks across the Channel. Derby, with Rolls-Royce based there, plus the railway Works and other heavy industries, was a specific target, first attacked in August 1940 and then regularly besieged well into 1942 and beyond. The haunting call of air raid sirens and a scuttling to shelters became a part of everyday life, as did the loss such warfare presaged and created.

Undoubtedly, war causes extreme stress and its effects are

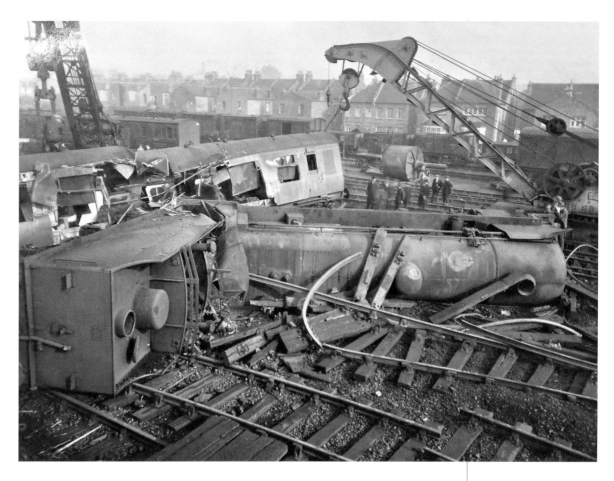

inescapable. The extent to which it touches each person is indefinable and almost impossible to quantify, but the slow grind of conflict and constant threat it generates is profoundly destabilising and will wear down even the strongest characters in time. And so, day by day, pressure grew and resilience began to evaporate, leading to exhaustion and illness, particularly amongst the older generation. In any life, a moment will come when the body and mind are no longer able to cope with demands placed on it. The greater the stress the quicker this point may arrive.

Fred Lemon had borne huge responsibility for many years

and his work at Crewe had been a cornerstone of the LMS's re-organisation and programme of locomotive building and maintenance for nearly two decades. By 1941, aged 62 and having spent all but nine years of his career at Crewe, his deafness had become so profound, and exhaustion at carrying such a heavy load so noticeable, that he was finding it difficult to meet the even more demanding needs created by war. Stanier, by all accounts, allowed him to continue as long as possible, but being a compassionate and sensible man gently persuaded his Works Superintendent that the time had come for him to retire.

Wembley, October 1940, another crash attended by Tom. The Liverpool-Euston service, headed by Patriot 5529, was derailed by a barrow that had run onto the track.

Fred Lemon's retirement photograph revealing a man gaunt and exhausted by his superhuman efforts in keeping Crewe Works running effectively.

Roland Bond, Fred Lemon's talented replacement.

The 32-year-old Roland Bond took his place and began work during the first week of May that year. In notes written for his biography, *A Lifetime With Locomotives,* he recalled these events:

'A few days before the raids on Greenock (Bond was then based at the St Rollox Works), I had received a confidential letter, handwritten by Mr Stanier, telling me he had decided the arrangements at Crewe must be revised. He had asked F.A. Lemon, my old chief there, to retire; and he wanted me to take charge.

'From the discussions that took place after my return to Crewe at the monthly Works Managers meetings at Derby usually chaired by Fairburn, I knew that Crewe had not been meeting their commitments. I had no inside information as to the causes of their difficulties. Knowing as I did from my experience as second-in-command for five years the very high standard of efficiency the Works had reached under Lemon's management, what emerged from my preliminary review of the general position concerning the output of locomotive repairs, Government works, particularly tanks, and new locomotive construction which took me a month to complete, was to say the least disconcerting. Things were really in a muddle.

'It was not difficult to diagnose the root cause of the trouble. The long established tradition at Crewe was always to take on anything and everything offered; and having done so, to do whatever was necessary, come 'hell or high water', to ensure the commitments would be met. But they had been unable to build up their resources to correspond. In the face of all wartime difficulties, this was understandable, and excusable. What was inexcusable was the failure to disclose the true position.

'No man, however able, can run a large Works single handed … My experience had taught me that running a Works is a team effort and without good assistants, whom one can rely on implicitly, it is an impossible job. I put the position bluntly to Fairburn, who took necessary action … and the Works had lost, without replacement, nearly a thousand men from its pre-war level of 6,440 staff, to the services and on loan to Rolls-Royce and many of these were highly skilled … I estimated that we needed a further 2,150 staff, but the net increase in staff over the previous three months had been only 20.'

So Fred retired, exhausted, to be replaced by a much younger man, who himself would struggle to make headway against such overpowering odds. A good team is essential, but war has a high attrition rate and diminishing resources inevitably get stretched to breaking point. Britain would have reached this point if the might of American industry had not been fully harnessed post December 1941 and the Japanese attack on Pearl Harbor. As it was, Fred managed at a time of the most profound and unremitting stress and his efforts over many years helped establish all that Stamp and his Board demanded.

Although his HQ team moved to Derby, Stanier's presence was required in London and, in the months before departing on secondment, he spent little time in the Midlands with them. There were regular visits, of course, and his senior managers often visited him to discuss progress on various projects, but few papers have survived to describe this management process in any detail. However, one example has come to light. In 1939, he and Coleman met at Derby to discuss the next two batches of streamlined Princess Coronations to be constructed. Tom kept a copy of the notes taken during this meeting, and the correspondence that followed, so we can get a fleeting impression of the way Stanier and Tom interacted:

'Visit of Mr Stanier to the Drawing Office on Wednesday 12th July 1939.
Proposed 4-6-2 Engines
Cylinders
Mr Stanier saw the arrangements for the inside and outside cylinders, and the shape of the exhaust passages and the wider exhaust ports – 2.3/8' wide instead of 1.3/4' wide – were pointed out to him.

Reversing Shafts
Mr Stanier mentioned that he wanted the reversing shafts carefully looking into as the existing ones are whipping.

Tender Axleboxes
Mr Stanier asked for the drawings to be prepared of an end thrust bearing for the old Midland Standard tender axlebox, on similar lines to the standard 4,000 gallon tender, and with Neoprene pads.

Cylinder Cocks
Mr Stanier asked to see the drawings of the cylinder cocks, and stated that a lot of trouble was being experienced in getting these cocks down, and wanted the matter looking into to see how much gear had to be removed

Charles Fairburn, acting CME in 1942, a promotion made permanent when Stanier retired in 1944. His premature death a year later ensured his tenure was short.

Even in wartime a Coronation could occasionally be turned out in a fairly clean condition, as seen in this photo from Tom's collection.

in order to get the cocks down. [Note added in pencil later 'Prefers 3 bolt flange']

PS I informed Mr Pepper to have all the engines examined to see what the difficulty was in getting to the valves on the cylinder cocks, and to have a report made out.

N.C.C. Engines. Smokeboxes and Deflector Plates

Mr Stanier was shown the drawing of the proposed smoke deflector plates fitted in the N.C.C. smokeboxes, and said this would meet his requirements, and would forward it to Mr Patrick for his information. I mentioned that if it were decided that the deflector plates should be fitted, we would make the necessary drawings.'

Within a week of the meeting, Tom and his team had submitted written briefs and revised drawings answering the points brought up by the CME. In one memo, dated 15 July, Tom himself reported:

The war disrupted and destroyed the harmony of family life. Tom captures his son-in-law during a period of leave with his wife, son and mother-in-law.

'Following a complaint made by Mr Stanier concerning the inaccessibility of the cylinder cock gear generally, investigation was made at the Running Shed to determine the nature of the complaints and possible methods of surmounting the trouble.

'It would appear that the principal trouble is that of difficulty in removing the cylinder cocks for the purpose of cleaning, or at mileage examination, after reports have been received from the drivers that the cylinder cocks are not closing. In many cases difficulty is experienced in removing the cylinder cocks, especially those carried on the elbow from the cylinder casting, due to the fact that the cylinder cock itself cannot be removed by unscrewing until the elbow has been disturbed to allow clearance between the cylinder cock and cylinder clothing.'

Tom then went on to describe possible solutions in some detail, weighing the potential of each one to solve the problem Stanier had briefly related. He ended by selecting removal of cylinder cocks at service or general repair and their replacement with a newly designed unit as the best option, attaching a copy of a newly prepared drawing to show what he meant.

In this one small example, we can see how the relationship between Stanier and Coleman had developed in the seven years since the CME's appointment. Absolute trust in someone else's abilities is a very rare commodity and only comes about when that

person has proved themselves beyond any doubt. And this is harder to sustain at a very senior level where political struggles are more commonplace and dictate a need for greater caution. Despite this it seems that the CME and his Chief Draughtsman had reached a point where trust was complete and, in truth, Tom never appeared to let Stanier down or sought to undermine his position in any way. In return the Chief Draughtsman was allowed tremendous autonomy and freedom in developing design solutions and so the Coronation Class was born whilst the CME was absent in India. It was a quite remarkable partnership with the most profound consequences for their company, for railway engineering and this country's history at a most gruelling time.

In many ways, what they achieved mirrored the work of Mitchell and Smith at Supermarine, which resulted in the 'Spitfire' fighter, that was as essential to Britain's survival and eventual victory as Stanier and Tom's locomotive designs. And this was a link made more remarkable by Tom and Mitchell's shared history. One can only wonder at his thoughts on the subject when Spitfires appeared in the Derby workshops for repair and assembly. I think that the depth of his feelings may be gauged from the photographs and souvenirs he kept of his association with Mitchell and his aircraft, from the Schneider Trophy onwards.

One sign of Stanier's faith in his Chief Draughtsman is revealed when reading through some of the letters and reports Tom signed on behalf of the CME, with the letter head revealing that the correspondence came directly from Stanier. If papers going out are routine in nature this is understandable – no senior manager wishes to sink under a pile of minor detail – but Tom was allowed to release items of some importance to the construction programmes. How others felt about this is not recorded, perhaps wary of the close working relationship that existed between the two men. And, of course, their way of working delivered great success, so other senior managers were unlikely to object. Did Tom ever flout this authority and overstep any established working principle because of the trust placed in him? It appears not. Until his retirement, Stanier held implicit trust in his Chief Draughtsman and Tom never sought personal gain by abusing the confidence placed in him. A strong sense of integrity ran deep in each man.

Throughout 1940 and '41, as allies crumbled before the Nazi onslaught and the war came to Britain's shores, the full effects of bombing and unrestricted submarine warfare were felt. For the most part, the country was fighting a defensive war, attempting to preserve itself and its Empire against a multitude of threats in the hope of gaining strength, and new allies, to begin the fight back. But standing alone demands huge sacrifices and a devotion to duty if attempts to conquer and subjugate are to be defeated. The newspapers and newsreels of the time paint a portrait of a country working together for a common good and a 'victory' was often claimed for a sound defence or a successful evacuation. Yet behind the headlines, the Government

grappled with a multitude of problems, inherited from its lack of preparedness, and struggled to find a clear path through this complex maze. But attempts to organise industry and seek to extend the production techniques and skills it had developed over the previous decade began to have an impact.

Some clarity of thought also became apparent as military requirements and the enemies' capabilities were better understood, allowing campaigns to be considered and planned. Adequate shipping and fleets of advanced aircraft, to defend and attack, were the key to the success of these strategies, whilst more effective tanks and guns would be needed if Britain's enemies were to be driven back on land, though the moment for such attacks was still in the future. But none of this would be possible if the railways could not

keep pace with all these changes and deliver supplies, war material, people to work or uniformed personnel to where they were needed in vast quantities. And as the years passed, so Ernest Cox's view of the different phases of Government control of the railways in the war began to evolve. Their primary policy of inhibiting the natural cycle of production and maintenance, from 1939 to '41, was clearly undermining the ability of each company to respond, just as the demand was increasing still further. There was also the requirement to provide locomotives for service overseas, which was a problem that soon found itself on Robert Riddles' desk, in his new role at the Ministry of Supply. In his authorised biography, written by H.C.B. Rogers, Riddles described, through his messenger, how these requirements evolved and the part

Toton 1942 and a line of Stanier-Coleman 8Fs await the call to arms.

Tom's war work included a new rake of coaches for the Royal Family amongst other things.

the LMS played in meeting the demands:

'The demand facing Riddles for locomotives was urgent, and he had to make up his mind as to how he was to get the quickest possible delivery. He realised that owing to the urgency he would have to select an existing type. He was tempted by the Robinson type [2-8-0 heavy goods engines designed during the First World War] on account of the large numbers already available in the country; but rejected the idea, because over the years they had been modified to suit the particular railways on which they were working and they could no longer be considered as constituting one standard class. There would therefore have to be new building based on an existing class of heavy freight engine.

'There was no question in Riddles' mind as to which was the most suitable. Stanier's 2-8-0s were well tried and had given excellent service on the LMS. Riddles accordingly went off to see Stanier and asked if he could help with drawings, patterns, press blocks, etc and if he would agree to T.F. Coleman discussing the problems with the North British Locomotive Company. Stanier agreed readily.

'As a result, a total of 240 Stanier 2-8-0 locomotives were ordered for the War Department, though only 208 were actually built, 158 by NBL and 50 by Beyer, Peacock. In addition to these, 51 engines which had been built for the LMS were transferred to the War Department, making a total of 259.'

In a press release issued by the Ministry in May 1940 the reasons

for selecting these engines was given prominence:

'The engine was chosen because of its simplicity of design, its known behaviour in service, its freedom from troubles in running, and its flexibility in that its gauge dimensions are such that it can run anywhere in this country and abroad.'

Riddles' request for Tom Coleman to become involved in this procurement programme is very revealing, because his biography barely acknowledges the part Tom played in designing the LMS's classic locomotives. In his position, as Stanier's technical assistant, he would have been only too aware of this contribution yet he wrote little and said less on the subject. There is also a suggestion, in the book, that Riddles played a larger part in developing the Coronation Class than reality supports. Yet it was to Tom that he turned when a pressing demand confronted him. We shall never know whether professional jealousy played a part in this relationship, but the Chief Draughtsman was arguably a greater, more gifted designer than Riddles could ever hope to be. Finding one's own limits can be disabling and realising that another person easily exceeds them can be provoking in the extreme. Perhaps Riddles was better than that, but a suspicion remains that his biography attempted to re-write history, except for this one clue which hints at Tom's great skills.

For his part, Tom saw this 'war work' as a natural extension of his day to day tasks with the LMS:

'During the war the 8Fs were built in considerable numbers and various modifications were made to suit the conditions in which they might run – even an oil burning version. I'm told they worked in Persia, the Western Desert, Egypt, Turkey and many more places (you will have seen them no doubt during your travels with the Army).

'Sir William, I'm told, agreed to let me advise various companies on the construction of this type and this went on throughout the war. There was even talk of being seconded to the Ministry of Supply for a time in 1940, but nothing came of this and I remained at Derby, spending time with the LNER at Doncaster, GWR at Swindon and the Southern Railway at Eastleigh and Brighton, when these companies built more 8Fs. At one stage I spent a considerable amount of time with Bulleid and was able to see

several of his Merchant Navy Class being constructed. He was quite disdainful of our efforts at streamlining, but seemed sure about his own efforts at 'air smoothing'.

'The war was difficult for everyone, but we got through, though by the end our engines and facilities were in a very poor condition.

'Looking back, I do wonder how engine design might have progressed if there had not been a war. In 1939 we were just getting into our stride and suddenly, for very good reasons, all this ended. It did surprise me that we were able to build 18 more Coronations during the war, but they were strong, reliable engines that had proved themselves, so were justified. Not so the Bulleid Pacifics though, which caused

Derby also produced armoured trains.

many raised eyebrows when they appeared.'

As the war progressed and many battlefronts demanded support, the requirement for more locomotives continued to grow. Whilst the Stanier 2-8-0s were ideal they had two drawbacks. Construction time was slow and production costs high, so Riddles was asked to consider a cheaper, more basic version that could be produced in great numbers more quickly. And from this, the Austerity 2-8-0s grew, with a 2-10-0 version added later to provide even more pulling power. The North British Locomotive Company began a partnership with the Ministry of Supply to

design and build these engines, with 935 2-8-0s and 150 2-10-0s being produced by the end of the war. Construction took place at NBL's Queens Park and Hyde Park Works in Springburn and Polmadie respectively, but the number required grew so quickly that the Vulcan Foundry in Lancashire also became involved, eventually building 450 2-8-0s.

Tom's involvement with NBL focussed on the Stanier locomotives, but amongst his papers he left detailed specifications of both austerity designs. There is no evidence to suggest he was involved in their production and no mention of this in Riddles' biography, but it is an intriguing

possibility that his valuable assistance might have been sought when working alongside NBL's designers in producing the LMS 8Fs.

Although a relatively small number of locomotives were built by the LMS in the early years of the war – fifty-eight during 1940 and '41 – munition production being given priority, in 1942 the company were allowed to begin manufacturing engines in larger numbers for their own use; nearly 400 by the end of 1945. At the same time, Tom Coleman supported the production of more than 500 8Fs by other manufacturers, 105 of which were built by the Southern Railway, in 1943, for the LMS itself, at their Ashford, Eastleigh and Brighton Works. The designs were not new, but at least the work kept the Drawing Offices and the shops engaged on more normal tasks. And to this was added specific projects relating to the war, including the design and construction of special carriages including three saloon cars for the Royal Family, converting goods wagons into twelve armoured trains and even some work on the production of 161 Mark V Cruiser tanks. So, the days may not have been so challenging for such skilled designers but they were busy nonetheless, and supported the war effort in no uncertain terms.

With all these tasks underway, there appeared little opportunity to test or develop ideas that, in pre-war days, had been central to their work. But both Stanier and Coleman were aware that the Royal Scot was capable of improvement and sought ways to achieve this within the restrictions placed on

As the war progressed the Derby and Wolverton workshops also tackled Spitfires, much to Tom and Frederick Johansen's interest and undoubted pleasure.

them by war. Work on rebuilding *Fury* into a conventional locomotive had shown how this might be achieved and now seemed the opportunity to put this theory into practice and seek an improvement to the 5X Jubilee Class in the process. Eric Langridge recalled how this was managed:

'I cannot remember how it was that Coleman had the idea of putting the "Scot" boiler (as designed for the "Fury" rebuild) on the 5X chassis; it may be that he thought that it would cut out one class of boiler and, at the same time, give the 5X class a little bit of a boost that sometimes they lacked … He came out one day with the order to see if it could be done and what sort of weights we should get. I gave Edleston the job to look at in detail and between us the best we could do without alteration to frames, etc, was practically nil. So we took the bull by the horns, and suggested lopping a bit off the taper "Scot" barrel and making a new cylinder pattern to suit. When Coleman said, "Cut up the taper 'Scot' inside cylinder pattern", I said to him, "What if 6170 (the 'Fury' in her new guise) wants a new cylinder?" He just said, "Don't worry about that"; I thought he had gone out of his mind! However, that is what we did: it was a bit rough on the 5X frame to load it up with a large boiler, but as only two were to be tried out I thought we might improve things later if re-boilering was successful.

'I never understood why Coleman did not give this job

to Crewe drawing office: the staff there had done the 6170 rebuild, when Coleman was chief draughtsman there, and G.R. Nicholson, now in charge, had done the boiler drawings.

'And so No. 5736 left Crewe shops in 1942 with a 2A boiler followed later in the year by No. 5735. New cylinders using the taper "Scot" patterns had been fitted … However, these two engines remained the only rebuilds … but it came back by word of mouth that the motive power people found them strong engines and liked them very much. Why, I am afraid I do not know. The little extra bit of grate could hardly have been the cause: was it the extra radiant surface in the firebox or the shorter barrel and smaller tubes?

'There was, nevertheless, an off-shoot. The original "Scots"

had run all this time in their as-built condition with their old parallel boilers, etc, and, as the 2A boiler had turned out to be a good steamer, it seemed logical that the time had come to bring them up to date. It would be interesting to find the minute authorising this work.'

In fact, the Mechanical and Electrical Engineering Committee considered a paper put forward by the acting CME, Charles Fairburn, though probably prepared by Stanier before his secondment began, and the Chief Operating Manager on this subject at their meeting on 26 November 1942:

'The smokeboxes at present fitted to the Royal Scot engines were of bad design, causing frequent loss of time in service and excessive maintenance at Sheds, and trouble could not

NBR Built 1941 oil burning version of the 8F.

As the demand for locomotives increased so other companies produced the LMS's 8F. Tom was seconded to them to help and kept this photo as a souvenir.

be overcome without major structural alterations, including new cylinders. Further, the engines were prohibited by their weight from working over the Midland Division where the class 5X three cylinder engines at present in use were overloaded.

'Certain of the engines were now falling due for renewal of boilers, cylinders and frames and it was proposed to alter 20 engines by fitting taper boilers – sufficiently lighter in weight to enable the engines to work over the Midland Division; new cylinders; and a new design of smokebox which it is anticipated would result in less maintenance and overcome smokebox trouble.'

Some broad costing information was provided and armed with this material, the committee were able to approve the proposal. Presumably they were content that the improvements noted when *Fury* was rebuilt justified this work and better performance would support the war effort more effectively. The remaining fifty Royal Scots and eighteen Patriots were approved for conversion in June and September 1944. But the programme had to be tied to the natural cycle of boiler replacements and this ensured that the task would take many years to complete. So, thirty-nine Royal Scots were rebuilt between mid-1943 and late 1946 and the other thirty-one between 1947 and 1955. The eighteen Patriots would emerge from the workshops bit by bit over a three-year period from 1946 to 1949, each one showing the benefit of the design work Tom Coleman and his Crewe draughtsmen initiated and undertook in 1935.

Even though the design teams under Tom were kept busy throughout the war on myriad tasks, there must have been a longing for the more traditional challenges of pre-war days. The Coronations, having absorbed so much energy and interest, inevitably remained in Tom's thoughts and the 1939 locomotive programme, approved in July 1938, had not been cancelled allowing some work to continue bit by bit. Twenty in one year was split over four separate years – 1939, 1940, 1943 and 1944 – so as not to interrupt other, essential, war work, and reduced by two overall. Tom recalled that:

'We pushed to have the extra locomotives built because they were strong and reliable and could pull even the heaviest troop trains of 600 tons or more without assistance, but it still surprised me that they went ahead. No one seemed to think

New Coronations continued to be built during the war, but the high gloss reds and blues were discarded in favour of unlined black.

it worth stopping construction or even questioning what was happening. But it was a "fits and starts" schedule.

'Remembering his involvement in both designs, I recalled that Johansen took a keen interest in the programme and like me found the prospect of building the engines at the same time as Spitfires were appearing at Derby curious and amusing. We toured the shops on many occasions together watching these two designs gradually emerge. There was talk of photographing a Coronation and a Spitfire together but nothing came of it, the need for secrecy being paramount.

'We did take the opportunity, when building 18 more Coronations, to consider modifications and the issue of

streamlining was discussed. There was no hard evidence that 'frocked' or 'unfrocked' was better from a performance point of view, but some considered day to day maintenance tasks of those streamlined more time consuming. Even so only four (the 1944 batch) of the new locomotives were built without casing.

'By this stage we were beginning to look beyond the war (the second and third fronts in Europe were in place and the Germans were slowly being forced back) and considering how to restore the railways to their pre-war condition. The locomotives were in a particularly sorry state and I remember that we looked closely at "unfrocking" the Coronations so built and standardising them. This came

during a discussion I had with Fairburn not long after Sir William's retirement in '44. The new CME was looking to the future of diesel and electric locomotives and saw steam as becoming a back number. So his attitude was to standardise them at minimum cost for the few years before other forms of traction took over. His interest after that was limited and he left us to get on with this work.'

There was talk, during a meeting of the Mechanical and Electrical Engineering Committee meeting on 24 April 1941, that two of these new Pacific engines be modified versions, though still streamlined. A boiler pressure of 300 lbs/sq.in., being mentioned, plus a steel firebox with thermic syphons, better draughting and a steam temperature of 750

Wartime conditions and lack of cleaners soon took their toll on looks.

6245 is named *City of London* at Euston in 1943.

degrees Fahrenheit. Certainly, it seems that Tom and his team considered a number of changes in a de-streamlined form, as his 1939 drawing suggests, but how much further this work went is difficult to assess so long after the event. But one thing is certain; the concept still beguiled those who had seen it emerge from the Princess Royal chrysalis and awaited the opportunity to keep developing these magnificent engines even further and tease more out of the design. For the moment though, they were allowed to construct eighteen more, of the twenty approved in 1939, with the other two held in abeyance as potential trials vehicles that might allow the concept to evolve still further.

Even as early as 1942, Ernest Cox and Tom Coleman had been asked to consider future steam locomotive needs beyond the war. In one paper, released in early 1943, the purpose of this work was made clear:

'The object is not to argue steam versus electrification or diesel, but rather to draw attention to the kind of development it is desirable to pursue with steam irrespective of these major decisions ... Indeed it is difficult to see complete elimination of the steam loco in this country in the next 20 years even under the most drastic decisions. This being the case it is highly important that they should not be ignored because of other developments, but rather that every effort should be made to reduce their cost of operation.

'Much has already been done and valuable work is continuing even under war conditions with such aspects as improved workshop methods. Much more can, however, still be done on the design and development side assisted by such expanded testing and resource work as will be thought possible after the war. Indeed, it is possible that development work on steam may itself have some influence in modifying the economic boundaries which circumscribe the most effective fields for the three alternative forms of traction.'

Their work then highlighted the areas considered and suggested where acceptance of these proposals might lead in preparing the LMS for future needs. Seventeen points were made reflecting their collective thoughts, reached quite amicably, or so it seems and occasionally uses words or phrases Tom often adopted based on his sporting and engineering background. In many ways, the report reflects many of the attitudes and issues he had promoted and pursued throughout his career – an open mind that was willing to learn, to work collectively towards common goals, to always seek the best most cost effective solutions, not to be hidebound by the past and to search for engineering excellence:

'A "close season" in new locomotive design immediately after the war, building only to already existing designs until new proposals are thoroughly worked out.

'That all existing designs which are likely to be retained, be "tuned up" by means of such alterations as are indicated by

Test Plant investigation and as can readily be made when major components are renewed.

'No inside cylinder engines of any kind be built in future in view of their unfavourable axlebox loading. A new 2-6-0 design is, therefore, called for to take the place of the 0-6-0 type.

'Existing range of engine sizes with modern improvements are likely to meet all traffic requirements for steam traction, except for heavy passenger and freight loads at high speeds, for which "superpower" 4-6-4 and 4-8-4 types are proposed.

'Bar frames, wide all-steel fireboxes, and roller bearings are the structural developments most-worthy of trial on normal type locomotives.

'Possibilities of water tube boilers, turbines and condensers are worthy of further investigation.

'More practical design to be obtained by keeping draughtsmen in closer touch with shop and shed practices.

'That a clear separation be made between research and mechanical experiment, the issue between the two departments being ill-defined at present.

'A plea for much better collaboration between Research and CME Departments, not only at the top but all the way down.

'That the anomalous position between mechanical inspection and drawing office be cleared up, and that this section be strengthened considerably.

'That both the Rugby Testing Station and Mobile Testing

Units to be completed and used, there being a separate field for both.'

Standard wartime conditions for footplate crew - the blackout, gas masks and helmet.

To illustrate their proposals, they attached three simple diagrams and two more detailed drawings, each bearing Tom's initials or signature – though on some copies these have been omitted or removed. The diagrams show an 'experimental Coronation type', a standard 2-6-4T modified to be a 2-6-0 tender locomotive and an 0-6-0 medium Class 3 freight locomotive, which bears a passing resemblance to a GWR Class 2251 engine. But it is the two drawings that capture the eye and reveal in great detail how

6250 *City of Lichfield's* naming ceremony in 1944 at Lichfield Trent Valley Station. Tom attended.

6251 is christened in her home city on a gloomy day in the Summer of `44.

the need for motive power, at the top end, might be developed. It would be interesting to know when these ideas first came to light and who initiated them. My feeling is that they bear the hallmarks of Tom's thought processes. Certainly, they seem to follow the evolutionary process that sets his work apart and confirm his ability to think independently. And, as has been seen with the Coronations, he was quite prepared to take the initiative and propose something quite different than that intended by senior managers. In Fairburn, he may have found a natural ally for this approach. The acting CME's background, as an electrical engineer, may have led him to give steam designers more freedom, recognising their superior ability in this field, preferring to focus his time on diesel and electric development schemes.

In this case, the new large passenger locomotive was a reworking of the streamlined Coronation Class, with a 4-6-4 wheel arrangement. This was an unusual development because this type of engine was largely unknown in Great Britain at that time. Two of the better-known examples were Hughes's 4-cylinder tank engine which was built for the Lancashire and Yorkshire Railway and Gresley's experimental WI 'Hush Hush' which had been rebuilt as a conventional streamlined engine in 1936. Neither had been particularly successful, so were unlikely to have been used by Tom as models for his proposal. So he may have looked more widely.

Although he hadn't visited the USA, unlike other senior

LMS managers, Tom kept up to date with all developments there, collecting many brochures, photographs and reports in the process. Amongst his papers are detailed accounts of the New York Central J Class Hudsons, with very favourable reports of their performances pulling the Empire State Express and the Twentieth Century Limited between New York and Chicago. Thirteen of these locomotives had been rebuilt, on the advice of the industrial designer Henry Dreyfuss, and re-appeared in a streamlined form during 1938, scheduled to pull these two premier express trains. It is tempting to think that this successful engine may have influenced his thoughts on a next generation of express locomotive for the LMS.

The proposal for a 4-8-4 large freight locomotive is easier to trace, there being no examples on British rails. But, once again, nearly 1200 were in use in the USA, and other examples appeared in other countries around the world. The 'Northerns' as they were called were described in American journals as 'exceptionally fine workhorses and have extraordinary pulling power as a result of the larger fireboxes they can carry supported by the four trailing bogies'. They were, by all accounts, free steaming at speed, particularly suited to fast freight, economical and contained all the latest developments, including Timken roller bearings and mechanical stokers. Once again papers relating to the locomotives built by Alco, Baldwins and Lima in America appear in Tom's items and may have influenced his thinking when

proposing such a design for his company.

Whatever the reason or the outcome, the plans produced were an interesting look ahead and suggested some thought-provoking avenues to be explored after the war. But it is always difficult to predict the future especially in the middle of a conflict, which could run on for an indeterminate period with little certainty about the future. Nevertheless, few doubted that the Big Four would still hold sway on the railways when the armistice eventually came, so planning to develop their existing locomotive stock would have seemed sensible. But though a fascinating look forward, the paper the two engineers produced remained simply that and no more.

Change after the war was rapid and took the railways in a quite different direction, sponsored by a new Labour government coming to power in 1945.

As the war slowly unwound and its stresses and strains took effect, effective management of staff and resources proved essential, but the results did not always prove popular as Eric Langridge described later:

'One day there appeared to be a lot of to-ing and fro-ing going on outside Mr Owen's [the Chief Locomotive Draughtsman at Derby]: he was in a bad temper saying something to the effect that Coleman had treated him badly and that he was moving down the passage.

6223 at Crewe North in 1946, her covers open to allow maintenance.

On the following Monday George Nicholson appeared and took up his stance in the chief draughtsman's office vacated by Owen. He informed me that he had been appointed chief, and that I should be his assistant on standard engine matters and that Durnford would be the same on other work, and that we should both be parked in the room adjoining his. All this was rather a surprise, the more so when he said that several of the senior men from Crewe would be coming too, and that our locomotive drawing office would have to house office copies of drawings to do with the then Standard engines, ie Stanier engines, Horwich "Crab", and one or two of the MR. So I was busier finding room for this influx and sorting the men out amongst the different sections than in any design work.

'Nicholson was not the sort of man one could get close to. At Derby he appeared always very smart. He strode into the office a quarter of an hour late and left early with his head held high. Evidently he was sure of staying and brought a house in a pleasant northern suburb. He had no car. He treated me fairly, but passed out most of his letters for me to draft replies to, and came round the office and dealt in a rather superior manner with his senior men. Tom Wright said, "He's like that", and I suppose they had got used to his manner at Crewe, but he was a very different man from Owen. What impressed Coleman when he took Nicholson at Horwich must have been his self-assurance, I presume, and that he could get on with a job quickly. He was not a neat draughtsman such as Coleman

had been, a point that usually appealed to him. Once he had been taken on, Nicholson, must have asserted himself by sheer personality and his determination to get to the top.'

Questioning the judgement of one's leader is a natural consequence of working in any organisation. Change when not explained or understood can cause resentment. Although Crewe and Derby Drawing Offices had a single head, the two organisations still saw themselves as being separate and independent. This was probably more the case at Derby, where the dominance and superiority of the old Midland Railway, in the first ten years of the LMS, had been a cause of some friction. By moving and promoting his protégé from Crewe to Derby, Tom risked the ire of staff there. The reasons for this change are lost in time, but could have been many and varied. Perhaps he needed an ally,

To celebrate the hard efforts of staff at Crewe during the war the oppoprtunity was taken for a group photo of the older workers, with Roland Bond, the Works Superintendent.

Aftermath of war: ex-WD locos awaiting disposal in the Middle East.

or felt that the design skills available to him at Derby were insufficient and needed to be boosted. It may even have been that Nicholson, as Langridge observed, was a little too easy with his time keeping, which can mean being a little slipshod in other areas. In wartime, when most were working an average of 62 hours a week, this could be an unpardonable sin. Even before the war, surviving records show that Tom visited Crewe at least twice a week and often wrote abrupt hasteners to Nicholson seeking progress on a number of projects he was involved in. But whatever the reason, its effects on the Derby team were deeply felt for a time. If so, the change only lasted for three years

and Nicholson returned to Crewe as Chief Draughtsman there when Burgess, the current incumbent, died suddenly in 1945. Yet even here Langridge hints at politics being played:

'It was a complete surprise when, after Nicholson failed to come into the Derby Drawing Office one morning, we were told by Coleman that he had returned to Crewe, and that Durnford and I had better carry on as usual. Who could have ordered this move? Certainly not Coleman, whose blue-eyed boy Nicholson had been for some years. More strange too when he told me that I had

better sit in Nicholson's chair, as it would give Durnford and myself more room adding some laconic remark that he expected he would be the next to go … Had Fairburn any plan, forestalled by Burgess' death? The fact is that he himself was taken ill, underwent an operation, and died suddenly in a Nursing Home on 12th October 1945.' His place was taken by Henry Ivatt.

Despite Langridge's conjecture, Tom was probably only seeking to move his resources where they were best suited and needed. At a time when his department was losing staff to the war, making best use of

The LMS came through the war battered but not defeated. The Coronations played a worthy part, streamlined or not, pulling all manner of loads and weights often with minimal maintenance.

those remaining was essential. So, Nicholson's transfer to Derby in 1942, and then his return to Crewe when the war ended, seems more a product of good management than of favouritism or politics. In any case, there is no evidence that either Fairburn or Ivatt interfered in the day to day running of Tom's drawing offices or sought to censure his behaviour in any way. And why get involved when he and his team were producing all that was required of them and

more? As Stanier had found years earlier, in Tom they had someone of exceptional ability as an engineer, but also a fine manager of great experience, as well as an astute team player.

But the world was changing rapidly and, as the war came to an end, new structures and ways of working would begin to rise. As in many fields of business, within four years a new generation would inhabit senior posts on the railways and a radical agenda of change

would be implemented that would sweep away Tom's generation, though many of their achievements would continue to influence the way design was managed. But most could only stand and stare as this evolutionary process rolled forward, unable to control any part of it. Yet in the few years left to him Tom would continue to participate very actively in locomotive design, wringing the last few ounces of potential out of steam power, and assist in the birth of diesels.

Chapter 8

A NEW WORLD

When the LMS's directors looked around their railway, in the months following the war, they found a system in an advanced state of decay. In truth, much of the network had barely recovered from its exertions in the First World War when the second conflict started.

If a casual observer had cared to look beyond the high-profile services that had defined the 1930s, and some cosmetic work to stations and track, they wouldn't have been greatly impressed by what they saw. Even without war it would probably have taken decades to fully modernise the whole system, but now the task facing the LMS was far beyond their capacity to respond. And soon the whole problem would be taken out of their hands as a wave of nationalisation swept through Britain's primary industries, sponsored by the socialist dogma of a new Labour Government. But change wouldn't happen overnight.

For the moment, though, everyday life began to return to normal. Demobbed servicemen and women returned home to pick up their pre-war lives as best as they could. Politicians were eager to support this transition and not repeat the mistakes of 1918, when recession and mass unemployment became the norm for many years. So, secure jobs became paramount as was the creation of the welfare state, but a near bankrupt economy could ill afford such 'luxuries' and these programmes only became possible with massive aid from the USA. But investment in the country's infrastructure was also essential, yet was only possible if industry boomed, creating trade, wealth and self-sufficiency. With much of Britain in ruins, or still tied to wartime production and needs, this was an almost impossible target to meet in the foreseeable future. This was nowhere more apparent than on the railways. In the immediate aftermath of war each company reviewed the state of its networks and tried to establish the cost of restoration, hoping that politicians would repay them for the unstinting service provided in times of great crisis. The LMS alone put the cost at £120 million (or £4billion today). But the Government's response was to nationalise the entire system in the belief that this would be the only way to ensure that the railways ran efficiently, effectively and economically.

In time, this change would be translated down, through Act of Parliament, to the hundreds of thousands employed on the railways. But until that happened the companies had no other choice but to carry on as before, trying to restore their networks to a fit level with insufficient funds and support. At Derby, Tom and his colleagues surveyed what lay around them:

'The engines were for the most part in a sorry state. Repair work had been minimal and quite often of poor quality. We had lost a lot of our best men to the war, so it's not surprising. When the survivors returned – and a lot didn't - they were faced with workshops in a very sorry state, worn out machinery and

Peace arrives and a new grandson, Michael, is celebrated with his paternal grandparents, his father, mother and older brother.

a backlog of maintenance work. But despite this new locomotive projects were put in hand within days of the war in Europe ending.'

In a memo to the CME, dated 28 May 1945, Tom listed forty-one significant items of work underway in the Locomotive Drawing Office spread amongst twenty-five members of staff. The first eight were:

'New design 2-6-2 tank locomotive.
New design 2-6-0 freight engines.
New design 3,000 gallon tenders.
New design 2-6-4 tank engine for NCC.
Conversion of 3-cylinder 5X engines with parallel boiler to take class 2A taper boiler.
New tender fitted with self-weighing apparatus for coal bunker.
Proposed diesel electric passenger locomotive.
Proposed diesel electric shunting locomotive.'

Michael with his mother and paternal grandparents.

And so the list gradually descended through new coal pushers, spark arresters, new design for motion with casehardened rod ends and plain bushes, and modified pony truck frames for Coronations, to a whole plethora of new designs for parts of Royal Scots, Black Fives, 2-6-4Ts and existing diesel engines. In addition, Ivatt had added a supplementary list of new items for attention. With work on carriages and wagons added to this list, Tom and his team were clearly kept very busy and appear to have met all these pressing demands successfully.

By December, and shortly after taking office, Ivatt was able to provide a clearer picture of future demands when the Board met and begun considering future building programmes. On 20 December, he wrote to Tom:

'I give below for your information preliminary particulars of the new locomotives it is proposed shall be constructed under the 1947 Locomotive Renewal Programme for which authority is being sought at the December Committee meeting. In addition to sanction by the LMS Board, this programme is subject to the authority of the Railway Executive Committee and the Minister of Transport.

Type No to be built
Class 5, 4-6-0 Mixed Traffic Tender 65
Class 4, 2-6-4 Mixed Traffic Tank 40
Class 4, 2-6-0 Freight Tender (new design) 20

Class 2, 2-6-0 Freight Tender 10
350 HP Diesel Electric Shunting Loco 10
2-6-4 Passenger Tank for NCC 6

'I am obtaining from the Chief Operating Manager particulars of special fittings which will be required on the locomotives for LMS stock and will let you have this information as soon as possible, but in the meantime Mr Fisher has asked for the 40 2-6-4 Tank Locomotives to be completely equipped with water pick up apparatus.

'I will write further respecting this programme as soon as the necessary authorisation is received.'

Just as the Railway Executive Committee stayed in place after the First World War until 1921, its Second World War equivalent did not disband immediately, but continued to exert its influence for several more years. So, the Boards of the four companies had to submit their plans to Central Government for approval before proceeding. Undoubtedly, there would have been dialogue early in the planning stage, so that CMEs and their Directors would not have faced censure by the Minister for showing an independence taken for granted in pre-war Britain. But, in reality, it is hard to say how much freedom they were allowed. And with so many other priorities, in restoring some order to post-war Britain, the Labour Party's favoured Nationalisation Plans could not immediately be brought to fruition. So, it was a time of some confusion – carry on as four single companies or seek some collective approach.

Tom's engines were noted for their balance and good looks, but under Ivatt's direction some ugly ducklings appeared, this 2-6-0 particularly.

A slightly battered *City of Leicester* emerges from the war still with her plain black, unlined livery.

In this situation, each company carried on with its own research and developed engines and rolling stock they thought would be required. And amongst these the Coronation Class would enjoy their final flourish in the hands of its designer.

Their programme had been a trickle feed of ideas turning into a slowly appearing reality. By 1945, a class of only thirty-three locomotives – twenty-four streamlined and nine 'unfrocked' – Coronations had appeared, in addition to the thirteen Princess Royals. It is hard to say how many more might have been built if war hadn't intervened. By comparison the LNER, which

had started building 4-6-2s much earlier than the LMS, eventually had 203 in service. Whilst the Southern Railway, despite the war, completed a programme of 140 newly constructed light and heavy Pacifics by 1950. So the LMS lagged far behind and now that peace had returned, and with it austerity, it was unlikely that more would ever be built in the numbers contemplated by other companies. There was also the issue of diesel locomotion to be considered. And here the LMS was taking giant strides towards producing main line engines capable of taking on the heavier traffic, making steam an ever-increasing irrelevance.

The four Coronations (6249 to 6252), authorised as streamliners in 1938, had eventually appeared from the workshops at Crewe between April and June 1944 without air smooth casing. By this stage of the war, it seemed

that any advantages gained by streamlining were negated by speed restrictions in place over the entire network. Added to this there were increasing concerns over the extra time taken to service these engines – sections of casing having to be opened or removed to allow access. So, the three tons of extra metal that streamlining necessitated were seen to be of minimal benefit and removal was authorised as a practical war time requirement. But to some, its loss was a long sought aesthetic improvement. Even so these four engines would appear with streamlined tenders, these having been built before a decision to drop the casing on the locomotives had been made.

In his last pre-war designs for the class, Tom had envisioned the 'unfrocked' Coronations being constructed with a number of modifications, the most noticeable being smoke deflectors. The first

five without casing had poor forward visibility caused by drifting smoke and steam, which could severely mask the footplate crews' view. Tom's plan sought to remove or reduce this problem, but for some reason this addition didn't find favour and so remained on the drawing board, until post-war research confirmed the need.

In November 1944, five more non-streamlined Coronations were approved, unexpectedly it seems, for inclusion in the 1946 Locomotive Renewal Programme put forward by the Mechanical and Electrical Engineering Committee. There was a simply stated justification for these extra locomotives, which raised the number of Pacifics to fifty:

'A number which it is considered will provide sufficient of the highest power passenger engines to meet the post-war accelerations.'

This seems to be an overly simplistic justification, based on little evidence of need at this stage of the war. But it was far enough in the future to be little more than speculation, so crept through each stage of approval. And so, Tom finally had the time and opportunity to consider how the improvements he had sketched in 1939 could be included in the design of these last five locomotives. He also had the services of Frederick Johansen to draw upon once again, the end of war meaning that the Research Department was once again available to consider the practical aspects of design. During the conflict, highly skilled scientists,

In the post-war years the streamliners lost their casing, but they kept the cut down boilers so giving them a unique and slightly unbalanced look.

Camden Shed post-war.

such as Johansen, had been drawn into armament related research, in his case aeronautical, and only returned to normal duties in late 1945.

As the Research team reformed and focussed on railway matters again, experience gained during the war began to inform other peacetime ways of working. Good management is the basis of any business. It drives best practice and sponsors the search for better performance, so that capacity can be exploited to the full. In war, this is even more important if the effects of restricted manpower and rationed resources are to be countered. On the railways, this was achieved by implementing speed limits, altering schedules and more effective firing of engines by footplate crew, so reducing consumption and deterioration. But better construction methods, using tougher materials and new products, that might last longer or be more resilient to wear, were equally as important. And here the LMS had learnt much, as Ernest Cox recalled:

'War experience had emphasised the deficiencies of existing design in several important directions. Shortage of staff made it increasingly difficult to clean smokeboxes and fires and empty ashpans by the old methods, which were laborious in the extreme, and yet if this work was not properly done performance could be badly affected. It had been fully appreciated that pre-war in the USA these servicing needs were adequately met by use, in combination, of the self-cleaning smokebox, rocking fire grate and hopper ashpan with bottom doors … they were now adapted to LMS design.

'The most valuable internal development of this period, however, was the introduction of the manganese steel liners in axlebox and horn guide surfaces … wear and deterioration in service which on the older engines required workshop attention at under 30,000 miles on average, was now contained sufficiently to double this mileage, with obvious benefits to availability and repair costs. A study at this time indicated that if the mileage could be raised to 100,000, between successive visits to main works, weekly repair output could be reduced as more engines were brought up to this standard, culminating in a possible £1m per annum saving.'

Cox, in his summary, lays credit for this work at Ivatt's feet and suggests that he himself also played a considerable part in the development of these cost saving modifications. Yet, the genesis of these design concepts seems to date back to pre-war work that Tom and his team initiated and developed, based on their observation of ideas being advanced elsewhere in the world and the results of extensive

Wartime precautions have been lifted and the crew can again 'enjoy' life on the footplate without blackout shrouds or gas masks.

testing of LMS engines. Long before Fairburn's tenure, then Ivatt's promotion to CME, the Locomotive Drawing Office had puzzled over these ideas quite independently and drawn Stanier into the debate.

Cox was undoubtedly a clever engineer and an ambitious man, but there seems to be a tendency in his books to use the period of tenure of each CME as justifying generic credit being placed on their shoulders for all work undertaken whilst they were in office. And this leaves to one side any consideration of self-publicity his accounts contain. It is true that as CME, each man took ultimate responsibility for all work undertaken on 'their watch', but it is misleading to assume that their involvement was, on many occasions, simply more than providing a watching brief. As Tom showed, over and over again, he was quite prepared

to initiate and develop new ideas independently, with little or no reference to those above him. He would then effectively sell these ideas to the powers that be. And the Coronations stand witness to his strength of character and sense of independence borne of superlative design skills and a clear understanding of need.

Stanier understood this and gave Tom his head knowing that it had and would again lead in a successful direction, and his trust proved to be well placed. But he was a very clever, perceptive man and one able to see those who worked for him clearly and delegate fully when his trust had been established, and would never assume credit for the work they did. But it takes greatness for this to happen and those who followed him could never hope to emulate these skills or approach.

Tom had worked under many good engineers and leaders, but it was his relationship with Stanier that defined his life as a designer. He would continue to work under two fairly effective CMEs until retirement, but it wouldn't be in such a mutually beneficial way. They in turn wouldn't enjoy the freedom of action that had benefitted Stanier when CME, strong constraints being imposed by war and then the confusing messages of their new political masters. The post-war years were defined by uncertainty and muddle and a struggle for dominance in the new order that the Government was driving. The ambitious, politically astute, but possibly less able, would rise to the surface and leave behind those who went before. Cox, by his own admission, was one of these

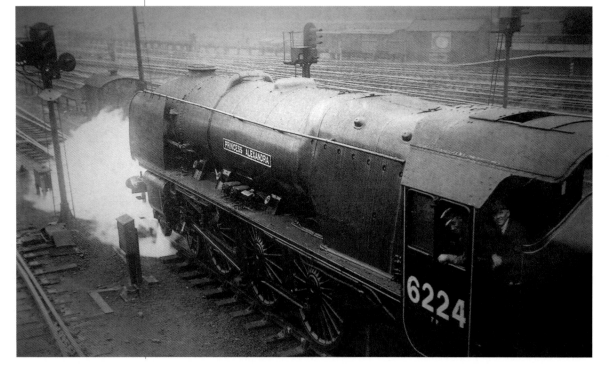

and so his recollections are, at times, a little self-serving.

It would be a time of considerable frustration for those used to a more supportive, progressive regime, as Tom recalled:

'There was great uncertainty in the post-war years. There was much to be done to bring the railways back to a fit state, but over everything hung the threat of nationalisation and there was much jockeying for position which made life very difficult. I don't think there were many 'old timers' who did not want to see the railway companies stay as they were. I think they might have managed change much better than the politicians and those they chose to manage the system after nationalisation. The LMS had very progressive ideas and would have brought in main line diesels much earlier and in greater numbers than BR if left to their own devices. The last four years of my career saw the company make progress, but it was made very difficult by outside interference.

'Many of Ivatt's plans were affected by circumstances beyond his control. However, we had worked together on and off for many years and got along well. He often voiced his frustrations at what he termed the 'politicians' inside and outside the LMS and the REC, then British Rail, but despite all this he tried to let each department under his control work with as much autonomy as possible.'

By early 1946, Ivatt had finalised his thoughts on the future management structure of his department, which he saw as needing nine separate, but interlocked groups. Amongst them were three Mechanical Engineer teams. The first, led by Roland Bond (who would also be Deputy CME), managed the works production, shopping and boiler inspection of locomotives, then came E. Pugson, covering carriages and wagons, whilst F.A. Harper took on the third role and managed 'all electrical engineering matters, including the development of electric traction'. Ernest Cox was Chief Technical Assistant responsible for developing testing and mechanical inspection programmes. Then there was the largest group, under Coleman as Chief Draughtsman, around which the whole locomotive and rolling stock design and development programme revolved. J.W. Caldwell and F.W. Gilbert were appointed Chief Loco and Chief Carriage and Wagon Draughtsmen respectively, whilst Eric Langridge became Development Assistant, in which role he supported both Tom and Ernest Cox.

Whilst these changes were being considered, and they awaited endorsement of the 1947 renewal plan, Tom and his team had been working up drawings and designs for the new 2-6-0 freight engine as well as improvements to other classes. By December 1945, when he signed off a series of preliminary sketches for the new engine, proposals covering a wide range of improvements to other engines had been completed and awaited Ivatt's agreement. The Black Fives, Coronations, Princess Royals, Royal Scots and Jubilees featured large in this work, but with finances in such a parlous state any modifications would only be undertaken when each locomotive entered the works for major overhaul. It would be a slow programme, but the target of achieving 100,000 miles between 'visits to the main works' was deemed an essential one that stayed fixed in the CME's mind.

In late 1945, Tom, who was considering improvements to the Coronations as well as the expected new build of five more, obtained Ivatt's approval for a series of wind tunnel tests on the de-streamlined version, as he recalled later:

'By this stage it had become clear that any new Coronations would be built without the casing and the original engines would be rebuilt. During the war, when manpower was short, the casing had proved to be an added burden, and after the war we didn't expect to have time or money to maintain the engines in their original form. Also, in many cases, the plating had worn badly and needed replacement as well. From the beginning the 'unfrocked' engines had a problem with drifting smoke and steam restricting the footplate crews' forward view, so the Research Department were tasked with testing different ideas. My pre-war ideas on smoke deflectors formed a basic part of this work.'

Johansen, now deputy head of the department, produced his report in March 1946, in it he wrote:

'This trouble is caused mainly by the exhaust steam, which

In early 1946 Tom obtained approval for a series of wind tunnel tests in a bid to improve draughting arrangements of the de-streamlined Coronations. Many shapes were tried by Frederick Johansen and his team and the most effective proved to be Coleman's design.

on these engines may cause obstruction of the driver's view when the engine is steaming lightly. The exhaust smoke and steam roll along the boiler top and eddies along the sides, and while side deflector plates have been fitted to 2 of the 9 engines of this class in an endeavour to cure this trouble, they are not regarded as being entirely satisfactory. At this same time, it was stipulated by the CME that no device would be acceptable which necessitated serious modification to the engine; such as extensive alteration to the shape of the smokebox or boiler profile.

'The behaviour of the exhaust smoke and steam in practice is very complicated, but it is considered that the wind tunnel gives a satisfactorily close reproduction of the actual conditions, and it can be taken as axiomatic that any improvement found by wind tunnel tests would lead to improvement on the full-scale locomotive.'

Johansen, when presenting papers on the benefits of wind tunnel tests and streamlining in one form or another, had faced criticism from locomotive engineers who doubted the validity of these ideas. Oliver Bulleid had been in the forefront of this and had voiced reservations that were probably felt more widely. His opinions, though, are a little disingenuous considering that he expressed them when working for Nigel Gresley, who was an advocate of these principles and was producing the streamlined A4s in a shape suggested by Johansen.

Interestingly, when CME of the Southern Railway, Bulleid would himself introduce a form of 'air smoothed' casing on his Pacifics. Yet he later spoke at an Institution meeting and stated that:

'I am quite unable to understand how a theory as to what would happen with a full-size train under working conditions could be built up from results from small models, obtained under such different conditions …There is a tendency to encourage engineers to think that streamlining would affect savings in train working which, in practical experience, would not appear possible. I feel, moreover, in view of the LMS's magnificent run from Euston to Glasgow in 6 hours with an ordinary train worked by a Pacific engine not streamlined, that the air resistances could not be anything like as high as the figures suggested in this paper.'

So, it is small wonder that Johansen began this latest exercise with a clear statement that underpins the scientific concept and its validity. His report then discusses the results of the trials:

'Wind tunnel tests have been carried out on a 1/24th model. Tests were made and photographs taken of a number of deflecting devices, with the wind at 0 degree yaw and at 20 degree yaw, the latter being the worse angle.

'The main features of the engine which contribute materially to the smoke trouble are:- large smokebox and boiler diameter, external steam pipe casing, short double chimney, only 7' high, top feed and dome on boiler top.

'The front end of an unstreamlined locomotive is of bad aerodynamic shape in that its irregular and bluff contours cause considerable air disturbance with pronounced eddy formation. Unless the exhaust steam can be discharged clear of the surrounding eddies, it is inevitably caught and diffused by these eddies and tends to cling to the top and sides of the boiler. The trouble is aggravated in a cross wind, when there is a particularly strong tendency for the smoke to be drawn into the low pressure region to leeward of the engine.

'With modern large boilered non-streamlined engines having small chimneys and low exhaust velocity, two principles may be followed in developing a smoke deflector. The first is to induce a flow of clean air along the sides of the boiler which counteracts the eddying tendency of the smoke (the principle of the side deflector plates) and the other to induce an upward current of air at about the position of the chimney, which causes the exhaust to rise vertically before moving along the boiler.

'Local devices, such as modifications to the chimney, which affect the airflow only locally, have been shown to be ineffectual.

'The standard engine gives a bad result, but the side deflector plates fitted to two of the engines effect some improvement. More effective devices have been evolved, at the expense of some complication. The side plates, and cross vane device, however, is both effective and fairly simple and appears worth a trial.'

Hanging over Johansen's paper is the unwritten thought that streamlining is the most effective way of designing engines and he describes the science in some detail. This was not the case when streamlining proposals were first considered in the 1930s. The papers produced then by the Research Department, for consumption by the CME and his team, contained little or no explanation. But Harold Hartley was in the chair at that time and drove the concept forward, presumably without debate or contradiction. During 1945, his association with

Tom, Harriet and Reg on holiday in 1947. Reg suffered ill-health after war service and his buoyant personality, captured in pre-war photos, seems to have slipped away.

July 1947 and 6244 at Grendon derailed by faulty track. Tom visited the site shortly after the crash, and studied the wreck for many hours. Five people were killed and many injured on the packed train.

the company had come to an end and the strength and role of his Research Department were significantly diminished, even with Riddles appointed into the post. Tom, however, remained a strong advocate of their work and found this latest paper of great interest and value. But he appears to have been alone in this. Ivatt noted the report but did not recommend continuing the experiments, so variations of Tom's deflector plate solution became a standard fit on the Coronations.

Meanwhile Johansen carried on with other tasks, but gradually began to realise that without Hartley's guiding hand and influence, scientific research within the LMS was in decline. The creation of British Rail held out some hope that he might be profitably employed in the future, but this too failed to materialised. However, Tom Herbert, the head of the team, was luckier, being appointed to the post of Director of Research for the Railway Executive.

So, Johansen carried on for a few more years, gaining his PhD, but growing increasingly frustrated by the lack of quality research work coming his way. For some unexplained reason, he resigned from the Institution of Mechanical Engineers in 1949 and, for a more easily understood reason, left the BR/LMS to become a director with W.T. Avery in the same year. This company specialised in producing weighing machines for industrial and domestic markets and employed around 3,000 people in the Birmingham area and London. In post-war years, they had begun growing their scientific arm and focussed on optical projection, digital encoding, fluid measurement and many other new technologies. Johansen was clearly attracted by the work they were doing and the status they offered.

He remained with the company, at their Clerkenwell Headquarters, commuting daily from his home near Etchingham, Sussex, for the remainder of his working life. He continued to write many learned papers and became a specialist in cinematography, a passion aroused by his work with wind tunnels. It was an interest that he and Tom shared. They remained in contact for many years until illness and infirmity intervened.

Johansen died in Dorking General Hospital on 4 November 1966, leaving a treasure trove of papers that highlighted his work and his hopes. In one letter, he mentions his days with the LMS and the frustration he felt in not being able to develop locomotive design in the direction he and Hartley thought best. With hindsight, he concluded that,' it

Engineers often looked to the USA for inspiration and amongst Tom's papers are many examples of this,including this fascinating picture of 8 4-8-4 engines.

might have proved more beneficial if I had stayed in the aero-industry … There were some at Derby who could see the future, but they were hindered by those with a much more blinkered view'.

With his continuous advocacy of their work, and evidence that the two men maintained contact years after they had left the company, Johansen probably placed Tom amongst the more progressive group. They were both scientists of some standing who met as equals unhindered by any differences in professional standing. Although from different and often conflicting worlds, it is interesting that both Stanier and Johansen saw in Tom a man of great talent and a designer of exceptional skill, finding him

both easy and effective to work with.

And, so, work on designing the last five Coronations, and modification of the older members of the class, continued. In fact, as the plans gradually emerged, the new, final set would evolve in two groups and in different timescales. But first, the question of restoring the Coronations, and the other LMS classes severely depleted by war, had to be addressed. In most cases it was simply a matter of re-instating a pre-war standard of upkeep and, longer term, seeking improvements when the cycle of major maintenance programmes allowed the work to take place. As Tom described earlier, this meant something more drastic

for the looks of the streamlined Coronations.

In October 1945, shortly after Fairburn's death, Ivatt, the new CME, drawing upon a memo from the Chief Draughtsman, raised the subject of these engines with the Mechanical and Electrical Engineering Committee, seeking their agreement to the removal of the casing:

'During the war the streamlined casing in the Coronation Class 4-6-2 passenger locomotives was a disadvantage both from the point of view of its maintenance and of the inaccessibility of the engine generally resulting in increased maintenance expenditure, and with the concurrence of the Chief Operating Manager, recommended that the casing be removed from 24 engines and that side deflector plates be provided at an estimated cost of £5,527.'

Work on converting these engines began in early 1946, with 6235 *City of Birmingham* and was completed in December 1947 when 6236 *City of Bradford* left the Works. Yet, strangely, these converted engines would continue to carry one last vestige of their streamlined form. The original boilers were built with a 'round down' at the front of the firebox to accommodate the curve of the streamlined nose. Presumably as a means of economy the boilers were not modified until they were due for replacement and major overhaul. This programme wouldn't be completed until 6246

(by then renumbered 46246) *City of Manchester* rolled out of Crewe Works in April 1960, following a heavy general repair, with a modified boiler.

In a letter written in the mid-1950s Tom recalled how these changes were received:

'By not changing the smokebox the engines were left with the look of a deflating football, or as one of my draughtsmen called it, 'a cushion sat on by grandma'. In answer to your question, no we didn't seek to wind tunnel test the de-streamlined locomotives to see how this new shape lifted the exhaust away. But there were no reports from the running department to suggest they were better or worse than those with completely round firebox openings. The

side deflectors did all that was required of them, no matter what the shape of the boilers.'

By the time construction of the next three began, all the engines had received smoke deflectors and been restored to their pre-war state. Even some of the premier services were being dusted off and put back into the schedules. Despite austerity for the majority, many elements of society could still afford some luxury and, now that the conflict was over, serving officers held an entitlement to first class travel paid for by the state. So there was a customer base that the companies could feed:

'In 1946 and '47, my last years as a Sub Lt(A) with the Fleet Air Arm, when not undertaking squadron duties, I ferried many types around the country – some to be scrapped and others to be stored in case hostilities recommenced. This often meant returning to air stations by train and the West Coast Main Line provided the best service from London, as it had during the war. Though travelling in blacked-out, grimy, over crowded, unventilated, smoke filled carriages had its draw backs. The constant stopping and starting, to let other services through, or even due to air raid alerts which carried on to the end of the war, whether enemy bombers were overhead or not, was also tedious. But that was all over now.

'In the post-war years, restaurant cars, reserved seats, cleanliness and speed returned. Trips from Euston to Liverpool,

Tom saw potential in the Chicago and North Western 4-8-4s and this may have influenced his outline design for a heavy freight engine of this type.

Manchester or Glasgow became the norm and Princesses, Coronations or Royal Scots provided motive power, occasionally in tandem.

'As an avid follower of the LMS before the war, finding a Coronation pulling the train was a bonus and happened many times. By this stage the wartime grime had been cleaned away and both streamlined and conventional engines were usually well turned out in either plain black or black with lining. I thought both suited the engines if clean and polished. The smoke deflectors on the non-streamlined locomotives also added a pleasing touch of balance to their lines.'

'One particular journey stays very clear in my mind. I was due to fly a life expired Hellcat II from Crail to Henstridge then bring a new Seafire 17 back. The Hellcat went u/s at 15,000 feet over the Lake District and there was no alternative but to put her down at Speke. Mechanics quickly wrote the aircraft off and I had to take the train to Euston, then, via Waterloo, to Wincanton to complete my mission. *Duchess of Montrose* was on duty and pulled 14 carriages south from Manchester, making light work of its heavy load. Her timings were good and the driver seemed to make full use of her power, streaking down from Rugby at a fair old rate that made standing up very difficult. We pulled into Euston 12 minutes early.

LM REGION CLASS 7 LOCOMOTIVE AND TENDER (Sir William Stanier)

extensively equipped with

TIMKEN

tapered-roller-bearing cannon-boxes and axle-boxes

BRITISH TIMKEN LTD., BIRMINGHAM, AND DUSTON NORTHAMPTON, ENGLAND

'I caught the Exeter train at Waterloo later in the evening and was pulled by a freshly painted malachite green Merchant Navy (*Channel Packet* I think) to the West Country. It was interesting to compare the two engines. My clearest memory was the speed of both and the amount of slipping as they pulled away.

'Flying the Seafire north the following morning thick cloud obscured my view, but I was able to pick up the LMS line near Tamworth and follow it to Scotland. In conditions like this such a method of navigation was simple and best, especially now that balloons and their cables and anti-aircraft guns no longer guarded the cities and

With some pre-war glamour restored to the railways, advertising was resumed and the Coronations continued to provide a potent image.

factories. There was no danger of being intercepted by fighters either and so a flight passed pleasantly enough, with the occasional express train being seen or overtaken to enliven the journey.

'The streamlined Coronations were easily the most recognisable from the air. I always felt it was the best way to view them because the designer's intentions were made very clear from up there. Throttling back and gently weaving allowed me to make a number of passes and enjoy the spectacle of a train running at speed. Their shape created the same scything motion to their forward movement as an aircraft in flight – though passing through two dimensions, not three in this case. The aerodynamic sleekness was amplified by the patterns of smoke and steam, as air resistance and speed did their work, and efficiently whipped them away. The non-streamlined locomotives were much more brutish when running at speed, even with deflectors.

'When I left the Navy and completed training as a Mechanical Engineer, then became a Design Engineer, I became closely involved in aero dynamics and the use of wind tunnels. By this stage the concepts were better understood especially in the search for supersonic speed. Mitchell's seaplane racers and Spitfires were still held up as good examples of the benefits of this science. What intrigued me most was the dual aspect of his S6 designs – through air and water. Because the floats faced greater resistance to forward movement and were profoundly affected by the constantly changing currents, eddies and flow found in open water, their shape had to be more sharply defined. Looked at in an inverted position they bore a very strong resemblance to the streamlined Coronation's shape. Their designer clearly knew what he was doing.

Sub Lt B. Graves RNVR'

The next three Coronations – 6253 *City of St Albans*, 6254 *City of Stoke-on-Trent* and 6255 *City of Hereford* – appeared from Crewe Works between September and October 1946 in LMS lined black livery. Even though the war was long over there was no immediate rush to restore red or blue colour schemes and some felt that black with yellow and maroon lining was the most striking of all, including Tom:

'All but seven of the class appeared with this colour scheme in 1946 and '47, with the rest being simply painted black. I forget who decided upon it, but to my mind it suited the locomotives in their non-streamlined form and showed them off to perfection. It would have suited the originals well too if any had been left by then. To some it seemed a strange choice, because it made them look like freight engines and appeared to be a leftover from the war. But when kept clean and polished there was no better colour scheme.'

John Powell, who served as a Mechanical Inspector and Technical Assistant with the LMS and then BR, and was involved in engine modification and maintenance, described the changes made to 6253, 6254 and 6255:

'By this time the LMS had adopted a revised policy on frame design; Horwich-type hornstays, bolted direct to frame extension legs, and manganese steel liners on axleboxes and horn faces to reduce wear, became the norm … The drop

The Spitfire theme continued in the memories of a young Seafire pilot who became a design engineer and understood the concepts Tom had tried to develop.

grate and hopper ashpan design which had served since 6229/34 was discarded in favour of a full rocking grate and a modified hopper ashpan with centre-hinged bottom doors. The standard back end frame arrangement under the firebox, and the plate frame trailing truck, were retained. In addition, the smokebox was fitted with deflector plates and mesh screens to make it self-cleaning. All these modifications were designed to reduce servicing requirements and thus increase utilisation and

mileage between shoppings. In the event this did not happen, though more for reasons of depot allocation than from engineering causes.'

As these three engines appeared, planning for the last two Pacifics – 6256 and 6257 – slowly gathered pace. At the same time work on designing two main line diesels advanced in the drawing office and the workshops at Derby. The casual observer might wonder why the Coronation design should be teased out even more when a next generation of motive power would

soon be available. But in parallel they would continue. Old and new sitting side by side, one increasingly a relic of a bygone age, whilst the other offered a new world of greater efficiency and power to suit a rapidly changing world. But the old guard weren't ready to release a science which they held so close to their hearts, presenting well-rehearsed economic arguments to justify this ever growing anachronism.

It was hoped that the changes incorporated in 6256 and 6257 would achieve the savings in effort and cost needed. These locomotives included much that had been learnt

The 242 A1 was completed in 1946 and was tested at Vitry, where this photo was taken. Tom and Reg, it seems, took the opportunity to ride on this engine when visiting France in 1947.

from the earlier engines, but to this was added a list of developments that Tom and his team initiated to tackle a number of other issues as John Powell recalled later:

'Five new developments were included:

'The four-plate structure spliced to the main frames behind the trailing coupled wheels was replaced by two bar frame extensions, 2in thick. These slabs made it possible to reduce frame depth while retaining vertical stiffness, and by setting them inwards over the trailing truck gave greater freedom in the ashpan design.

'The plate-frame trailing truck was replaced by a one-piece steel casting. The weight transferred to the truck by side

bolsters positioned behind the wheels on the rear cross-member straddling the side control springs. While neat and simple, this truck was not a success, suffering cracking due to defective casting, and it was replaced during 1948 by a revised frame made up by welding smaller cast sections.

'The ashpan was redesigned with a single commodious hopper; even with the new rear-end frames the side slopes could not be inclined sufficiently to be self-cleaning, however, and so raking doors were re-adopted. It was surprising with an engine of this size to have only one front damper.

'Roller bearings were fitted on all axles (as had been the case with 6202 Turbomotive

in 1935). Except for those on the crank axle where, to accommodate flexing of the axle SKF separate boxes with grease lubrication were fitted, they were of Timken manufacture, oil lubricated, the coupled boxes being of cannon type. The bogie, trailing truck and tender bearings were of the same size as those of 6202.

'The unsatisfactory superheat of the 'Duchesses' led to the use of the Superheater Company's Type '5P4' elements: these consisted of four 1in diameter finned tubes from the downcomer pipe towards the firebox, the return being via a single 1 ½ in diameter pipe. There was a marked increase in superheater surface, to 979 sq ft.

'There were also changes in the reversing gear and other details; the reversing aids of 6253-6255 were also included.'

In appearance, the new locomotives looked little different to the others in the class, except around the trailing bogie and the cut down cab sides. But more importantly it was hoped that the largely unseen internal changes would have the desired effect on their performance. Tests would soon reveal if this hope would be translated into reality. During their first few outings, Tom rode on the footplate, or in the trailing carriages, gauging their performance and keeping extensive notes. In one brief summary he recorded, 'Ran well and to time. Coal and water consumption as good as the rest of the class. The ride on the footplate was

Tom kept this photo of engine 241.101 that was converted by Chapelon into 242 A1. Though unsuccessful it provided valuable information on the 4-8-2 configuration.

Another locomotive that interested Tom was the 4-cylinder compound Pacific 231s series F and G.

uncomfortable, more so than the others. More tests needed.'

When they entered service, the explanation for their existence was officially recorded as offering a comparison to the two new diesels, in availability and maintenance costs. Managers at Camden Shed, where they would be based initially, were given instructions to work them intensively and attempt to get the required 100,000 miles a year from them. In reality, the LMS and then BR LM had a plethora of good express locomotives at the time and it would be a struggle for any one engine to reach an average of 75,000 miles, let alone the higher total. 6256 did manage 88,219 in 1949 and 6257 achieved 88,441 in the same year, but this was the high spot and other years were significantly lower.

Tom followed the development of the two new Pacifics and the main line diesels with great interest and involved himself very closely in both designs. Although Stanier had sought to limit his work on diesels in the late 1930s, so as to keep his task list within bearable limits, neither Fairburn or Ivatt found this necessary. Presumably the pressure of post-war work was less and allowed their Chief Draughtsman to become more closely involved and use his undoubted talents to push this high-profile project forward. It had, of course, been in gestation since the early 1930s and had moved closer to reality in 1937 when the cost of designing and building main line diesel engines had been estimated. But for the war, construction would probably have started much earlier. As it was,

City of Leicester now with smoke deflectors but still attached to its streamlined tender. An odd mixture to say the least.

some plans had been considered and outline schemes prepared by the Drawing Office well before the conflict came to an end. In a memo written in late 1944, Tom outlined the key issue involved and some of the possible solutions:

'The first scheme to be investigated was for a locomotive of the rigid wheelbase type, having a 4-6-4 wheel arrangement. Several difficulties with this layout presented themselves, one of which was the inaccessibility of the intermediate traction motor, etc.

'But the principle difficulty was due to the unusual length of the vehicle and excessive throw-over, causing the buffer heads to foul the structure

gauge when on a five chain curve. Consequently, a locomotive having two six wheeled bogies was considered to be a better proposal.

'With the motor arrangement as shown on English Electric Drawing No. 13041/030, great difficulty would be experienced in accommodating the bogie bolster with centre casting in the space available between the intermediate motor and underframes, without building up the underframe … It is recommended that the alternative suggestion made by the English Electric Company Ltd be adopted, that four traction motors only be fixed, one to each of the first and third axles of each bogie.

'On the layout under discussion accommodation is made for approximately 5 tons or 1,320 gallons of oil fuel. This would be sufficient for about 30 hours with an average engine of 1,000 horse power.

'At this stage it is difficult to give an accurate description of total weight, but an approximation for this has been made and is in the region of 104 tons in working order. It is essential that a vehicle of this description should be as evenly balanced as possible, because bridge bending moments will be determined from the bogie which carries the greatest load.'

An expanded version of this memo appeared late January 1945. The surviving copy is unsigned, but it is possible to assume it was written by Tom, Ernest Cox or Ivatt. Either way, it underlined the serious intent

that now inhabited the project, gave this development some meaning and set out the basic planning assumptions and principles. And by slow degrees, the design of the new diesel gradually emerged in its final form from the Drawing Office, with contributions from English Electric, their joint venture partner. It was programmed that final assembly would take place at Derby in 1947, although at that stage a completion date was more a matter of conjecture than certainty.

Once these assessments had been completed and construction authorised, a project team was set up to oversee development. Roland Bond was appointed to be its chairman and he held regular meetings, two or three times a month, with the key players in attendance. These included Ivatt sometimes, Tom full time, Langridge an occasional member when the Chief Draughtsman was unavailable, Harper, Cox, J.A. Ellison, A.E. Robson, the Derby Works Superintendent, and other ad hoc members. From the minutes that have survived it is possible to see the level of influence each member exerted on the project and where most actions seemed to lay. Although Bond and Ivatt drove the project forward, Tom and the Drawing Office were clearly at the centre of all developments, and as the work gradually evolved became the chief focal point for English Electric and the workshops at Derby, resolving problems as they arose in this cutting-edge design. Undoubtedly without their input and control there would have been delays. But Tom, in particular, had vast experience of locomotive project work against a tight

timescale and was ideally suited to the role of co-ordinating all the related activities.

From the first, Ivatt emphasised the urgency and importance of the project as Langridge recalled, 'Without fail the engine must be ready for the Directors' inspection at Euston on 17th December next.'

With the Railway Act, authorising the nationalisation of that industry, having passed through parliament, the changeover was programmed to be enacted on 1 January 1948. It is commonly believed that Ivatt wanted to have the new diesel in service when still under the LMS banner, as a last 'hoorah' for the company and all it had achieved. Less prosaic may be

the reality of building such a new, untried locomotive against any sort of realistic deadline.

But appear she did on the due date, to sit alongside her 'rival', 6256, very shortly to be named *Sir William A. Stanier FRS*, at Euston. The Pacific had rolled off the production line at Crewe on 12 December with probably less fanfare than the diesel, now numbered 10000, had at Derby. But 6256's naming ceremony, with Stanier officiating, drew great interest and Tom, most unusually, travelled to London to be there. By nature, he was reserved and loath to attend public events, but it was different when his ex-CME was concerned. To put this in

6255 undergoes heavy maintenance in 1948.

6236 is prepared for another turn of duty. The locomotive sparkles in the sunshine and dwarfs her driver.

France in mid-1947, possibly on some private mission. He was accompanied by his son, now back from the war and working as a railway engineer again, though suffering the effects of gastric ulcers; a common condition amongst veterans of conflict and hardship.

It is known that they visited the locomotive test centre at Vitry, near Paris, and examined several new locomotives then coming into service. But they may also have met Andre Chapelon, the French locomotive designer, whose reputation for building cutting edge steam engines was second to none. In the papers he left, Tom alludes to this visit and includes photographs and reports on Chapelon's 242 A1 3-cylinder compound 4-8-4 locomotive, rebuilt from a 4-8-2 design, and others including the 241P and 141.

The 242 A1 is considered to be the most advanced and effective steam engine ever built and drew admiring glances from engineers around the world when it appeared in 1946. But such plaudits had been gathered for much of Chapelon's career. Nigel Gresley could be numbered amongst his many admirers and incorporated elements of his work in the A4. Undoubtedly, Tom was aware of the French engineer's work and seems to have taken a keen interest in his post-war designs. He, himself, had advocated developing 4-8-4 and 2-8-4 engines during his and Ernest Cox's mid-war review of future needs, and may still have thought these realistic possibilities. If so, he could have learnt much from French railway development, then beginning to recover from wartime occupation and damage. He later wrote:

perspective, the only other times he felt moved to attend were 6220's unveiling at Crewe in 1937, then when 6254 was christened *City of Stoke-on-Trent* in honour of a city that had played such an important part in his life, and 6250 *City of Lichfield*'s naming ceremony in 1944, for reasons that are unclear.

As these two projects came to fruition, and before testing got underway, Tom had much else to keep him busy. For some unrecorded reason, he visited

The LMS wished to complete construction of their new main line diesel before nationalisation became a reality so it had to be rolled out in December 1947, a few weeks before the LMS disappeared.

'The visit to France was an eye opener. Much good work was being undertaken on steam designs, but the powers that be saw the need to change the system from steam to electric as soon as possible. Of course, as you will remember from your time in France in 1944, their railways had been left in a very sorry state by the Germans and the RAF, so it was easier to think in terms of modernisation than here.'

He and Chapelon had much in common, although their aesthetic sense was different, Tom having a much better eye for such things. One look at any Chapelon locomotive soon reveals that he saw little merit in simplicity of line or reducing the visual impact of pipes or ancillary equipment – a look reminiscent of the Lloyds Building in London, where the design makes a virtue of appearing to be inside out. Tom, on the other hand, believed in simplicity of line and produced well balanced, elegant engines. But, otherwise, their approach to locomotive engineering was to gather information, careful analysis by testing, studying and comparing locomotive behaviour and riding properties, then applying clear ideas on such things as thermodynamics and gas flow. In essence, they both had open, enquiring minds which understood new ideas and scientific developments very clearly. However, Chapelon was probably more wedded to steam designs than Tom, who could look more openly and assess the value of other forms of motive power.

Although their achievements were of equal note, it is interesting to observe how these two designers were treated in their own countries. Chapelon was awarded national honours for his work and is revered to this day, whilst Tom, who conceivably produced better engines in more substantial numbers and to greater effect, has been forgotten or simply overlooked. Such are the vagaries of life.

To a certain extent the construction of the last five Coronations, and the first two main line diesels, proved something of a distraction from the core business of the Drawing Offices. Once nationalisation came into play their role would change, but in the last two years of independence many other projects were in hand. So developments appeared to go ahead largely ignoring the coming changes. The Railway Executive Committee still tried to oversee building programmes, until the new management structure was in place, but it is unclear how much influence they actually exercised.

In 1946, ten of the new 2F 2-6-0 mixed traffic locomotives made their appearance at Crewe and this was followed by another ten the following year. Production would continue, year by year, until 1953 and result in 128 engines, the last sixty-three being built at Darlington and Swindon. These were seen as replacements for Class 2 0-6-0s that had been constructed before the LMS came into existence and were now well past their prime. In roughly the same timescale, Crewe and Derby turned out 130 new Class 2P mixed traffic tank locomotives, whilst nearly 100 modified 2-6-4 Class 4P passenger tank locomotives and about 100 Black Fives were built in 1946/47. Also during 1947, the first three Ivatt-initiated Class 4F 2-6-0 engines came into existence to replace the numerous 0-6-0 freight locomotives of the same power

Whilst 10000 was being constructed the last but one Coronation Class engine, No 46256, was being completed at Crewe.

46170 *British Legion*, now re-numbered and bearing few reminders of her previous experimental guise as *Fury*.

rating. By 1952, another 159 would be added to stock. In addition to all this there were the continuing programmes to rebuild the Royal Scots and eighteen Patriots, as well as modifications to the streamlined Coronations to manage.

The continuing Class 5 4-6-0 programme was of particular interest to Tom. The original concept had been his first real design task for Stanier and he retained a strong affection for these highly successful engines. But post-war, with Ivatt as CME, some of these engines would undergo change and be used for experimental purposes. Those that now appeared included modifications that other LMS types would also receive – self-cleaning smokeboxes, rocking grates and self-emptying ashpans. But for some,

Timken roller bearings, double blastpipe, double chimneys and Caprotti poppet-valve gear would also be added. In one solitary case, a Stephenson link motion was also tried. To some many of these changes smacked of 'gilding the lily' and did little to improve performance or the looks of these classic engines. Tom, apparently, remained silent on this issue, and quietly managed all the changes suggested. Yet having a good eye for design he must have marvelled at the ugliness of the engines that came out during Ivatt's tenure. Amongst rail enthusiasts the 4Fs became known as 'Flying Pigs' or 'Doodlebugs', which may well be an affectionate description of their looks.

So the last months of the LMS saw a heavy workload for Tom and

his team, whilst uncertainty over the future must have caused them all some concern. Change tends to be accompanied by rumour and political manoeuvring, as different people jockey for position or benefit, and this would only have increased their feeling of being disconnected from reality. In Tom's case he seems to have played little part in these games, preferring to work, as he had always done, to achieve engineering excellence in the design of locomotives and rolling stock.

And so, British Railways was launched with much fanfare on 1 January 1948, but for Tom and his family this change was soon overshadowed by a personal tragedy of the greatest intensity and pain.

Tom and Harriet's son Reginald had, when his war service came to

The war is over, but the grime and struggle of life with steam engines changed little as witnessed by these two hard worked Black Fives.

Reg's grave in Derby.

IN AFFECTIONATE REMEMBRANCE OF A DEAR SON REGINALD GEORGE COLEMAN 8TH JANUARY 1948, AGED 34 YEARS.

an end, moved to Bradford to take up a post as a railway engineer there. As with many veterans, re-acclimatising to civilian life wasn't easy, but finding a job could be a stabilising influence after so much uncertainty. Once peace arrived so the possibility of sudden death diminished and families could again look forward to a less worrying future. But this wasn't to be. On 7 January Reginald's poor health was exacerbated by the sudden onset of peritonitis and the longer term effects of a perforated ulcer. He was rushed to St Luke's Hospital for emergency surgery, but this was too late and he died early the following morning. He was buried the following week in a cemetery close to his parent's home in Littleover, Derby.

Chapter 9

THE LAST LAP

There are no depths to the despair or pain you feel when your child dies. No balance remains to your life and its rational core is stripped away by the most profound grief. There is no comfort or escape and words of sympathy have little effect. Only one thought pervades the grieving mind, 'I have lost my child'. There is a natural order to our being – life and death by generation, as age relentlessly strips all bloom of youth, strength and purpose. To lose a child breaks the symmetry of our existence and casts us adrift; our hearts and soul mortally wounded. There is no recovery, though time can seem

to blunt the barbs and provide passing distractions. But even then, a transient, unexpected thought can take you back to grief in the twinkling of an eye. And so Tom and Harriet had to cope, as best they could, with the shock and anguish of the death of their son.

Work can provide a distraction and this is one of its strengths, especially if your colleagues respect

Companionship and shared grief helped Tom and Harriet cope with the loss of their son.

your privacy and quietly empathise. And in 1948, the Colemans were not alone in having lost a child – the war having claimed so many young lives and the severely injured were still dying. Tom didn't have to look far to see more tragedy. Dudley Sanford, one-time Chief Locomotive Draughtsman at Derby, and in 1946 appointed to be Mechanical Officer of the soon to be revived Test Centre at Rugby, had lost his son in the Far East during the war. By all accounts, ill-health dogged him after that and in late 1947 forced him to give up work. His decline was rapid and irreparable. He died on 28 August 1948, at the comparatively young age of 58, still grieving for his lost son, leaving a wife and daughter to cope as best they could.

Tom returned to work, but as Eric Langridge recalled, in notes he wrote much later, the effect of his loss was only too clear:

'Coleman, upset over the sudden death of his son, retired more into his shell. He said he was only staying on as he had promised Ivatt not to retire before he went.'

Photographs taken at the time show a man shaken to his core, with zest and self-belief stripped

Tom's retirement photograph shows a pensive and withdrawn man showing the effects of grief.

away, revealing someone cast adrift from life, whilst trying their best to cope. So 1948 became a year of great personal as well as professional change, as British Rail came into being and the 'Big Four' disappeared. If his son had survived, it is probable that Tom would have sought and been offered a senior position in the new organisation. His skills, knowledge and accomplishments were, after all, well known to Riddles, Bond and Cox, who would dominate the senior positions in BR over the coming years. But the extent of his loss took away any desire for advancement. However, Riddles and Cox sought Tom's advice on locomotive design and testing on many occasions during 1948 and '49, as surviving correspondence reveals. So clearly, he had gained and retained their respect.

To aid nationalisation, the Government set up the British Transport Commission to manage rail, most road haulage concerns and other forms of transportation. Beneath this sat an executive body for each, with rail coming under the chairmanship of Sir Eustace Missenden, late of the Southern Railway. Then there were heads of specialisations – civil and mechanical engineering and so on, with Riddles appointed, 'member of the Railway Executive for Mechanical and Electrical Engineering'. To all intent and purposes, he was BR's first CME. Roland Bond described how he then structured his senior team:

'Riddles based his organisation on the familiar lines of three main divisions of responsibility for locomotives, carriages

and wagons, and electrical engineering respectively, with a Chief Officer directly responsible to him for each. He also appointed a senior officer to take the lead in the design of locomotives and rolling stock, and to co-ordinate the work in the drawing offices of the CME s' departments in the Regions, where it was intended that the actual work would continue to be undertaken. There was no question of setting up a centralised design office at Headquarters (in the old Great Central Hotel at Marylebone).

'Two of the three Chief Officers, Ernest Pugson and myself, came from the LMS … Cox, in charge of design, also came from Derby. A fourth key man in the new organisation, the administrative assistant, was George Hussey, also from the LMS at Euston HQ.'

In the immediate aftermath of bereavement, it was this new structure to which Tom returned. As word got around, it would have undoubtedly been a major talking point of those at Derby, and all the other rail centres across Britain. In some ways, the predominance of well-known LMS names might have reassured many of their old colleagues, but it was still a radical change from the world which they had served for so long. There was also the impact of tighter Central Government control to consider. But as funds had been restricted, due to war and recent austerity, there was a hope amongst some that this constraint might be lifted. However, this was counter balanced by real concern that there might be large scale redundancies if true modernisation were to be accomplished and road haulage continued its inexorable rise, this despite having a socialist

The second to last Coronation and the first main line diesel stand side by side at Euston in January 1948, 6256 soon to be named after Stanier.

Stanier poses on the footplate after the engine's naming ceremony.

government with the closest links to a trade union movement growing in strength and will to resist. With so many rail centres inherited from the 'Big Four' operating, duplication was unavoidable. It took only a small step of imagination to realise that some rationalisation was inevitable.

As with any new organisation the early months are usually a time of confusion, as new systems are developed and imbedded. As Eric Langridge recalled, change raises many questions of varying degrees of importance:

'The first indication of the change was an enquiry from St Rollox as to what they should put on the tenders in place of "LMS"? The Scots seem to like being precise and St Rollox were our great friends. We thought the best thing was to paint "BRITISH RAILWAYS" in the absence of instructions from on high … In due course when people had settled down at Marylebone a small drawing of the lion emblem came down.'

Much more of importance, plus greater central control, would follow shortly, but for the moment, the construction and development programmes already agreed remained in place. And so Tom immersed himself in this work and found in locomotive testing programmes a particularly effective distraction; it was something that had always absorbed him and would do so again. Movement and activity, at times of great emotional stress, can temporarily bring some calm, though it may only offer some fleeting respite from grief. Politics and jockeying for position, which had never been his strong suit, became of even less relevance and BR's early days would be full of such things.

With the new diesel electric locomotive, as well as the two new Coronations, now in service, their capability needed to be observed and analysed. How the new BR organisation would view these two developments, and which way they would direct engine strategy, was unclear. But for the moment both might contain ideas that could direct future policy, so were pursued. One thing is certain, though, Tom would work hard to establish the merits of these and other schemes, but whilst he did, the central focus of the new organisation rapidly moved on leaving him behind. It seems that he didn't have the will or desire to keep up. As Langridge observed, he placed a protective shell around himself, so as to shield a grieving heart. He seemed to lose his driving ambition and spur to design new and better locomotives. In some ways, the change to BR allowed him to do this and some believed that he had lost heart because the old order was fast disappearing. In this they mistook the reason for the gradual erosion of his strength of mind and interest. But only those who experience such a death can truly understand the melancholy and corrosive effect of loss.

So in the months that followed, Tom became a frequent presence on the footplate of many locomotives, recording performances, seeking the opinions of their crew and welcoming the numbing effect of movement. He also visited sheds at Camden, Willesden, Crewe, Liverpool and Glasgow on many occasions. He talked to staff at each place and watched the process of locomotive preparation and disposal, taking many photographs, which he developed later in his temporarily converted kitchen – war time blackout measures aiding the transformation.

In mid-June, he began taking an increasing interest in 'Turbomotive', then still plying her trade as a singleton engine, but gradually reaching a time when scrapping or conversion would become real possibilities. He pulled out the modification proposals left to one side when the Princess Royals were transformed into Coronations during 1937. In isolation, he began working on these schemes again, seeing the turbine locomotive as a worthwhile recipient of these designs, often taking the plans home to consider the changes during the long nights. And he took the opportunity to travel with this unique engine on several occasions, taking the controls on the faster sections between Euston and Liverpool. He later recalled his thoughts in a letter:

'She was a magnificent locomotive, but came too late to be developed in bigger numbers or types. The crew I spoke to seemed to prefer her to the Royals, Coronations and Scots. Some believed, including me, that more should have been built, with 2-8-0s being modified to take turbines, as they had in Sweden. But for the war this might have happened.

'I met Henry Guy [of Metrovick and the engine's chief architect] on many occasions when 6202 was being built and then afterwards when the engine was undergoing test. He was, with Sir William, a strong supporter of building more,

The Loco Exchange Trials of 1948. *City of Bradford* working on the old LNER lines.

but felt that [Ernest] Lemon and Urie actively sought the end of the experiment and even placed obstacles in its way.

'But despite some problems in service, which could take a long time to fix, there being no pool of spare parts for the turbine units, the engine was kept going, but always under threat. From Spring 1947 to April 1948 the engine ran a creditable 60,000 miles or so, but then entered the works not emerging again for 12 months. It seemed that her days as a turbine might be over and so my mind turned to her conversion, but back into service she went until 1950 when she was mothballed. But my plans were eventually dusted off and the engine would appear in 1952, part Royal and part

Coronation. In this form I rode on her twice as a passenger and was very sorry to see that the Harrow crash ended her life before having a chance to prove what she could do.'

In January 1948, the first tests with 10000 began, before she entered revenue earning service. LMS Report No 91 appeared shortly afterwards and Tom's heavily inscribed copy still exists. These initial tests had a single purpose, 'To obtain full particulars of the performance, and fuel consumption of the Diesel-Electric engine when working under conditions designed to test the full capabilities of the engine.'

The tests took place on 14/15 January between Derby and St Pancras, then to Manchester before returning to Derby, each time pulling a special train of

393 tons. With only a few days between his son's death and these trials Tom was unable to attend and Langridge deputised for him, providing his chief with extensive notes and assessments. Considering that the locomotive was unfamiliar, with a driver having only worked the engine for thirty minutes or so before the tests began, the results were satisfactory:

'Sectional times were maintained without difficulty on the severest sections of the route, and 21 minutes were gained on the scheduled running time (8 hours and 18 minutes) for the whole test.

'The test schedule demanded sustained high power development, and the engine was worked to full capacity for long periods, giving a consistent 900 to 950 HP at the drawbar over a speed range of approximately 20 to 75 mph.

'The diesel electric engine appears to be approximately three times more efficient, in terms of fuel per Drawbar Horse Power per hour, than the steam locomotive.'

Testing carried on through to February, with Tom riding in the cab on occasions. The engine's performance continued to be satisfactory, with teething problems seemingly easy to correct. Tom's experienced eye quickly saw potential faults in the design and, when not attending himself, left Langridge, or whoever from his team might be present, a list of items to be observed. Each person was instructed to report back to him as soon as possible after

In April 1948 46251,pulling a mail train,crashed into an express pulled by 6207 at Winsford. Tom again attended and kept notes.

46257: The last Coronation and the only one to be constructed under the BR banner, appearing in May 1948.

each run. And so, by degrees, he began to assemble a large body of research data essential to the programme and future development of diesel traction. But his interest in this project, although shared by Ivatt and others at Derby, was not universally applauded or welcomed, especially with the new central team set up by Riddles in London. Their primary aim was to bring the four companies together, to work as one and implement a single development policy. Yet each still seemed pre-disposed to follow independent lines. As H.C.B. Rogers observed in his biography of Robert Riddles:

'The erstwhile CMEs at this time were variously engaged.

Ivatt was busily occupied with his diesel locomotives and the troubles that arose around them; Bulleid was trying to make a success of his controversial "Leader" class of steam engine and was busy as well with double deck carriages and other imaginative projects; the amiable Peppercorn was happily turning out lots of Pacifics; and Hawksworth watched approaching events in the comfortable knowledge of Great Western superiority.'

So Riddles, Bond and Cox had to pick their way through this political minefield and establish a common approach, which had to recognise financial constraints as well as the difficulty of initiating change. Rightly or wrongly, the new team laid great emphasis

on constructing more steam locomotives, believing that the cost of electrification and dieselisation too great to bear in post-war austerity hit Britain. Whether this decision was influenced by their own preference for steam is difficult to assess. But with rapid advances in diesel design being made by the LMS, in particular, and the example of steam replacement taking hold in most developed countries, their decision is open to question. Research into alternative forms of motive power didn't stop, but it seems to have taken a back seat. And so, the new management group set about developing their own locomotive programme, hoping that this would draw together the best that each region could offer.

Ernest Cox described what happened next:

'Quite unashamedly, and with deliberate intent, Riddles at once initiated a fact finding process which involved the work of a lot of people split up into several different committees. Amongst these a locomotive testing committee was set up to draw together the testing sections of each of the former companies, and to administer the use of new equipment which was now becoming available. More immediately this group was asked to organise, and report the results of, a comprehensive series of interchange trials in which the principal locomotive classes on each Region would be tested over the main lines of its own and of the other regions in order to see what happened.

'We were mercifully spared one possible embarrassment. With the exception of Bulleid's "Leader" design, a diagram for a Doncaster design of small 2-cylinder 2-6-0 and a proposal for a pannier tank with low axle loads for the Western, there were no new projects from the former companies which required any decision on whether to continue or to stop them.'

Despite progress being made on diesel design, no place was found in this new BR world for its immediate expansion or development. This must have come as a blow to Ivatt, who had become one of its major advocates. As he pointed out in a letter written in late 1948, 'with potential fuel efficiency three times greater than steam engines, the difference in fuel costs would have been quickly balanced or bettered

19 November 1951 and 46252 derails at Polesworth. Although retired, Tom still followed the investigation that followed and acquired a report and photographs.

An echo of pre-war glamour returns.

The first BR standard Pacific under construction at Crewe in 1951. Tom played an active part in their evolution and visited the works to see them under construction, although retired by then.

by lower consumption rates per mile and better DBHP PH.'

But his words fell on deaf ears and diesel and electric traction began to lose the impetus Derby had given these developments. When interchange trials took place the presence of 10000 or its sister engine would have provided an interesting comparison. As it was, Tom did his own analysis, by comparing the diesels to the last two Coronations; partly privately and partly in the hope that attitudes might change:

'It seemed to be short sighted to ignore all the work undertaken on main line and shunting diesels by the LMS. They proved themselves to be efficient and only needed a little more refinement to resolve teething problems and make them generally available in greater numbers. Fuel costs and production costs were put forward as reasons to delay development, but these arguments were spurious, especially when considering the cost of Riddles' standard locomotives. The high cost of building the first two diesels was taken by some to mean they would have all cost the same amount, forgetting that a larger number would make cost per unit significantly less. It would have been better if the Railway Executive had simply continued building the best in each field that the

The scene of indescribable carnage that met rescuers at Harrow on 8 October 1952, captured in this photo that Tom kept in his files.

four new regions could offer, giving priority to diesels until electrification could become a reality. My overseas visits and all I saw there convinced me that this would have been the best way forward.

'Stanier's locomotives had taken steam as far as it was possible to go and this became even more obvious when comparing the best of steam – the Coronations – with the new main line diesels.'

Coming from such a gifted designer of steam locomotives, this assessment carries great weight. But, by nature, he looked to the future, even when the past threatened to overwhelm him, and his enquiring mind always sought better ways of achieving change. In essence, he was a realist, with an eye for good design and the

needs of an advancing world. One wonders if he had been selected to guide the new organisation, rather than Riddles, where the drive for change might have led. It seems likely that Tom would have been more creative and forward thinking, looking for more than another range of obsolescent steam locomotives that would soon be scrapped. But it wasn't to be and Riddles' comparative trials went ahead and the charade was played out. And, perhaps, if the Labour Government hadn't been so tolerant of trade unions, growing more radical and ever more powerful, plus their desire to make a success of a nationalised coal industry, Britain's political masters might have looked beyond a steam solution.

Although not selected to be part of the team that managed these trials, which ran from April

to September 1948, Tom followed events very closely. Three classes in which he had played such a large part in creating were well represented – a Coronation, a Black Five and an 8F – and a rebuilt Royal Scot was also included. These locomotives would be matched against the best the other three regions could offer. Amongst their number would be an A4 and a B1 from the LNER, a Merchant Navy and West Country Class from the Southern, whilst the Western Region would turn out a King and a Hall, amongst others. And, according to their intended role and power classification, they would perform in one of three groups – express, mixed traffic and freight – with all performing over routes in each region.

Even before all the trials had been completed, Ernest Cox produced a report outlining the aims of a future standardisation programme and the types it should champion. In many ways, it reflected the work he and Tom had undertaken during the war when considering post-war steam locomotive development. Cox described his report as becoming, 'the blue print upon which the ultimate design of the standard engines was closely based' and listed twelve basic designs to be pursued. And behind these assumptions he laid credit on the work undertaken by the LMS, through Stanier and Ivatt's leadership. He later wrote, in his book *Locomotive Panorama*:

'Firstly, the recent work under Ivatt had shown how essential it was to develop in the direction of easier maintenance and more

46242 slowly emerges from the debris, her dead crew being deemed responsible for the accident. The engine survived, not so 46202 which was scrapped.

9 April 1956 and *City of Lichfield* pulls easily away from Lancaster with a fairly light 11 carriage load for a Coronation.

study of other peoples' practice, plus the illuminating example of Stanier's 2 and 3-cylinder 2-6-4 Tanks, showed little if any advantage for multi-cylinders up to the point where their use became inescapable due to loading gauge considerations.'

In reality, a broad cross section of ideas and concepts were drawn from each region, but, as Cox confirmed, seventeen major design elements, introduced by Stanier and Tom, appeared on the new engines, though three of these could be said to be adaptions of ideas brought by the CME from the GWR. There were far fewer contributions from the GWR, LNER and SR.

It is entirely within the bounds of possibility that Riddles and Cox had a natural bias towards anything with an LMS stamp on it. But, if this was the case, they could simply have adopted the company's engines in their entirety without

miles between shop repairs, not only for the obvious economy, but also to combat labour shortages. Secondly, experience with the LMS Pacifics greatly favoured for the larger engines the straight-sided wide firebox clear of all

coupled axles which gave best firebox life, ashpan capacity, and access for combustion air. The lower combustion rates made possible under heavy working were also considered an important contribution to efficiency. Thirdly, the closest

City of Salford, the last Coronation Class
engine, well into her stride.

The guts of the new BR were freight trains that competed with
road haulage for business. Here two 8Fs pass at Lichfield.

debate and not have bothered about
comparative trials. Most LMS types,
other than the Pacifics, were already
operating over the other regions so
were well known and appreciated
and, of course, the 8Fs had been
manufactured in the other regions
during the war.

Design work for these new
engines was spread amongst the
four regional centres – Swindon,
Doncaster, Brighton and Derby –
with each being given a twin role.
However, by this stage the drawing
offices' functions had been split up,
so Tom no longer oversaw work on
carriages and wagons. He expressed
no opinion on this change, though
seems to have enjoyed the challenge
managing both centres of design, so
may have seen the change as part of
the gradual erosion of his role. Cox
described how the new dual tasking
arrangement worked:

'Each design office was first
of all made "parent" for a
particular locomotive type
or types for which it had to
undertake the completed
production drawings.
Superimposed upon this, each
office was made responsible
for a range of components
applicable to all types. Thus, for
example, the Class 7 4-6-2 under
Derby sponsorship carried
bogies and trucks, wheels, tyres,
axles and spring gear designed
at Derby for the whole series,
but at the same time drawings
of steam fittings and boiler
and smokebox drawings came
from Swindon. Coupling and
connecting rods and valve gear
drawings from Swindon, and
brake and sanding gear details
from Brighton. Although this

Black Fives continued to play a significant part in BR's operation and were still being built in 1951.

sounds complicated it worked like a charm.'

In time, Derby would lead on scheming five standard classes, but it is interesting to note that the first two would be Class 6 and 7 Pacifics. With Tom's reputation for excellence in designing locomotives of this type, it is likely that he was entrusted with this programme because of his record of success. In time Derby would also take on a Class 8 Pacific, a Class 2 2-6-0 tender engine and a Class 2 2-6-2 tank engine. Their 'dual role' in the new organisation would also

see Tom's drawing office design tenders, axles, axleboxes, springs, wheels, two axle trucks and bogies for engines across the entire range. In addition, they kept responsibility for any modifications to existing LMS types. So, the programme of work was a substantial one, but with a level of control unseen in pre-BR days.

Even though grief would afflict Tom for the rest of his life, work continued to act as a distraction as the months passed. To some, he may have appeared unchanged and he certainly involved himself actively in the new locomotive

programme, but there was an increasing tiredness in his actions and a notable absence of his old vigour. Yet he still managed to embrace change and keep abreast of new developments, even though frustrated by an apparent lack of original thought by Riddles and his HQ team. He also took the opportunity to visit France, for the second time since the war ended, and then Switzerland to view developments there. This trip began as a visit to the Swiss Locomotive and Machine Works, at Winterthur, to discuss rotary snow ploughs built there. But whilst there, he took the opportunity to assess locomotive development as well, with particular interest in their electrification programme. This would give him a flavour of the future beyond his own working life. As always, he was interested in all he saw and kept notes of the engines he witnessed in operation and details of their performances. The habits of a life time were hard to break, even so late in the day.

One other key issue that drew his attention was progress being made towards building the long-awaited Locomotive Test Centre at Rugby. Finally, the pre-war plans carefully fostered by Stanier and Gresley had come to fruition. On 19 October 1948, Alfred Barnes, the Minister

The Coronations ploughed on through nationalisation, here at Wigan, their performance never being bettered by the new Pacifics.

The eventual scale of BR's standard steam loco programme, many of which drew heavily on Stanier and Coleman's work.

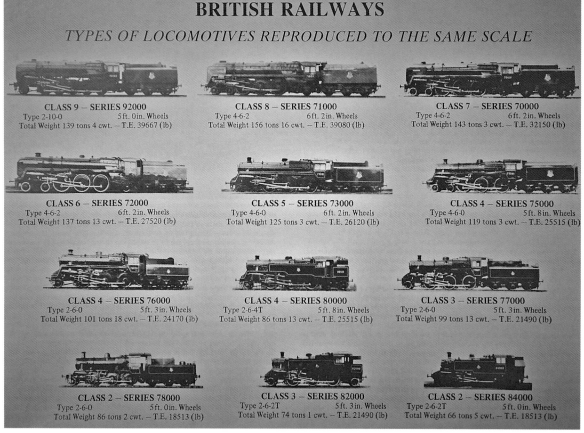

BRITISH RAILWAYS
TYPES OF LOCOMOTIVES REPRODUCED TO THE SAME SCALE

CLASS 9 — SERIES 92000
Type 2-10-0   5ft. 0in. Wheels
Total Weight 139 tons 4 cwt. — T.E. 39667 (lb)

CLASS 8 — SERIES 71000
Type 4-6-2   6ft. 2in. Wheels
Total Weight 156 tons 16 cwt. — T.E. 39080 (lb)

CLASS 7 — SERIES 70000
Type 4-6-2   6ft. 2in. Wheels
Total Weight 143 tons 3 cwt. — T.E. 32150 (lb)

CLASS 6 — SERIES 72000
Type 4-6-2   6ft. 2in. Wheels
Total Weight 137 tons 13 cwt. — T.E. 27520 (lb)

CLASS 5 — SERIES 73000
Type 4-6-0   6ft. 2in. Wheels
Total Weight 125 tons 3 cwt. — T.E. 26120 (lb)

CLASS 4 — SERIES 75000
Type 4-6-0   5ft. 8in. Wheels
Total Weight 119 tons 3 cwt. — T.E. 25515 (lb)

CLASS 4 — SERIES 76000
Type 2-6-0   5ft. 3in. Wheels
Total Weight 101 tons 18 cwt. — T.E. 24170 (lb)

CLASS 4 — SERIES 80000
Type 2-6-4T   5ft. 8in. Wheels
Total Weight 86 tons 13 cwt. — T.E. 25515 (lb)

CLASS 3 — SERIES 77000
Type 2-6-0   5ft. 3in. Wheels
Total Weight 99 tons 13 cwt. — T.E. 21490 (lb)

CLASS 2 — SERIES 78000
Type 2-6-0   5ft. 0in. Wheels
Total Weight 86 tons 2 cwt. — T.E. 18513 (lb)

CLASS 3 — SERIES 82000
Type 2-6-2T   5ft. 3in. Wheels
Total Weight 74 tons 1 cwt. — T.E. 21490 (lb)

CLASS 2 — SERIES 84000
Type 2-6-2T   5ft. 0in. Wheels
Total Weight 66 tons 5 cwt. — T.E. 18513 (lb)

of Transport, officially opened the facility, an event attended by many famous names in locomotive engineering, including Sir William himself and the other CMEs. A whole host of senior London Midland men were also there, but Tom declined his invitation, leaving a very noticeable gap in the ranks of key figures. But his ever-present need for privacy, and as little fuss as possible, remained intact, magnified now by loss. Nevertheless, he followed all these events very closely, eager to see the facility he and the CME had thought essential for so many years, open and ready for business.

For demonstration purposes, one of the A4s, appropriately 60007 *Sir Nigel Gresley*, was run on the rolling road once the opening ceremony was over. But it would be another seven months before the first engine underwent full testing. Essential commissioning work on the centre's equipment had to be completed before the locomotive evaluation programme could begin in earnest. But if a long productive future was predicted for Rugby it was a hope destined to be stillborn.

Ten years later, the last steam engine would pass through the hands of these specialists. The centre would then be mothballed, any need for it having been erased by rapidly changing circumstances. Whilst it lasted, only twenty-six locomotives underwent test, barely enough to justify the cost of the facility. Some would call it a 'white elephant', whilst others, including Tom, regretted that it hadn't been built decades earlier. Churchward, in the west, had been more perceptive and forward looking. In 1904, the GWR opened their own test plant – in the heyday of steam when there was much to be exploited and improved. By 1948 the end was in sight and potential gains from testing steam engines had been all but exhausted.

In retirement, Tom followed the work of the centre, through magazines and newspaper articles and contact with old colleagues at Derby, but didn't have the opportunity to see a locomotive being tested there. But he did acquire by some means a copy of test data after a series of his Class 5s had passed through the centre's hands in 1950. He may also have listened to a BBC live broadcast on 18 May that year when 45218 was tested on the rolling road at high speed.

Although he wouldn't see the construction of the new BR Pacifics before retirement, or even the end of the planning stage, he actively participated in the design of both new classes. One wonders

Black Fives could be found all over the network. Here at Paddington on a 'special'.

A photo taken by Tom, apparently, during one of his trips following retirement.

if he saw them as an evolution or merely a superfluous shadow of the Coronations. He expressed no view that has come to light, so we shall never know. But with such an excellent class of engine available, supported by Jubilees, Royal Scots and Black Fives, it may have seemed an unnecessary development. And, of course the other regions had their own very effective engines still running. But such criticisms were unlikely to find a voice when BR's senior management were determined to pursue their own dreams of steam locomotion.

Eric Langridge probably summed up what others felt about these changes when he wrote:

'In 1948 Coleman brought into Derby Development Drawing Office the first diagrams of the proposed range of the new BR steam locomotives. They had been drawn out at Marylebone HQ. No doubt Riddles had obtained the agreement of his fellow members of the Railway Executive and the approval of the BTC for his general designs. They appeared to be very much what one would have expected from him, remembering his Crewe works background; simple and straightforward for manufacture and maintenance. I have read since then that the Commission were of the opinion that the Executive were too conservative in their proposals and would have liked to see them make more effort to explore other types of traction before embarking on a series of new designs of steam engines that should last for 30 years or more.

'Riddles must have got the goodwill of the Regional MEs, who were formally the CMEs of their own railways. These men were mostly waiting for retirement to come along or on the look-out for other jobs: it was the second line men, who would succeed to their positions, who were more critical of the dropping of multi-cylinder designs and were more vociferous.'

Despite these objections and disagreements work on the new designs slowly progressed, but as Langridge again recalls a sense of independence still beat in some hearts:

'As Marylebone were using Ivatt's Development Drawing Office it was natural that Coleman should be invited to look over the designs. There was no love lost between him and the executive design officer at Marylebone HQ, in fact he said to me that Ivatt had persuaded him to stay on until he [Ivatt] retired, otherwise he himself would have retired.

'So we started off on the development of the Marylebone proposals. Coleman was of course our boss, and he saw and initialled practically everything that came in and went out: the letters were signed over Ivatt's name. Coleman was not playing second fiddle and had few comments to make unless something in particular irritated him, as for instance the boiler ratios, and then he would have something to say to HQ.'

In his writings, Langridge suggests that Tom didn't enjoy the best of relationships with either Ivatt or Cox. But in reality, he worked

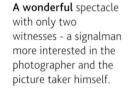

A wonderful spectacle with only two witnesses - a signalman more interested in the photographer and the picture taker himself.

Two BR Pacifics found their way to the Rugby Test Centre - 70005 in 1951 and 70025 in 1952. Tom procured both reports, his interest undiminished in all railway matters.

closely with both men over a prolonged period successfully. There may have been differences of opinion – inevitable when strong people work together in a dynamic, pressured environment – but when each spoke or wrote of the other it was in terms of respect, not hostility. In fact, it is in Ernest Cox's writings that we find many positive descriptions of Tom and references to his great skills. Riddles and Bond barely mention him and even Stanier did not feel moved to write on the subject. So one is left with the impression that

Langridge was mistaken or was revealing a level of dislike he may have felt himself towards Ivatt and Cox. He did, after all, condemn Stanier when writing, 'I came to the conclusion that he was no designer'. And he was also critical of a number of other colleagues, including the Chief Draughtsman. So perhaps his memoirs should be treated with a little caution in certain respects.

Tom, as one would expect of such an experienced designer, took the opportunity, offered by the new management structure, to look more

closely at Pacific engines on the other regions. Amongst his papers there appeared new assessments of Gresley's A4s and Bulleid's Merchant Navy Class and his light Pacifics. Although products of a different age, and constructed with air smoothed casing, the engines underneath these shrouds offered much for the open minded to consider.

During the early stage of planning for the new Pacifics, he visited Doncaster and Brighton to gather information and drawings, then rode on several examples to

Finally in 1955 a Coronation went under test at Rugby. A rather pointless exercise on such an established class. The report proved of little value.

gauge their post-war form. It is difficult to assess what effect these engines had on the design of the new Pacifics, but as ever, even in this late stage of his career, he was prepared to look more broadly for ideas and solutions. Disillusionment

may have been creeping into his view of the railway world, but it didn't stop him being a good scientist and engineer.

It is rumoured that he prepared rough sketches of an A4 and Merchant Navy stripped of their

casing in his search for better form and function. If so, these haven't come to light yet, but there is an echo here of earlier work to defrock the streamlined Coronations.

Although conjecture, he seems to have predicted the rebuilding of the Merchant Navy Class, and many of the light Pacifics, by Ron Jarvis, an old colleague of his at Derby, within a few years. And some would later comment on the resemblance between the rebuilt Southern Pacifics and the new Class 7.

Ernest Cox oversaw the preparation of the new designs and continued to consult Tom as the process gradually evolved, as he recalled in a letter:

> 'On Coleman's advice, the boiler diameter [of the new Class 7] was increased at the throat plate from 6ft 1½ in to 6ft 5in, giving a total free area through the tubes equal to 16.2% of the grate area, a feature which ensured that the cylinders could never beat the boiler. He also suggested that the use of bar frames be abandoned, the cost and the weight being too high, whilst available machine capacity and handling space in workshops was insufficient. We turned instead to 1¼in plate frames set centrally over the axleboxes in a manner successfully applied by Bulleid to his Merchant Navies.'

As the 50s passed so all the old streamliners received new boilers without the cut down smokeboxes. *City of Manchester* was the last to be modified in 1960.

And so 1948 passed into 1949. If the new structure seemed to be working, it was probably more by luck than judgement, with many fault lines barely concealed below the surface. But such a radical change would always be traumatic and leave a bitter taste in many mouths. As the new year progressed there were those, including Tom, who decided that enough was enough and the time had come to sever their links with BR. Some would seek pastures new, whilst others would leave to enjoy well-earned retirements. But even in the short period before he departed, Tom still commanded the Drawing Office and all that it did and was an immensely strong presence, as Alan Rimmer described in his book *Testing Time at Derby*. As a recently qualified engineer, he was temporarily assigned to review the Interchange Trials records and then came into Tom's orbit:

'The work lasted for about 5 weeks and took us to within a week of Christmas 1948. Vic Roberts asked the head of the drawing office, a formidable fellow called Tom Coleman who had only to come into the drawing office and stand and glower down its length to have every pencil hard at work, whether we should be sent back whence we came. Mr Coleman replied that surely Vic could find us some work to do for a time, which was really an order. So it was that we were put to sorting out a storeroom full of old drawings and all sorts of bits and pieces that the test-section had accumulated. A couple of drawings I remember well were linen-mounted prints of the *Great Bear* and the associated valve gear; odd things to find at Derby.

'After the cupboard, we then started on a mass of tracings in

about five big drawers. Some of these were really fascinating as they were engine diagrams for 'might have beens'. Such as a 2-6-2 version of the rebuilt Scot, various 0-6-0 tender engines with bar frames, outside cylinders and other ideas obviously replacements for the 4F, a 2-8-0T made by grafting tanks and bunker on to a Stanier 8F, and many many more. There was a vast variety. I seem to remember a 4-8-2 passenger engine and a dainty little 2-4-2T, rather like the large boilered Stanier 3P tank.

'In due time, all the tracings were sorted and stored away and still Mr Coleman would not let Vic send us back – not that we were pressing, mind you! "Find them a job, Roberts. Surely you can make good use of them can't you". And so it was that we were found a permanent place in the drawing office, at the end of a long row of boards down one side, right outside the chief draughtsman's office'.

Despite the normal comings and goings of office life, there was still design work for Tom to do; a small flurry of activity to mark the end of his long, distinguished career.

One type of locomotive suggested during 1948 had been a class of freight engine with a 2-8-2 wheel configuration. Both Cox and Tom had long advocated this idea, seeing it as a natural development of the LMS 8Fs. Basically a new engine capable of pulling heavy, fast freight trains. This had been

Power and elegance at speed. The epitomy of Stanier and Coleman's work.

City of Lichfield gets underway, her fireman keeping a careful watch on the lineside photographer.

number of fitted brake wagons per train. One day before we started on this job, Coleman said to me, "They are asking me what is the maximum speed a Class 8 2-8-0 should be allowed to travel at?" When we came to the new design we naturally thought of using the Class 7 boiler on a 2-8-2 wheelbase and the minutes of the Chief Draughtsmen's meeting recorded that a 2-8-2 was to be developed. It made a nice design, using Class 7 motion as well, and by this means boilers could interchange and much of the front end design could be similar, saving money on jigs, tools and castings. Coleman had had diagrams drawn out of such proposals in LMS days, but the CME would have none of it. Back it came from Riddles: he wanted a 2-10-0. Coleman tried to persuade him against that, but Riddles was adamant and I regard the 9F 2-10-0 as a true Riddles effort.'

The first 9Fs began appearing in 1954 and proved to be one of the most successful steam locomotives ever to run on British railways. By 1960, 251 were in service alongside fifty-five Class 7 and ten Class 6 Pacifics, plus another 683 standard engines of various types. Although his part in their evolution may have been small and most of the new BR designs may not have equalled the quality of his LMS work, he still followed the programme with great interest. In a short letter written in 1956 he offered a brief tribute to Riddles' standard designs:

'The 9F is a particularly fine locomotive. The Britannia Class can also perform well, but doesn't have the strength or endurance of Gresley's A4s or Stanier's Coronations, but they were exceptional by any standards, so to fall short, by comparison, is not a failure. Riddles may have been remiss in following a programme of steam to the exclusion of diesel and electric developments, but his engines were still creditworthy.'

But Tom must also have realised that the effort expended was ultimately wasted, because the end of steam couldn't be long delayed. As it was, these locomotives fell far short of their planned lives by an embarrassing margin of at least twenty years in most cases. But trying to plan any long-term capital programme when politicians are in the driving seat, as they were with nationalised industries, was difficult in the extreme.

Work on diesels and other forms of motive power hadn't gone away though, even allowing for the low priority given to it by Riddles and BR. But most projects that existed in 1949 pre-dated the creation of BR, so may have been regarded as an unwanted inheritance. And the LMS hadn't been alone in developing new power sources. Gas turbine technology, as well as diesel concepts, were being explored by the Western Region. The Southern, already well advanced in developing electric traction, including three Co Co electric engines built during the war, were now in the process of designing a Co Co diesel, with three shortly to be built. Meanwhile, the London North Eastern had

an ambition for many years, but development took an unusual turn as Langridge recalled:

'The powers that be had been trying to speed up freight trains for some time by increasing the

invested in electric locomotives and electric multiple units. And all four companies had developed diesel shunting engines of various types and numbers for some years.

And in the last few months of his career, Tom would be involved in two other diesel projects, both initiated before nationalisation and each in partnership with a private company. The first of these was an 0-4-4-0 Bo Bo diesel electric locomotive constructed to meet secondary level services usually rostered to tank engines. North British Locomotive Company were commissioned by the LMS to design and construct the unit with diesel and electrical equipment being provided by British Thompson-Houston. The locomotive appeared in mid-1950,

Busy days and a mixture of different carriages, a scene typical of the last few years of steam.

In the last few years of steam many enthusiasts pursued these engines armed with colour film, recording the soon to depart Coronations in all their glory.

numbered 10800, but proved to be a fairly lacklustre performer. Even so, it remained in service until 1959, before being converted into a mobile test bed for the 'Hawk Project'; a joint Brush-BR collaboration to test an alternating (AC) generator. This work proved to be a great success and would in time become a standard item of equipment in a new generation of diesel electric locomotives and the power cars of HST 125s.

The second project involved the construction of a trial 4-8-4 diesel, with 6 engines; four producing tractive power and two auxiliaries that drove pressure chargers for the main engines – allowing a higher torque at low crankshaft speeds to be achieved. The idea was cultivated jointly by the LMS and Fell Development Ltd, in co-operation with Davey Paxman and Co and Shell Refinery and Marketing Co. Planning proceeded, with Tom chairing meetings between interested parties, whilst his drawing office produced plans. In many ways, this work was more conceptual than practical and construction hadn't been approved by the LMS when BR came into being. Nevertheless, and surprisingly to some, the Ministry of Transport gave permission for a prototype to be built and it appeared in 1950. Testing followed, interspersed with some revenue earning service, but it never found broader acceptance or application and was withdrawn in November 1958.

In many ways, Tom's role in both projects was simply to be a facilitator. He found the work interesting and kept extensive notes on each engine, but by this time his enthusiasm and energy were quickly ebbing away. Grief and a growing sense that his day had passed were keenly felt and retirement seemed to offer a blessed release. If he had promised Ivatt to remain in post until the CME himself retired, then it was a promise he was unable to keep.

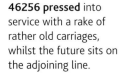

46256 pressed into service with a rake of rather old carriages, whilst the future sits on the adjoining line.

As a compassionate, understanding man, Ivatt would have been only too aware of Tom's predicament and was unlikely to stand in his way. And so, in August 1949, at the age of 64, he retired without fanfare or celebration.

The following month BR produced the briefest of items for the *Railway Gazette*:

'Mr T.F. Coleman, Chief Draughtsman, Chief Mechanical Engineer's Drawing Office, London Midland Region, British Railways who has retired, was born on May 28th 1885, at Endon, Staffordshire. After serving an apprenticeship at Kerr, Stuarts, Stoke-on-Trent, he joined the North Staffordshire Railway in 1905. In 1926 he was transferred to Horwich, LMSR., as Chief Draughtsman, Locomotive Drawing Office, and seven years later he went to Crewe as Assistant Chief Draughtsman, HQ, and Chief Draughtsman, Crewe Locomotive Works. He was appointed Chief Draughtsman HQ, Derby, in 1935. During his period in office at Derby the designs of many notable locomotives came off the drawing board.'

From the papers that have survived it seems likely that Tom drafted this short item for publication. If so, it is typical of his modesty and self-effacing character. He wasn't one to seek or expect recognition, but, in his careful selection of words he suggests something else – his leadership of a good team. It is also interesting to note the reference to Endon being his birthplace, when Gloucestershire should rightly claim him. He only arrived in the Stoke area when 11 years of age, but clearly felt the strongest of bonds with the city and chose to be regarded as a Staffordshire man. Perhaps he had a pressing need to belong and this helped fulfil that ambition.

46254 *City of Stoke-on-Trent*, was one of Tom's favourites celebrating as it did his adopted city

Fred enjoys his well earnt retirement with his wife and son, his partly read *Times* resting nearby.

And with this slightest of acknowledgements he slipped away, into obscurity, his reputation and achievements being a matter for private contemplation, not public consumption. Only one brief reference to his departure appears in the few accounts that have survived of that time and it fell to Eric Langridge to recall his impressions of the day:

'Coleman retired with a rather queer speech to the drawing office that seemed to hint that the high level that it had reached in his time was now on the decline and the drawing offices were left like sheep without a shepherd.'

Although he quickly disappeared from view, railways remained a central feature of Tom's life. Regular contact with Fred Lemon, through their combined family, must have fed this continuing interest. Their occasional meetings must have evoked a time now past which had enthralled and enveloped them both completely. One wonders if they reminisced about the engines they had built, the battles fought and the companies they had served. Sadly, we shall never know. Yet being in positions of such great authority, where their actions echoed widely, it is hard to believe that these events were not constantly in their thoughts and their conversations.

Tom, as had long been his custom, never joined an institution or other professional body. Fred, on the other hand, remained a member of the Institution of Locomotive Engineers, though attended meetings less frequently as deafness and old age restricted him to his home in Somerset. But even without the bond created by these groups, the results of their work were still around them, to be seen and enjoyed. Steam was gradually disappearing but for a while in the 1950s it enjoyed an Indian summer, to be savoured by professionals and amateurs alike. Tom would often take the opportunity to travel up and down the old LMS routes, photographing engines in all states and locations. He also maintained an interest in their performance and evolution, especially the advance of diesel and electric units.

There were significant events on the railways to be observed and followed with interest and Tom collected items relating to them. New engines were noted, but so were the problems that beset the system, particularly on the old LMS. The most notable of these was the Harrow Rail Disaster of October 1952. With over a 100 dead, and many more seriously injured, no one could avoid the news coverage or the sense of horror such an event arouses. But Tom had a particular interest, three of the locomotives involved having come from his drawing office – 46242 *City of Glasgow*, 46202 *Princess Anne*, the converted 'Turbomotive', and Jubilee Class 45637 *Windward Islands*. In due course, he obtained a copy of the crash report, plus some photographs of the two Pacifics, wrote down a number

of observations and probably wondered if their design had contributed to the accident.

Whilst no one welcomed accidents, they could still be a useful source of information for designers. Learning by experience was essential and it was an age where scientifically testing an item to destruction was in its infancy. So engineers would visit crash scenes to assess cause, see if their products were responsible and how a design might be altered to make it stronger or safer. And Tom had made this a regular practice throughout his career, so seeing it stretch into retirement was hardly surprising.

Aviation also continued to fascinate him, especially in the early 1950s when Britain had entered a new golden age of flight, powered by jet engines. Air displays, not unknown in pre-war

Even grime could lose its deadening affect in a downpour of rain. *City of Lichfield* passes under the ever spreading masts and wires of the electrification system.

The driver takes a 'breather' whilst the engine works hard.

days, were now commonplace. At RAF Stations around the country and at Farnborough, particularly, displays galvanised a public eager to view the latest and fastest jets. Mitchell's Spitfires were rapidly becoming museum pieces, but they, and the next generation of aircraft, remained a constant and treasured presence, and drew Tom and many thousands more.

So he slipped into a well-deserved retirement, to enjoy photography and fishing, probably relieved that the stresses of his last few years at Derby were behind him, but still fostering an interest in science and the railways. He

also had two grandsons to enjoy as Mike, his youngest, recalled:

'The Coleman family were very close to each other. He was a wonderful grandfather who appreciated my interest in all matters of engineering and would take me train spotting and to such places as Ironbridge. He used the kitchen as a dark room for his photographic exploits and I remember the brilliant photos he took of locomotives.

'Until I was 9 years old my family home was Orton Longville outside Peterborough, where Tom and Harriet visited us.

One of these times occurred when mum and dad went to New York on business travelling west on the *Queen Elizabeth* and east on the *Mauretania*. Tom would take me to the LNER line at a crossing which I think was near the village of Holme and take many photos. We would always have lunch somewhere. My first Prep School was very near Long Buckby through which the line ran and also the Grand Union Canal. I was often taken to one of the entrances to the Kilsby tunnel and a picnic would ensue.

'During the time he lived at my home outside Bridgnorth, Tom would take me out in his car to various railway locations where we would chat a lot whilst waiting for a locomotive, camera in hand, to pass by. Then he would give me much information about the loco which would include the name of the designer and builder. During this period he would also take me into Wales where he was particularly interested in the Llangollen area – I well remember being fascinated by the aqueduct – and also Betwys Coed. We would take a picnic and I believe a lot of hot air floated around. I felt totally comfortable with him and my interests were very similar to his.

'If my mum and dad were away on business it would always be Tom and Harriet who honoured an exeat. I was so very much at home with them and believe that they were wonderful company.'

But life never runs smoothly and loss has to be endured. Tom's brother,

Reg, died suddenly in Canada during 1953 and then Harriet fell ill in 1957 and passed away shortly afterwards. One can only imagine his thoughts at losing his wife of forty-seven years, having experienced and borne so many things together, including the death of their son. Only they could begin to understand the depths of despair they had endured and offer comfort and support to each other through this darkest of times. And now Tom had lost that mutual and supportive understanding, with its warmth and solace.

In the months that followed he gave up his home in Littleover and moved to be with his daughter and family near Bridgnorth, in Shropshire, suffering another loss when his half-brother, Harry, died in February. Tom's health was declining and atrial fibrillation of the heart was diagnosed. Today, with modern medical support, such a condition is dealt with by minor surgery, fitting a pacemaker and drugs. But in 1958, although the first external pacemaker was tested in the USA that year, these treatments were far in the future and rest was the only advised course of action. Without better intervention, the course of the condition was downwards and in late May Tom suffered acute cardiac failure and was admitted to the Infirmary, in Bridgnorth, where he died on the 27th.

There were no obituaries written in the weeks that followed or tributes expressed, except by his family, but this, I expect, is something he would have preferred. The wording on his death certificate probably best summed up what he felt about his working life. Under 'occupation' is written, 'Chief Designer, LMS Railway (retired)'. His daughter registered Tom's death on 28 May and, I suspect, used this term because it was probably the way her father saw himself. This seems to me to be the best possible description of his modesty and the enormous contribution he made to railway engineering and the LMS.

Some years later Tom's son in law, George, also a noted engineer and member of the Institution of Mechanical Engineers, met and befriended William Stanier. With a father and father-in-law so well known to the retired CME, and central to his greatest successes, the conversation turned to their work. George recalled the great man saying that, 'without Tom I would not have succeeded on the LMS'. What better memorial could there be than the praise and recognition of someone you hold so high.

Tom and Harriet, towards the end of their lives, at home in Derby

Tom's grave in Bridgnorth

In April 2017, I visited Tom's grave in Bridgnorth. The distant sound of preserved steam locomotives working along the Severn Valley Railway was carried by the wind across the valley to where I sat. Great endeavour has faded, but still echoes thanks to all the people who give so unstintingly of their time and energy to conservation and education. In 1958 few would have thought this possible and now, because of this work, many of Tom's locomotives survive to pay homage to his life, creativity, leadership and labour.

A fitting memorial to Tom's work - a preserved Black Five working hard and without assistance in March 2017 outside Westbury.

Chapter 10
STEAM'S INDIAN SUMMER

Within ten years of Tom's death all that he had worked so hard to achieve had been swept away. It was a very short period of time for such dramatic change, but he probably wouldn't have been shocked by the velocity or intensity of the transformation. He was, after all, a moderniser, his scientific curiosity provoked by new possibilities and an ever-present search for engineering and aesthetic improvement. Yet despite this, he would probably have been saddened by the demise of steam, as would anyone losing touch with long familiar elements of their world. But he wasn't noted for sentimentality or a yearning for the past, so the effects of change probably aroused no more than a brief backwards glance. And, even before he retired, clear signs of change were all around him and had absorbed much of his creativity.

One thing is certain though, the demise of steam was well advanced when he left British Railways in 1949. Riddles, and his distracting programme of new standardised steam locomotives, gave the science one last flicker of life, but this wasted effort did little to hold back the torrent of real change. His ideas, whilst nobly based, did not fit into a modern world and led to the

ludicrous position of new steam locomotives virtually being taken from the production line straight to the scrapyard. Though an admirer of steam it is hard to imagine Tom making this mistake, seeing change as inevitable and to be embraced. Steam was the power source of his generation so had to be exploited, but it wasn't his religion, which one feels it was to many of his contemporaries. Common sense, practical application, an appreciation

of new developments and careful analysis were the cornerstones of his creed. He wasn't hidebound by convention or the restrictions of lesser men.

When the end of steam came, in 1968, the last engines were restricted in use as the infrastructure that supported them disappeared. Hard running Pacifics had a last fling over Southern metals until July 1967, then disappeared like phantoms almost

Steam and diesel mix for a short time.

City of London always seems to have been in pristine condition, perhaps a reflection of the care and attention lavished by staff at Camden then Willesden.

Two Coronations awaiting the call to duty, enthusiasts seemingly given open access to the locos and sheds.

overnight, whilst a few of Riddles' standard Pacifics kept running to the end. But the engines that survived into the last few months of steam on BR were dominated by old LMS designs – Black Fives, Jubilees and 8Fs. The Coronations could have been there at the end, but west coast electrification and dieselisation had advanced so rapidly that their end came in 1964, all but three being consigned to the scrapyard. A fourth nearly survived, but efforts, by the Mayor of Lichfield and the Town Council, to buy the engine named after their city, came to nothing and only one nameplate was purchased instead. But few could then predict or foresee the monster that the preservation movement would become only a few years later and the new religion this created. If steam was disappearing now, it is probable that all the Coronations

would have been bought and restored, such is the intensity of demand. However, many might have languished in sidings or corners of sheds, used for spares, neglected and gradually running to rust for lack of funds. Still it would have been nice to see a few more preserved.

So, thankfully, some signs of great endeavour remain to mark the lives of very creative engineers and designers. And Tom Coleman must, by any standards, rank amongst the foremost champions in this field. The years following his retirement saw the engines he did so much to produce run to great effect, performing as they were intended even when maintenance standards declined and their condition left a lot to be desired.

In some ways, the 1950s were a long goodbye to steam and a time in which they dominated the railways. The Coronations, in particular, continued to gather

headlines and plaudits. For train spotters and the general public alike they retained a glamour only equalled by Gresley's A Classes and Bullied's Pacifics in many people's eyes. Yet they all came at the end of a long period of evolution in which every conceivable element of steam design had been considered and exploited to the full. In reality, they were magnificent dinosaurs that should have been replaced by new, far more advanced concepts sooner. Tom Coleman was aware of this, but was restrained in helping develop new forms of motive power by lack of time and the limited aspirations of other beings. Ernest Cox, towards the end of his life, saw all this and wrote:

'We were woefully slow to learn from experience in practical matters, and although better materials and improved machines and processes have latterly made possible what was impossible before, the first 130 years of the steam locomotive were hardly acts of God, but arose from our lack of perception or lack of ability to draw the right conclusions from what we saw. These are judgements which we must pass upon many of our predecessors from today's standpoint……

'However, the fact remains that by the end of steam, and in particular over its last 30 years, the various blind spots in locomotive design were one by one made clear, and there finally emerged an end product, as distinct from the theoretical, possibilities of steam traction. To such men as Gresley, Stanier, George Ivatt and Riddles, the historian must rightly accord the direction and authority which made this possible. To the lesser names of Tom Coleman, Bert Spencer (LNER), James Clayton (SR) and Sam Ells (GWR) goes the credit for the original thought and application which ensured its success.'

In these words, Cox perceptively described the way Tom, in particular, supported his greatly admired CME. He used his strength of purpose, great intellect, scientific skills and leadership to ensure that the locomotives that emerged, no matter what their source of power, could rarely be bettered. In his last few years, he was able to witness the final flourish of his wonderful steam engines, but also take pleasure in seeing the next generation begin to blossom.

It seems that he had a particular fondness for Pacifics, Turbomotive,

Two red Coronations pass but only one is identified - 46225 *Duchess of Gloucester*.

The Lakes Express pulled by 46236 *City of Bradford*.

The 8Fs were such strong reliable performers that they went through to the end of steam in 1968 and could have gone on much longer being so well built and reliable.

8Fs and the 2F Dock Tank engine. Why this should be he didn't explain, though the reasons aren't hard to discern from his papers. The first were the highest profile projects. The second teased his sense of scientific curiosity, as it did Stanier. The third because of its wide practical application and huge construction programme, across all regions, in peace and war. And the fourth, simply because it was his first, significant design scheme. Yet of all these the Coronations stand head and shoulders above all the others and will be remembered as his and Stanier's greatest achievement long after everything else is forgotten. And in the fifteen years from Tom's retirement to

their final demise they continued to shine, even though their evolution came to an end with the final two of the class.

They have received plaudits from many sources, but as Tom always realised, it was the drivers and firemen who knew best what the engines could do. He valued their thoughts and opinions as highly as anyone's and sought them out whenever he could, on the footplate or in the sheds. He also saw the value of visiting the workshops, discussing the engines with those who managed and maintained them. And carriages and wagons received the same level of attention. After overcoming some initial reserve, he found that

most people were eager to talk about their experiences, to impart their knowledge and contribute something that went beyond their everyday tasks and Tom's notes include many references to this. He seems to have realised, very early on, that no matter how advanced the design it is the skill of individuals, and their ability to adapt, that makes it work and allows potential to be exploited to the full. This was nowhere more apparent than on steam locomotives where so many variables can affect performance and the Coronations epitomised this best.

Sadly, very few first-hand accounts of life on the footplate or sheds have survived. For the most part, these weren't sought or if they were, the men themselves lacked the words to adequately describe their memories or feelings. So the few that exist may be restricted in number and content, but still reveal a great deal about life with Coleman's Coronations. And it was often their first exposure to these iconic locomotives that revealed their true feelings about the engines and their creator, though at first they often struggled to get the best out of them. But a great racehorse needs a highly skilled jockey and the Coronations were racing thoroughbreds.

Peter Johnson probably left the best description of footplate life on these machines:

'It was October 1952 when I first rode on the footplate of a Coronation, or "Lizzies" as all Stanier's Pacifics were called. I had only transferred from the ex-GWR shed at Crewe, to the ex-LMS North Shed, so was used to Granges, Halls and other GWR types.

'On making my way to the shed I began to have butterflies. I had never been on the footplate of a Lizzie before, let alone have to get and keep steam on one. On arriving at the roundhouse I looked up at the biggest piece of machinery I had ever seen. "Sir William A Stanier FRS", blazed the nameplate on the huge boiler side. I climbed aboard and was amazed at the size of the cab, there seemed enough room to ride one's bike around. I looked into the firebox – it looked more like a bottomless pit, with little fire in it yet. I had heard

Black Five number 44890 in a classic pose beloved of enthusiasts or just those with a strong engineering and aesthetic sense.

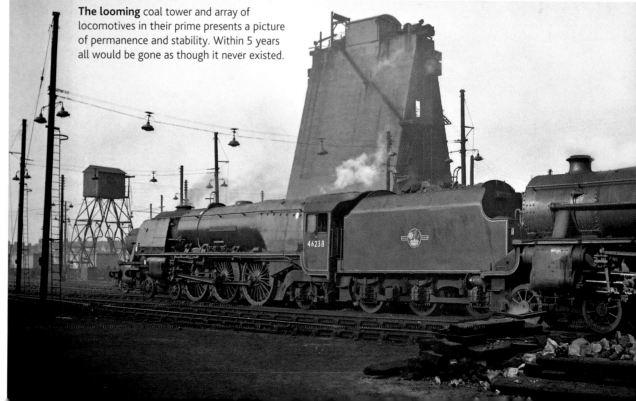

The looming coal tower and array of locomotives in their prime presents a picture of permanence and stability. Within 5 years all would be gone as though it never existed.

several of my new-found mates say, "A Lizzie firebox will hold about three tons of coal."

'The blower was applied and drew up the fire, preparatory to my levelling the fire all over the box with the fire iron. This done I threw a dozen or so shovels full of coal in, but to my consternation I didn't seem to be getting anywhere, the bars still looked bare. The Carlisle preparing fireman was still on the footplate and was rather amused at my puny efforts. He volunteered to show me how to fill the box and undid the catches that held the tender doors shut. Immediately all the coal cascaded down onto the footplate, lumps, cobbles, slack, the lot. Grabbing hold of the biggest lumps he proceeded to sling them into the firebox. Gradually the coal pile was diminished and I looked into the firebox expecting to see not

a glimmer in there after all that coal had been put on. I needn't have worried, the Carlisle man was experienced and knew what he was doing, the fire was burning nicely and the steam was rising.

'As we left the shed and made our way, tender first, towards Carlisle Citadel Station, the pegs were off on the up line and making her non-stop way, London bound, was No 46244, "*King George VI*", her exhaust going sky high as she lifted the "Scot" out of Carlisle. I heard the deep throated beat of the "Lizzie" as she was put to the climb out of the station. The whole air seemed to vibrate and pulsate as she pounded past us.

'It was our turn now. Once again I heard the beat of our "Lizzie" as we moved out of the station. As my mate had only just put some coal on I thought it would be alright for a bit.

How wrong I was. We were hardly out of the station before I noticed the steam pressure dropping alarmingly. I had no sooner got a shovelful of coal in the firehole door when "Whoosh" it had gone. The driver kept saying, "get some in the corners". That was easier said than done. It just wouldn't stay there, no matter what I tried. This went on for the whole of the journey, even with the driver helping all he could. I'm afraid I didn't reckon much to Stanier Pacifics at that time and was wishing for a more familiar Grange or Hall which I was convinced could do a better job. Suffice it to say we did eventually arrive and my driver softened the fireworks when a footplate inspector had a quiet word with me.'

But with help and experience Johnson began to understand these engines and with this growing expertise his appreciation of the class developed:

'The following week we were rostered on a Crewe to Carlisle parcel train. The loco we got was No 46227 "*Duchess of Devonshire*", once again a "Lizzie". Going to the shed my driver saw a gang of cleaners and recognising one he called him over and offered him a pack of cigarettes if he "could show my mate how to get coal in the corners". He jumped at the offer and was only too pleased to oblige. He set about levelling the fire all over the box and, picking up the shovel, he deftly put a shovelful of coal right into the back corner, the shovel blade

Greater access to sheds by lay people in the early 1960s led to the production of some of the best locomotive pictures. 46245 is again the star.

A scene reflecting the contribution made by the Stanier-Coleman partnership - a rebuilt Scot, Black Fives and an 8F.

City of *Salford* passes by.

being nearly at right angles to the Firehole door. I suddenly realised what had gone wrong the previous week, the back corners had been completely bare, no wonder I was down the nick for steam. I was eager now for another crack at a long distance express and was rostered to a night sleeper from Glasgow to Euston.

'A set of Crewe men brought the train, headed by No 46249, "City of Sheffield", in from Carlisle and we relieved them at Crewe. The engine was in tip top condition with the firebox full and water in the top nut. Clear of the Junction my driver opened out for the climb up Whitmore. Grasping the shovel eager to try out my new found knowledge, I found it worked like a charm. I began to wonder

if I was dreaming as I kept testing the level of water in the boiler and examining the steam clock every few seconds. My mate, with a knowledgeable smirk on his face, enquired what was the matter, he hadn't heard me swear once yet! When the "Lizzie" is fired correctly, they are indeed marvellous engines.

'In 1957 I was promoted and looked forward to my first Pacific as a driver. It came in the form of No 46246 "City of Manchester" on a Crewe to Glasgow relief to the Mid-Day Scot, rostered to work to Carlisle, returning the next day with the Glasgow to Euston. I remember the feeling of pride as I prepared my engine.

'The "City of Manchester" was always considered to be a good

locomotive and on this trip was no trouble whatsoever. That was the thing about a "Lizzie", if fired correctly and the coal was of average quality they would do everything asked of them. There never seemed to be a limit to their capabilities, they always had an ace up their sleeves as it were. I've seen "Lizzies" loaded up to the hilt and they have still kept time. Towards the last they were relegated to goods work, but even on such unglorified work such as this they still gave of their best.'

And the other accounts of those privileged to ride on the footplate of these superlative locomotives were peppered with such words as, 'you became part of the machine', 'their ride was superb, no rolling, vibration of axle knocks', 'worked effectively at low or high speeds', 'we never discovered their limits they were that good', 'they weren't for the faint hearted', 'no vicious kicking on the curves, no matter how tight', 'plenty of steam', and so on. They truly earnt this praise, despite their tendency for wheel spin when starting and the sheer hard work needed to keep them moving effectively.

As with any thoroughbred, their care and maintenance could be difficult especially when in streamlined form. But this seemed to raise few complaints from hard-pressed shed staff, as Alfred Ewer, who was in charge of Camden and Willesden during the heyday of the Pacific, recalled:

'When the first four Coronations arrived at Camden in '37 most believed they'd be more

Sisters back to back and still looking in good condition in the last two years of their lives. 46206 and 46233 on shed in 1962.

Princess Royals and were quite surprised by their look and performance. Contrary to what many believe little was known about them before they appeared. Any press reports were seen when the locomotives were already on shed. All the footplate crew had seen or read about the Gresley A4s and there was a certain amount of grumbling about the company's lack of a rival to the 'streaks'. So the streamlined engines were well received.

'The drivers soon adapted to the new engines, especially those who had worked the Princesses, but some of the fireman struggled to get sufficient steam from those massive boilers at first. Word did get back to Urie, then to Euston and Derby, that firing and coal consumption weren't as they should be. Instructions were issued quite smartly and things improved very rapidly. The likes of Tom Clark and his regular fireman had no problem from the start, but they were an exceptional crew. It's not surprising that they took the first 'Coronation' on the press run in June. Clark was a bit of a daredevil and his speed record attempt on the 29th wasn't unexpected. Though when he got back the poor old chap looked much older than his 65 years of age and took a few days off to recover.'

'Much was written later about the problems created by streamlining – making day to day maintenance more time consuming and difficult. There

46254 at Carlisle awaiting her next duty. The yellow diagonal stripe on the cab side suggest this is 1963 or 64, shortly before she was withdrawn.

A strange pairing - a Stanier-Coleman 8F with a Fowler tender.

Lancaster **and** *Edinburgh* side by side possibly at Crewe North Shed.

The Stanier-Coleman influence continues. The filial ties are only too apparent.

is no real evidence to prove this. They may have taken slightly longer to prepare and access to the smokebox was a little trickier, with those big hinged doors, but there were no complaints that I heard. All steam locomotives were difficult and time consuming to work on. It was all hard and dirty, but, at least with the Coronations, shed staff had the prestige of working on the best we had. This counted for a lot to those men and it was a matter of great pride to prepare these engines to the highest standard. Better that than the thankless task of working on freight locomotives.

Duchess of *Buccleugh* begrimed and in poor condition but still capable of great things. She was withdrawn in November 1963 and cut up a month later.

'With streamlining all I can say is that when polished and in fine fettle the drivers felt the performance to be better at speeds over 50mph – with headwinds or cross winds – than the unfrocked engines. The casing also lifted smoke and steam away more effectively than the others, even when fitted with deflectors, so gave better forward visibility. But whether streamlining produced better coal or water consumption on fast long distance services was never really put to the test.

'For many it was a question of looks. The traditionalists didn't tend to like the casing. But I and most crew did.

'When war came we soon lacked the men to prepare these engines properly and their looks quickly suffered, though not their performance. It wasn't unusual to see 600 or 700 tons up, pulled without double heading. They were without doubt the most remarkable engines. Later I transferred to Doncaster under BR and had many types of Gresley Pacifics under my control. They didn't compare to the Coronations.'

The years that followed the war saw these engines restored to their former glory, with the streamliners losing their casing, bringing the class nearer to a standard look. With other locomotives to assess none found their way to the new Test Centre at Rugby in the first few years of its existence, although 46256 *Sir William A. Stanier FRS* was present for the opening ceremony. But in 1955, 46225

Duchess of Gloucester was selected for a prolonged period of trials there. Why, when the class had been in service for eighteen years, they were chosen is far from clear and the test report doesn't reveal a pressing reason. One can only assume it was to compare their performance with other similar classes, particularly the BR Standard Pacific, two of which had passed through their hands in 1951 and 1953, followed by a Merchant Navy. Alternatively, the centre was running out of work and needed to boost output to justify its existence. One thing is certain though, there was little or no scope to improve the design at this stage of its life and little will to do so in BR.

Tests at Rugby ran from 31 January until 16 May and included seventy-six separate runs on the rolling road to determine, 'general efficiency and performance'. An interim report was published in August of that year. The locomotive was then returned to duty with the London Midland Operating Department, to meet pressing traffic needs, with tests resuming in January 1956, and running to May. This second period saw 46225 pulling a series of test trains, the heaviest consisting of a dynamometer car and seventeen carriages, weighing 640 tons, over the Settle and Carlisle line.

When the results of tests at Rugby and 'on the road' were compiled and analysed, a significant difference was found between power outputs achieved. This disparity caused a certain amount of head scratching, followed by

The Black Fives carried on until the end of steam and then became the ever reliable work horses of the preservation movement, 18 having survived.

46248 at rest, made permanent a few weeks after this photo was taken in the Summer of `64.

In 1964 it was hard to believe that a green liveried locomotive was hidden under all that dirt. 46257, the last of the class, would be cut up a few months later.

extensive correspondence between D.R. Carling, the Test Centre Superintending Engineer, Ernest Cox, the Locomotive Testing Joint Committee Chairman and J.F. Harrison, the LMR's CM & EE at Derby. A compromise was eventually reached, allowing the final report to be drafted in 1958, not long before the Test Centre's activities were curtailed. The report's summary suggested that the different readings were a result of the time lapse between both sets of tests, 'the condition of the engine was inevitably not quite the same on both occasions. Application of the methods described in Report L116 of December 1957 to adjust results brought the two sets of tests within the normal limits of experimental error'.

After such prolonged correspondence and discussions, one would expect the report to reveal some dramatic differences and conclusions, but it didn't. It was true that the engine produced a high steam rate of 41,500lb/hr at Rugby, reducing to 40,000lb/hr on the road, but the locomotive's liability to slip was given as the primary cause of this. So after considerable time, money and effort the final report made fairly inconsequential reading:

'The locomotives of this class are fully adequate for the operation of any express in this country, at least with the better qualities of coal at present available, but may need redraughting to counteract the effects of any serious decline in coal quality in the future.

'The boiler efficiency is very similar to that of comparable locomotives tested with South Kirkby coal, eg BR Standard Class 7 and SR Merchant Navy 4-6-2 types and also with Blidworth coal agreed well with that of the LNER V2 2-6-2.

'The cylinder efficiency is rather lower than that of either the 2-cylinder Class 7, the 3-cylinder V2, or the 4-cylinder GWR King. This is believed to be mostly due to the use of four cylinders instead of two and a little to the slightly larger clearances.

'Providing the adhesion is sufficient the locomotive could sustain 2,700 IHP at express speeds, for as long as the fireman could keep up the firing rate of over 7,000 lb/hr of South Kirkby coal.'

When the preliminary report appeared, Cox very thoughtfully sent Tom a copy, with a short message of thanks and goodwill, plus a brief comment on the, 'continuing good performance of your engines'. In fact, before the trials had begun Roland Bond, now BR's CME, HQ, and Cox had contacted Stanier and Tom Coleman, respectively, to invite them to attend some of 46225's tests at Rugby. But both declined being 'indisposed at present'. Carling suggested holding the engine over until they were fit, but Bond thought this unnecessary. It is impossible to say if this was a 'diplomatic' indisposition or a real case of ill-health on Tom's part; his dislike of public occasions was unlikely to have changed with retirement.

Even though he maintained little or no contact with his ex-colleagues, Tom still avidly

Grimy, but her red colour can still just be seen. *City of Coventry* was withdrawn in September 1964, but not cut up until March the following year.

Even at the end a Coronation could be given a good clean, certainly better than the unnamed standard class engine behind.

Jubilee Class engine 45721 '*Impregnable*', on a special towards the end of her service in 1964, captured here in a scene typical of Britain at that time.

followed developments on the railways, here and overseas. In December 1954, BR published its long-awaited Modernisation Plan. This was followed two years later by a Government White Paper, which sought to electrify many principle lines, see a large-scale diesel building programme in place, the end of steam, closure of some lines and the construction of large freight marshalling yards. All this Tom absorbed and, it seems, welcomed, although it sounded the death knell for his steam engines. But in a short note written at the time he recorded that:

> 'Change has been too long delayed. We have lost nearly

a decade of time in which the railways could successfully have made great leaps in producing diesels in great numbers. All those new standard engines now look to be what they always were, a distraction from the main business.'

But it wasn't simply Riddles' 999 steam engines being constructed at this time. Each of the regions kept developing engines from their pre-nationalisation days and by 1956 this totalled 1538 new locomotives, 690 built by the London Midland Region alone. So the cull, when it came, was even more dramatic and costly than it might have been

if politicians and railwaymen had grasped change and innovation much earlier. So two conflicting idealisms met head on and the outcome was neither sensible or well planned. Steam would linger on for a few more years, but even in accountants' eyes, their demise was handled badly. Asset depreciation was deemed irrelevant, whilst the huge capital expenditure on locomotives, with projected lives stretching into the 1990s, was simply written off in the way that only politicians seem able to do. And then you had the destruction, rather than evolution, of perfectly good and effective motive power. State imposed vandalism seemed to be the order of the day, with only scrap merchants and locomotive builders ever likely to benefit.

Yet the world didn't change overnight and these new strategies would take some time to become reality. Whilst this transition slowly passed, steam locomotives enjoyed a brief spell of hard running before their night fell and the Coronations were at the forefront of this late blooming show. With the end in sight, footplate crew would push the locomotives as far as they could 'legally' go, and occasionally over the limit. Shed staff, reducing in number as recruitment and retention became increasingly more difficult, could often be relied upon to turn out the premier expresses in top condition. So pre-war days were recreated for some if not all of the services, with occasional high spots still able to produce headlines.

One of these occurred on 5 September 1957 and resulted in a half page spread on page 5 in the *Daily Express* the following morning. In some ways, it captured a caustic attitude towards BR, but also its admiration for the footplate crew who attempted to make the service work:

'Photonews, always on the alert for the significant, presents here an event of great importance to all who this morning will catch the 8.10 (a symbol not a certainty).

'For certainly the most significant event captured by camera yesterday was on the railways. A train arrived 37 minutes early. And it was hauled by one of those beautiful, supposedly obsolescent things….. a steam engine. For the incredulous, it must be stated that there was no cheating. It was an ordinary time table run. It was indeed a post-war record.

'The first sign that anything unusual was this flash on the arrival indicator at Euston. The Caledonian Limited express thundering down from Glasgow was signalled 30 minutes early at Watford – 13 miles from Euston. By the time the eight coach express steamed into platform 3 it was seven minutes earlier than that. The whole journey took six hours three minutes….. fastest on the London Midland Region since the Coronation Scot's run in 1937 (for which the line was specially cleared).

'Said William Starvis, of Kingsbury, Middlesex, a railwayman since 1916: "My fastest run. It was almost a clear line. We touched 92-93 mph."

'The official explanation: "Just normal service – but a

By the end cleaning and maintenance standards had slipped considerably as effort was focussed on diesel and electric traction.

After long and distingushed service an 8F awaits an inglorious end in the flames of cutters' torches.

clear line". Oddly enough, not one passenger thought of thanking the driver. But then, maybe, nobody could believe it.'

Under the main photo was written, 'Record breaker of the old school – the Caledonian Express, Euston bound, hauled by Duchess class engine *King George VI* …. Built in 1938, long before the modernisation plan and the impersonality of the diesel locomotive were conceived'. It was a sentimental view shared by many, although not always the fare paying public, who were growing increasingly tired of the 'old school' – its dirt and grime.

Bill Starvis became something of a celebrity in the last few years of steam whilst working on Coronations, just as Tom Clark, Laurie Earl and Fred Bishop had before him. They were a tough breed of no-nonsense drivers, who spent their working lives rising to the top of their profession. Starvis, unusually, kept diaries listing the duties he was given, the locomotives he drove and any incidents occurring during each run. And these now form a rare record of steam's last years.

He was well qualified to comment on each class of locomotive, having driven most types regularly over the years whilst based at Camden; a shed he joined, from his home in Newmarket in 1913, aged 16. Two years military service proved to be only a brief diversion in his career and during the 1920s he became a fireman, then was passed for driving in 1933. And it was in the years that followed that he became an expert on Stanier's Pacifics, including Turbomotive.

In his records, Tom Coleman mentions his name on occasions and was apt to join Starvis when seeking a footplate ride to assess an engine's performance. There were many others, of course, but their memories have, for the most part, been lost to posterity.

His diary entry for 5 September 1957 is brief and to the point, containing no hint of pride or self-congratulation:

'Thursday September 5. 1019 Ex-Carlisle. 6244. J.Tumalty (Fireman). Insp Woodruff. Signals Penrith, Scot Green, Norton Crossing. Permanent Way Hest Bank. Arrive Euston 2/33. Official Run.'

Each daily report follows a similar pattern. A Royal Train pulled by 6245 (Starvis always used the old

A very dirty and anonymous Black 5 trundles past with a mixed but heavy load towards the end of steam on BR.

Driver Starvis and Fireman Tumalty celebrate their record run.

46253 still working hard shortly before withdrawal in late 1962. She was broken up at Crewe in May 1963.

LMS numbering system), rates no more than, 'Signals at Hatch End and Crewe. 10 minutes late'. But other entries are peppered with references to Princess Royals and Coronations as their condition slowly deteriorated as maintenance standards began to slip. Retirement in 1962 meant that he was saved from witnessing first-hand the final days of these magnificent engines. But, like Tom Coleman, he followed them faithfully to their end, being happy to recall his days on their footplates, up until his death in 1975. In early 1970, he gave a brief talk describing his feelings as he looked back:

'The Lizzies were best. I couldn't have asked for more and whether streamlined or not they were always a pleasure to drive. They were strong and did well in all conditions, even when poorly maintained and dirty, as they were in the war and at the end of steam. They never let me down.

'They were designed by a master, who knew a thing or two about his trade. I always felt that on the right track they would easily have beaten *Mallard's* record and not broken down shortly afterwards as that loco did. The old LMS lines just weren't suitable for this though. How fast could the "big uns" have gone if pushed I can't say. We always joked that we couldn't have got coal into the firebox quick enough to find out.'

And so the last few years of steam gradually passed, the number of locomotives slowly diminishing year by year as diesels took over their duties. But as the total shrank, interest in them grew, many lineside enthusiasts wishing to observe the last few locomotives before they were gone. I was amongst them, chasing them down,

46251 was withdrawn in September '64 and cut up that December. Such a magnificent machine could have lasted another decade.

The new world in close up. The Coronations, and other LMS express locomotives, highly efficient, but not so enigmatic replacements.

taking photographs or simply sitting watching them flash by. It was a fairly harmless, but stirring pursuit that absorbed countless numbers of people. They were mostly schoolboys of varying sizes and degrees of expertise in slipping round station and shed staff to get close to the engines or take illicit journeys with them. Souveniring towards the end became commonplace and was rarely discouraged by the powers that be. With so much to dispose of in so short a time, and those in authority unable or unwilling to consider careful sifting and preservation of historic material, some were happy

to see it go by any means. By this route a vast amount of material was saved, some finding its way into national institutions, supplemented by a huge number of photographs.

As a teenager at the end of steam, with a growing awareness of the world around me, I couldn't help but wonder about the men who designed, maintained and drove these engines, as they disappeared from view. What sort of people were they? What skills did they possess? Why did the railways attract them and many other questions, that the passing of years have only served to enhance and emphasise? In many ways, it was a search for the reality of their lives in a world that had readily absorbed me and which I wished to recreate. But it was a search made difficult by so many things. A lack of first-hand accounts, a preponderance of technical and engine performance detail, a scarcity of material describing their

lives and an inability amongst those who were there to describe in a meaningful way the events that shaped them – Stanier and Tom Coleman particularly. So, machines we can understand from what has survived, but not the people who created and sustained them. If we are to truly appreciate their world the two parts should be set in a reasonable balance.

Tom personifies this dichotomy more than most. A man of huge talents, enterprise and achievement who has literally slipped through the cracks in history. Whether by design or accident he has avoided the historian's glare and stayed firmly in the shadows long after his death and long after the credit that was due to him should have been expressed. But, it seems, he wasn't a man to court popularity or fame, preferring the quiet satisfaction of a job well done. This modesty, and the shortage of eyewitness accounts, has ensured a high degree of anonymity and little recognition. Yet there was much to uncover, helped by a friendship which allowed Tom to express some of his thoughts. But even here he was muted in expressing strong opinions or views, choosing a degree of diplomacy and obduracy in avoiding contentious issues. From the first he had been a team player and this principle remained with him to the end.

Many of the strengths that stayed with him were a product of a Victorian childhood and attitudes prevalent at the time. He was also helped by having educated parents, who encouraged their children academically, supported their ambitions and gave them a position in life slightly more comfortable than most enjoyed at the time. Yet none of this would probably have counted, in terms of becoming a railway engineer, if the family hadn't moved from Shere to industrial Staffordshire when Tom was 11. This proved to be the catalyst for significant change in his life.

It is interesting to consider the simple fact that when questioned, he claimed Staffordshire as his birthplace, suggesting the depth of his association with the area. It seems to have fed a wish for something within him; a sense of belonging perhaps, or simply that he was happy there. There are several accounts of his personality that describe Tom as a 'rough diamond', with a slightly gruff way of expressing himself. Yet as a headmaster's son, who was well educated and would undoubtedly have espoused middle class as well as Victorian values, the 'rough diamond' label doesn't quite ring true. One wonders whether it was a front he adopted to survive in the

The Coronations were laid up and made melancholy viewing in sidings as they awaited scrapping. 46226 and 46225 await their fate in late 1964.

46256 still looking good, but soon to receive the yellow stripe and then be consigned to Cashmores to be cut up in December 1964.

heavily industrialised world in which he found himself. If so, it worked to a certain extent, but probably didn't do justice to the very talented, diplomatic man that lay behind this image. His lack of interest in joining professional institutions, and his footballing activities, also fed this illusion in a world coloured by social climbing and snobbery.

From an early age science, engineering, drawing, the railways and sport were Tom's passions and remained so for the whole of his life. It was this combination of talents and interests that fed his fertile mind and imagination. Down to earth he may have been, but he had higher aspirations than most

around him, and found a ready outlet for his burgeoning skills in the world of design engineering. In a later age, he would undoubtedly have attended university and developed as a scientist, but in those days, it was apprenticeship schemes that provided a primary access point to higher education. And when coupled to an ever-increasing number of colleges offering evening classes, this route became the gold standard for establishing a sound career. Tom took full advantage of these opportunities and rapidly made progress, driven by scientific curiosity and a love of learning, towards his true calling.

Even with talents such as his, success could not be guaranteed. Fate and chance will always play a part and Tom enjoyed much good fortune in his career. Moving to Staffordshire gave him access to many engineering concerns offering sound apprenticeship schemes. Kerr, Stuart, who recruited him, were noted for their training regime and once qualified, fledgling engineers had a number of sound companies around Stoke in which to seek employment. At the North Staffordshire Railway, he was again in luck and blossomed under the guiding hands of men with great influence and stature, such as John Adams, John Hookham and Arthur Tassell. He even began his long and positive association with Henry Ivatt whilst with the NSR. Promotion followed, guided by these men. And when opportunities in Stoke diminished, following amalgamation of the railways in 1923, Tom found favour in the new regime and became Chief Draughtsman at Horwich. Undoubtedly his great skills demanded this recognition, but luck still played a part. Yet the greatest element of his good fortune still lay ahead, as it did for William Stanier.

And so we turn to the most interesting twist of fate, one that could so easily have been missed if Stanier had chosen to stay at Swindon and not risk his reputation by joining the rather dissipated, conflict-strewn world of the LMS. Stanier without Coleman is unthinkable in railway history terms. It was this developing relationship, which mixed their exceptional and complimentary talents, creating so much that is important in railway history.

Two anonymous Coronations-though one is either 46256 or 57- barely attract a backwards glance from the youngsters passing by, though still ready for service.

City of Salford's last few days in service.

If Fowler had stayed in charge, or Lemon had remained as CME, it is more than likely that the design explosion, that followed Stanier's arrival and Coleman's promotion, would not have happened.

Once in a position of authority, and retaining Stanier's implicit trust, Tom established a centre of excellence, in locomotive and rolling stock design, that few could equal. But here again, he was lucky, because the teams of draughtsmen under his control were exceptional by any standards, although most have now been lost to history, even more effectively than Tom himself. Luckily, we have Eric Langridge's memoirs and correspondence to provide a small, though sometimes biased reminder, but there is precious little else. Yet without their support and ideas Tom could not have achieved as much as he did.

In 1966 Ernest Cox wrote:

'Sheer luck enters into how it is possible to progress – to have been in a particular place at a particular time, to have been sent to Derby and not Crewe, to have had Stanier or Ivatt as boss and not a Thompson or Bulleid. Such things help or hinder a career entirely outside the sum total of one's own endeavours.

'Apart from a few bright spirits however, destined by exceptional gifts or advantages to soar to the top in any case, there are few of us who have much cause for self-satisfaction. Who can be said, for example to have designed a locomotive? The name of the reigning CME is rightly attached to it, but with few exceptions it is an amalgam of ideas and pieces of individual effort to which technical officers at many levels have contributed. There have been designs which more or less grew from the bottom upwards, while others, imposed from the top by some strong character with original ideas, have missed their true intention by the limiting capacity of those who had to work out the details.'

Stripped of nameplates but with tenders still full, 46231 and an unidentified Coronation stand and wait for a call that didn't come. And so Coleman's legacy passed on.

Great endeavours fade, soon to feel the cutting torch and oblivion.

Tom's greatness rested in his ability, no matter whether at the top or bottom of an organisation, to see clearly what was needed, take all he knew and observed and turn it into the finest designs possible. He led those above and below in a search for excellence and drew out potential where none seemed to exist. The steam locomotives he helped create were arguably some of the finest ever built and were produced in huge numbers to meet company and national needs, at times of great crisis. What greater accolade could be there be and how little such a modest man sought such an honour. No locomotive was named after him, but Coleman's Coronations stand as his true memorial.

The 21st Century version of Tom's streamlined Coronation Class powers through Lichfield, showing the clear lineage of its shape and aerodynamic strengths.

KEY BIOGRAPHIES

John Henry Adams. Born on 10 September 1860, the third son of William Adams, a noted railway engineer who rose to become Locomotive Superintendent of the London and South Western Railway. John Adams was educated at Brighton Grammar School, Thanet College then by private tutor in Brussels before being apprenticed to his father with the Great Eastern Railway at its Stratford Works, East London, in 1877. He completed his engineering training at the LSWR's Works at Nine Elms where his father had transferred two years earlier. He also, most unusually, qualified as a fireman then driver. Appointments around Great Britain and Brazil followed, at increasingly senior ranks, before being appointed to the North Staffordshire Railway in March1902 as Locomotive, Carriage and Wagon Superintendent, a position he held until his death on 7 November 1915.

James Anderson. Born on 3 April 1871 and died on 15 January 1945. After serving an apprenticeship with the Great North Railway of Scotland, he gradually rose to become Assistant Chief Draughtsman for Robert Stephenson Ltd of Darlington. A move to Derby followed in 1903, where he was promoted a little later to Chief Draughtsman. Between 1915/19, during Fowler's absence on war service, he was acting CME. Post-war, he reverted to the position of deputy and was awarded the CBE for his work during the conflict.

When the LMS was created in 1923, Anderson was appointed Motive Power Superintendent and in this role strongly advocated a small engine policy, although he was flexible enough to agree that the 'Lickey Banker' should be of an 0-10-0 design and the needs of the Somerset and Dorset Railway were best served by a 2-8-0 class of engine. But he virtually vetoed the construction of two Pacific designs for the LMS put forward by Fowler and Hughes, when they were each CME. Ernest Lemon, realising that Anderson's influence did not suit the changing climate in the company with Stanier's arrival, eased Anderson out by enforced retirement in 1932.

Hewitt Pearson Montague Beames. Born on 9 May 1875 near Taunton, Somerset, though often recorded as Monkstown, near Dublin. His personal entry in the 1911 Census confirms Somerset. It seems that his father was a serving officer in the Army so the vagaries of the posting system may account for the disparity. He died at his home in Crewe on 5 March 1948. He was educated initially at the Corrig School, Kingstown, then Dover College and finally Crawley's Military Academy, Dublin. For a time, he was a private pupil of F.W. Webb. In 1895, he began a five year apprenticeship in the LNWR Works at Crewe before becoming a draughtsman then junior assistant to the Works Manager there. He volunteered for service in the Boer War where he saw action as a trooper and then a sergeant with Paget's Horse, across the West Transvaal. He returned to Crewe in 1901 and was appointed as Assistant to the Outdoor Superintendent for machinery, where he remained for eight years before being selected to be Personal Assistant to the CME, C.J.B. Cooke. From 1914 to 1916 he was commissioned, despite being 39, and served in France, being given command of the 110th Railway Company. He was released from the Army in April 1916, due to age, and became Chief Assistant to the Works Manager at Crewe. Promotion to Deputy CME followed in 1919, then, a year later CME, following the death of Bowen Cooke.

In 1921, he was elected to the Institution of Mechanical Engineers and, a year later, to the Institution of Civil Engineers. His proposers included George Churchward, Henry Fowler and Vincent Raven, which underpins the very high regard in which he was held in the railway industry. Many expected him to become the LMS's first CME, but he was passed over on four occasions between 1923 and 1932; in favour of George Hughes, Henry Fowler, Ernest Lemon and finally William Stanier. He served each man with skill and good grace and helped the passage of change enormously. He retired on 30 September 1934 and later became Chairman of Cheshire County Council and was awarded a CBE in 1946.

John Robert Billington. Born on 18 April 1873 in Freckleton, Near Kirkham, Lancashire and died at Horwich on 22 March 1922. He was educated at Clifton-with-Salwick National and Kirkham Grammar School. He completed a Mechanical Engineering Ord in 1896 with the Lancashire and Yorkshire Railway at Horwich, where he had been employed as a draughtsman in 1894. He then achieved an honours grade in his City and Guilds exams before becoming a Whitworth Exhibitioner in 1897. During this period, he worked under John Aspinall and George Hughes on such tasks as the design of locomotives, workshop cranes, pumping and electrical installations. Promotion followed. In 1902, he was placed in charge of the Testing and Inspection Department, then in 1904 became head of the Gas Department, before becoming the company's Chief Draughtsman, a post he held until his death.

Roland Curling Bond. Born on 5 May 1903 at Ipswich and died in 1980. Educated at Tonbridge School, he became an Engineering Apprentice at Derby Locomotive Works and then a pupil under Sir Henry Fowler, the LMS's CME.

Once qualified, he specialised in overseeing locomotives built by contractors for his parent company. He so impressed managers at the Vulcan Foundry Locomotive Works that he was 'head hunted' and became their Assistant Works Manager in 1928. A return to the LMS followed in 1931 with a posting to the Horwich Works, then to Crewe as Assistant Works Manager. Despite his comparatively young age he was picked out for rapid promotion and by 1946 had become Deputy Chief Mechanical Engineer for the LMS. Nationalisation of the railways did not hinder his progress and he succeeded Robert Riddles as BR's CME Central Staff in 1953. Before retiring in 1968 he held the post of Technical Adviser to the British Transport Commission before becoming General Manager of BR's Workshops Division in 1965. In recognition of his great contribution to engineering, he became President of the Institution of Locomotive Engineers (1953/54) and the Institution of Mechanical Engineers (1963/65).

Herbert Chambers. Born in Derby during 1885 and died in September 1937. On leaving school he became an apprentice at the Midland Railway Works in Derby. Once qualified, he found employment in the Locomotive Drawing Office, before being recruited by Beyer, Peacock in Manchester in 1911,

returning two years later to Derby. In 1923, he was promoted to Chief Locomotive Draughtsman and four years later to Chief Draughtsman of the LMS. In 1935, he became William Stanier's Personal Assistant at Euston, a post he held until his death. As Chief Draughtsman, and then Stanier's technical assistant, he played a leading role in the planning and construction of the Princess Class, Turbomotive and the standard locomotive designs introduced by the LMS.

Thomas James Clark. Born in Southport, Lancashire, during 1872 and died at his home in Crewe during February 1954. He joined the London and North Western Railway in December 1888 as an engine cleaner. Near the end of his working life, having risen to the 'top link' as a driver, he was chosen to take charge of Royal Trains, but also drive Stanier's new Pacifics. This work culminated in the high-speed test, with 6201 *Princess Elizabeth*, between Euston and Glasgow on the 16/17 November 1936, to prove the validity of the big engine policy. A year later, on 29 June 1937, he pushed a brand new Coronation Class locomotive, No 6220, up to 114 mph, then a record in Britain. Very late in his life he was able to enjoy the status this work conferred on him and was awarded the OBE shortly after his record run by King George VI.

Ernest Stewart Cox. Born in Lanarkshire on 17 June 1900 and died on 19 September 1992 at home in Berkhamstead. His father was a Principal Clerk with the Customs and Excise Department and so the family often moved. Ernest's younger brother was born in Yorkshire and they both attended Merchant Taylors School in Crosby, Lancashire. In 1917, he began an apprenticeship at the Horwich Works of the Lancashire and Yorkshire Railway, under George Hughes. A gifted engineer, he was soon promoted and by 1934 was Assistant Works Superintendent at Derby, quickly moving on to become Personal and Technical Assistant to the CME at Euston. During the war, he was seconded to the Railway Executive and post-war his star kept rising until he became Assistant CME for British Rail.

He held a number of unique positions within the LMS and BR and was one of only a few chief officers to record his memories of those days. Many historians have questioned the veracity of his recollections, but they still contain many eye witness accounts of Stanier and Coleman, their way of working and the locomotives they produced, that seem to be above question so are extremely valuable.

Alfred Ewer. Born during 1895 in Fulham, London, died at his home in Rochford, Essex, in 1963. He served an engineering apprenticeship with the LNWR company from 1911. In 1921, he was appointed Assistant Locomotive Superintendent at Holyhead. Three years later he was transferred to Widnes as Running Shed Foreman, before moving to Swansea as Assistant District Locomotive Superintendent. 1929 saw him transfer to Kentish Town and five years later to Camden. From June to November 1938 he was seconded to Derby, then returned to Camden and Watford as Locomotive Superintendent, where he remained until 1948. Whilst in this post he came into close contact with all the LMS's senior managers as well as manage the day to day work of all Stanier and Coleman's locomotives, but particularly the Pacifics. He was in a position of great responsibility and the records he left illuminate in great detail many aspects of life on the LMS at that time.

On leaving Camden he moved to Llandudno Junction Depot, then under BR management, and ended his career at Doncaster.

Charles Edward Fairburn. Born in Bradford on 5 September 1887 and died suddenly following a heart attack on 12 October 1945. Educated at Bradford Grammar School before winning a scholarship to Brasenose College (Oxford), in 1905. He achieved a 1st in Mathematics then read Engineering Science in which he also gained 1st Class Honours. A two year tutelage under Henry Fowler then followed at Derby before he joined Siemens Dynamo Works in Stafford, where, from 1913 to 1916, he was Resident Engineer on the Shildon-Newport electrification project for the North Eastern Railway. Service with the RFC and RAF followed and on leaving the service he joined English Electric, again being involved in railway electrification work. From here, Harold Hartley led in recruiting him to the LMS and in 1934 he became the company's Chief Electrical Engineer. During 1938 Deputy CME was added to this role. When Stanier was seconded to the Ministry of Production Fairburn stepped up to be temporary CME, taking the role permanently when Stanier retired in 1944. It was a promotion he enjoyed for only a very short period. It is probably fair to state that he would have achieved much more if electrification and dieselisation had been developed more actively in pre-war years. Steam locomotion was not his natural area of competence.

Henry Fowler. Born on 27 July 1870 at Evesham. Died at his home, Sponden Hall, Derby, on 15 October 1938. Educated at Prince Henry's High School, Evesham, then Mason Science College, where he studied metallurgy. He entered into an apprenticeship with the Lancashire and Yorkshire Railway, under John Aspinall, in 1887 at their Horwich Works. A growing reputation led to him being appointed Assistant Works Manager, now of the Midland Railway, then deputy to Richard Dealey in 1923, whom he succeeded two years later, now under the auspices of the LMS. The company followed a 'small engine policy' which many have argued set the company back in its battle with its chief competitor, the LNER. In this role Fowler was responsible for the Royal Scot Class, but had an ambition to build a Pacific engine, but was thwarted in this by an Operating Department, over which he had no control, dictating need and types. Nevertheless, his work on a 4-6-2 design prepared the way for Stanier and Coleman and highlighted the need to control any opposition to such a development.

In 1930, Fowler became assistant to the Vice President for Works, replaced by Ernest Lemon as CME, who in turn gave way to William Stanier. For his services in peace and war Fowler became a Knight in 1919.

Edward Mellor Gass. Born in Openshaw, Manchester, in 1861 and died at home in Bolton on 2 May 1942. Following a general education at the Endowed School, Gorton, he took technical courses in machine drawing, geometry and mechanical design under William Rose before becoming an apprentice with Beyer, Peacock. He was then employed as a draughtsman by Sharp Stewart in Manchester and Glasgow. In 1888, he was appointed to Horwich as Assistant Chief Draughtsman where he remained until retirement in 1926. After John Billington's death in 1925, he became Chief Draughtsman, but retired soon after, leaving the way open for Tom Coleman.

Harold Brewer Hartley. Born in London on 3 September 1878 and died on 9 September 1972. Educated at Mortimer College, then Dulwich College. He graduated from Balliol College 'Oxford', with first class honours in natural sciences in 1900. He remained at the College as tutor and lecturer and married the Master of Balliol's eldest daughter. During the First World War, he rose from junior officer with the 7th Leicestershire Regiment to Brigadier-General, Controller of the Chemical Warfare Department. He was awarded the Military Cross for gallantry and was Mentioned in Despatches three times. He advised different governments on the development of chemical weapons until 1950.

Although returning, part time, to the academic world in 1919, he combined this role with work in different industries. But in 1930, he resigned his tutorial fellowship at Oxford to become the LMS's Vice-President for Works and Ancillary Undertakings and Director of Research – a move encouraged and sponsored by Josiah Stamp. His influence on many areas of railway work was immense, not least of all in the design of locomotives. But a man of his drive and ability would be frustrated by the poor business sense and hidebound tradition of the LMS in the early 1930s. He and Stamp saw in William Stanier a man who could move things forward and set out to recruit him. His arrival in 1932 provided the long sought for catalyst for change and they gave 'their man' complete support and huge freedom to develop effective locomotives. He had a long and active career with the LMS, retiring in 1945, but continued in many roles advising government and industry.

He was elected a Fellow of the Royal Society in 1926 and was knighted two years later. In 1944, he was awarded a KCVO and a GCVO in 1957.

Thomas Martin Herbert. Born in Temperley, Cheshire, on 19 March 1901. Attended Marlborough College before studying an Honours Degree in Engineering Science at Cambridge between 1919 and 1922, where he achieved 1st Class Honours in studies concerning heat, structures and metallurgy. This was followed by a two year tutelage at Derby and a period of further study at Kings College, London. By 1926, he was undertaking exploration work for the Ferrous Metals Association in Birmingham, whilst, concurrently, completing research for the LMS on a range of subjects. He became an Associate Member of I Mech E, his proposers being Herbert Chambers and Sandham Symes. Harold Hartley's appointment to the LMS in 1930 led to the creation, two years later, of a larger, more expansive research department and Herbert was appointed its first head. He held this post until BR was formed and continued on in the new organisation until his retirement in 1961. He died at his home in Harpenden, Hertfordshire, on 5 December 1963.

John Albert Hookham. Born in Clapham, London, on 9 November 1863 and died in Exmouth, Devon, on 24 January 1934. Educated at Durnham House School then the Birkbeck Institute for three years. He became a pupil at the London and Chatham Railway Locomotive Works at Longhedge under William Kirtley. On qualifying, he was employed as a draughtsman at this works then by the Pulsometer Engineering Works at Nine Elms. In 1887, he moved to the Gengall Ironworks, Millwall, followed by a period at Ashford before taking up the appointment of Locomotive Superintendent to the Donna Thereza Christina Railway in Brazil. On its nationalisation in 1902, he returned to Britain to become the NSR's Works Manager at Stoke, becoming Locomotive Superintendent in 1915 when John Adams died. He held this post until grouping in 1923 when his post was re-designated Mechanical Engineer, Stoke Works. He retired shortly afterwards as the tasks assigned to this works gradually dried up and was transferred elsewhere. His grand-daughter was Dame Margot Fonteyn, the ballet dancer.

George Hughes. Born on 9 October 1865 in Cambridgeshire. Died in Stamford on 27 October 1945. He began his apprenticeship at Crewe in 1882 and became a fitter with the Lancashire and Yorkshire Railway at Horwich Works in 1887. By 1895, he had risen to become Chief Assistant in the Carriage and Wagon Department at Newton Heath, before returning to Horwich as Works Manager in 1899. 1904 saw him promoted to CME, having served for a short period as Chief Assistant, and then, on the creation of the LMS, he became that company's first CME. Under his guiding hand, locomotive development was dominated by a small engine policy and his designs stayed within this framework, but he and his team did explore the potential of the Pacific configuration and planning for such an engine reached an advanced stage before being dropped. It seems that James Anderson was again responsible for dictating and managing these development proposals.
Hughes retired in 1925 due, in part, to the intense pressures imposed upon him. Nevertheless, he had begun the process of changing minds in the company which smoothed the path for Stanier and Coleman's Pacifics.

Henry George Ivatt. Born on 4 May 1886 and died on 4 October 1972. He was the son of a famous locomotive engineer – Henry Alfred Ivatt – who was Locomotive Engineer for the Great Southern and Western Railway when his son was born. He rose to become the GNR's Locomotive Superintendent in December 1911, carefully fostering his son's engineering

career in the process. Henry junior was educated at Uppingham School before beginning an apprenticeship at Crewe in 1904, which ended in 1907, during which he spent time with the Electrical Testing Department, Rugby. Promotion followed and before the First World War had started he had worked as Assistant Works Manager at Crewe on experimental locomotive work then as Assistant Manager of the Locomotive Outdoors Department. During the war, he was commissioned and served on the staff of the Director of Transport in France.

On leaving the services, he was recruited by the NSR at Stoke as Assistant Locomotive Superintendent. In 1928, he became Works Superintendent at Derby, before moving to Glasgow as Divisional Mechanical Engineer. In 1937, he moved south again to become Stanier's Principal Assistant for Locomotives. Following Fairburn's death in 1945, Ivatt was appointed CME, a post he held until nationalisation, when his empire was severely denuded. He carried on until 1951 and retired on his 65th birthday and was offered work as a consultant with Brush Bagnall Traction. He then became their Director and General Manager, working on well into his seventies.

Frederick Charles Johansen. Born in Goole during 1897 and died in Dorking General Hospital on 4 November 1966. He gained his BSc and MSc at Kings College, London. After working for the Yorkshire Electric Co he was appointed to a research post at the National Physical Laboratory (NPL), Teddington, to study

aspects of fluid motion, which led to experiments on air and liquid flow around solid, but moving, objects. This work was relevant to many branches of engineering, including aviation, maritime and locomotive design. In the late 1920s, he produced a series of papers outlining the results of this research and worked closely with Supermarine and R.J. Mitchell in designing their fast monoplane seaplanes for the Schneider Trophy.

He became an expert in the emerging science of aerodynamics and the use of wind tunnels. In 1934, the Royal Aeronautical Society published their *Handbook of Aeronautics* and Johansen was its major contributor. His research also resulted in an I Mech E paper entitled *The Air Resistance of Passenger Trains*, which although published in 1936, was based on his research going back to the 1920s. Some of his work had informed the development of Gresley's 4-6-4 experimental engine 'Hush Hush', the P2 and the A4 Class, and associated carriages. Johansen was sponsored by Gresley from 1929, on an ad hoc consultancy basis, to test various shapes at the NPL and final designs were heavily influenced by the scientist. As early as 1932 Harold Hartley identified the value of his work and recruited him to the LMS (based nominally at Euston to remain close to the NPL test facilities). Concurrent employment by the LMS and its chief rival, the LNER, appears unusual to the casual observer.

Johansen and Coleman worked closely together in formulating the design of the Coronation Class. During this period, the scientist maintained close links with the

NPL and continued to work, part time, on aircraft development, being involved in the design of the Spitfire and Hurricane.

Johansen left the LMS in 1949 following nationalisation and became Director of Research at W.T. Avery and completed his PhD. His work on air flow, though largely rejected by steam locomotive designers at the time, now has great relevance and is seen as groundbreaking.

Eric Arthur Langridge. Born on 20 May 1896 in London and died in Polegate, East Sussex, on 18 May 1999. Educated at St Olave's School. He began an engineering apprenticeship at Eastleigh Locomotive Works in 1912, with part of his training being undertaken at Hartley College, Southampton. Subsequently he worked in the Drawing Office at Eastleigh, but it seems that the London and South Western Railway could not offer him longer term employment and he was recruited by the Midland Railway at Derby. He began work in 1920 and remained in the Drawing Office there for thirty-nine years.

In the years that followed he worked on the design of many locomotives, but eventually specialised in boilers and in this role worked on the Princesses. Two years later, he worked on proposals for an improved Princess Pacific - plans that were then shelved when the Coronation Class came into being. This work was resurrected in 1952 when Turbomotive was converted to a conventional, reciprocating engine.

He holds a unique place in railway history having served

for so long in one of the most important centres of locomotive development. In so doing, his work encompassed some of the major steam engine developments of the twentieth century and embraced the future beyond steam traction. In retirement, he wrote numerous articles about the work in which he was involved, which were, in time, made into two books, entitled *Under 10 CMEs*.

Ernest John Hutchings Lemon. Born in Okeford Fitzpaine, Dorset, on 10 December 1884, the youngest of 6 children, and died in Epsom, Surrey, on 15 December 1954. He was apprenticed to the North British locomotive Company in Glasgow, and completed his training in 1905, before spending two years at the Heriot-Watt College, further developing his engineering skills. A brief period of employment with the Highland Railway at Inverness followed and then three years with Hurst, Nelson and Co at Motherwell (wagon builders).

In 1911, he became chief wagon inspector for the Midland Railway, then, in 1917, Carriage Works Manager at Derby, followed, in 1923, by promotion to Divisional Carriage and Wagon Superintendent.

When Sir Henry Fowler retired in 1931, Lemon became the LMS's CME, despite the fact that he had little or no experience of locomotive engineering. But it proved to be a stop gap measure only, the post being filled by William Stanier in early 1932. Lemon became Vice-President in charge of the Railway Traffic, Operating and Commercial Section. Whilst CME he had not

been idle though, having completed a major review of locomotive stock, identifying and recommending future engine policy and needs. He also oversaw major changes in the way locomotives were maintained and repaired. In so doing he laid valuable groundwork on which Stanier could build the loco modernisation programme.

In 1938, Lemon was seconded to the Air Ministry, in recognition of his considerable skills of management and industrial manufacturing. He was appointed Director General of Aircraft Production, his primary responsibility to sort out the many problems that beset aircraft construction. He remained with the Air Ministry until April 1940, when his secondment came to an end. A knighthood was his reward. Three more years service with the LMS followed before retirement in August 1943.

Although retired, he continued to be involved in various scientific and engineering studies, the last as Chairman of the Committee for the Standardisation of Engineering Products for the Ministry of Supply. Their report, published in 1949, was Lemon's final project. After this his health declined and he died five years later.

Frederick Arnold Lemon. Born near Castle Cary, Somerset, and died in a Watford Nursing Home on 23 October 1961. He successfully completed an apprenticeship at Crewe and after several appointments entered Works management there in December 1920. His association with this Department would last until his retirement in 1941. By the time of

Stanier's appointment, as the LMS's CME, Lemon had become Crewe's Works Superintendent and so was responsible for the construction and maintenance of Stanier's engines during the most dynamic and pressured time of his tenure as CME. Without Lemon, the level of success achieved might have been considerably less.

Robert Arthur Riddles. Born 23 May 1892. Died 18 June 1983. His engineering education began in 1909 when he was taken on as an apprentice by the London and North Western Railway at Crewe and then found work as a fitter in the Erecting Shop at Rugby. When war came he volunteered for service and saw action on the Western Front with the Royal Engineers, becoming an officer in the process. Post-war, he rose rapidly through the ranks and he began to specialise in streamlining and improvement of production processes. His first major success in this field was as part of the team that re-organised Crewe Works between 1925 and 1928, now part of the recently created LMS. He then moved to Derby where he undertook a similar exercise.

Such success did not escape Stanier and a year after his arrival, having carefully assessed his staff, he promoted Riddles to be his Locomotive Assistant and then Principal Assistant in 1935. In this supporting role, he played a significant part in the development and testing of new engine designs, including Turbomotive. But as a 'rising star' he had to gain wider experience and in 1937 was transferred to St Rollox to become Mechanical and Electrical Engineer,

Scotland, though for such an ambitious man this move felt more like demotion. He had hoped to be promoted to Deputy CME, a post which went to his rival, Charles Fairburn. He need not have worried unduly because shortly afterwards he was selected to go on a high-profile visit to the USA, with a new Coronation Class engine and her rake of coaches.

The coming of war changed the course of his life, as it did for the whole population. His skills in production techniques were sorely needed and, under Harold Hartley's guidance, he found himself seconded to the recently formed Ministry of Supply to become Director of Transportation Equipment. To meet wartime needs his principal responsibility was to produce new engines suited to military needs. As a result, the LMS's 8F 2-8-0 was selected and 240 were ordered. Later he led on the design of two simplified austerity engines – a 2-8-0 and a 2-10-0 - and the construction of 935 of them.

He was awarded a CBE in 1943 and then returned to the LMS as Chief Stores Assistant, by which time Stanier had retired and been replaced by Fairburn. On his death in 1944, Henry Ivatt became CME and a year later Riddles was promoted to Vice President to replace Harold Hartley, so became Ivatt's boss.

With nationalisation of the railways in 1948 Riddles became BR's first CME, though initially this post went by other names. He took Roland Bond and Ernest Cox from the LMS with him as assistants. Before his retirement in 1953 he led the major programme of steam engine design and production and

attempted to bring together the diverse groups that had run the Big Four companies. It is said by some that his primary focus on producing more steam locomotives diverted attention away from the development of diesel and electric alternatives, hindering BR's progress by many years. In the years that followed he became a Director of Stothert and Pitt in Bath, finally retiring at the age of 75.

Dudley William Sanford. Born in London on 17 April 1890 to William and Ada Sanford, butchers and pub proprietors in Walton-on-Thames. He died in Derby on 28 August 1948. Educated at Uppingham School between 1905 and 1909, he then went to Cambridge to read Mechanical Science, receiving his degree in 1912. A two year period was then spent as a pupil at Derby before war started and he was commissioned into the Royal Engineers. With hostilities over, he returned to Derby as a draughtsman. On the formation of the LMS he was promoted and posted into the locomotive experimental group and four years later became Senior Technical Draughtsman. Under Herbert Chambers, Sanford was promoted to be Chief Locomotive Draughtsman in 1934, a post he held until 1943 when he became Technical Assistant to the CME. Post-war, with reactivation of plans to construct a locomotive testing facility at Rugby, he was appointed its first Mechanical Engineer, but in 1947 ill-health intervened making this posting impossible. An early death followed and his great promise was lost at a time when BR was about to take a leap into the future, where Sanford's undoubted scientific skills could have proved extremely useful.

Josiah Charles Stamp. Born in London on 21 June 1880 and died on 16 April 1941. Following education at Bethany House School in Kent, he joined the Inland Revenue in 1906 and, by 1916, had risen to Assistant Secretary level. An avid scholar, he studied economics as an external student at London University, obtaining a 1st Class Degree in 1911. His thesis on incomes and property became a standard work on the subject and made his reputation as a leading economist of the time.

In 1919, he left the Civil Service to pursue a more ambitious career in industry, first with Nobel Industries then as Chairman of the LMS in 1926. At the same time, he served on many public bodies and became a Director of the Bank of England. His career was one of the highest office and immense achievement. He was appointed CBE in 1918, a KBE in 1920 and raised to the peerage in 1938, becoming Baron Stamp. He was also a prolific writer on many economic issues and rose to become Colonel commanding the Royal Engineers Railway and Transport Corps.

A man of drive and huge talent, his role in the development of the LMS and guiding it to success from a group of uncoordinated and conflicting companies was immense. Though not an engineer he understood the needs of business and set out to recruit a team of specialists from many spheres who could take the company forward successfully. Stanier's appointment was a key part of this process. He backed his CME and allowed him free rein to create some of the most potent steam locomotives ever constructed.

Sadly, Stamp, his wife and son, Wilfred, were to die when their bomb shelter took a direct hit during a night time attack in April 1941. His passing was a significant loss for the LMS and his country.

William Arthur Stanier. Born on 27 May 1876 at 10 Wellington Street, Swindon. Died at Newburn, Chorleywood Road, Rickmansworth on 27 September 1965. He was the eldest child of William Henry Stanier, an employee of the GWR, who was educated at Wycliffe College, Stonehouse, Gloucestershire, before becoming an office boy at Swindon in 1892, then taking up a five year apprenticeship in the works there. On qualifying he then spent two years in the Drawing Office before becoming Inspector of Materials. Under the guiding hand of George Churchward, then C.B. Collett, rapid promotion followed from Acting Divisional Locomotive, Carriage and Wagon Superintendent to Principal Assistant to the CME in 1923. In this role, he led the way in the design and construction of two of the GWR's finest classes of locomotives – the Castles and Kings.

By 1931, it was apparent to Stanier that he was unlikely to become the GWR's CME and when an offer from the LMS was made by Josiah Stamp, later that year, to become their CME, he jumped at the chance, being appointed in January 1932. And so the greatest challenge of his career began.

The LMS was a colossal business (created at Grouping from many often competing companies) greatly in need of modernisation if it were to meet the challenging business targets set by its Board. Through the late1920s, great advances had been made, but when Stanier arrived its locomotives left much to be desired, reflecting as they did, the outdated and often limited requirements of the LMS's constituent companies. Stanier's target was to establish standardised design and construction methods and to provide a fleet of new, more powerful and efficient locomotives. And this he did, with the aid of some very able assistants, principle amongst them Tom Coleman.

Such was his and Coleman's success that two of their designs – the Class 5 and Class 8F – were still in service when the last steam locomotives were withdrawn from traffic in 1968. Their work also greatly influenced British Rail's standardisation programme in the 1950s.

The coming of the Second World War led to a great increase in his duties on the LMS, but also in the wider service of his country. In the early years, he oversaw the construction of weapons in LMS factories and in 1942 was seconded to the Ministry of Production, as one of three full time Scientific Advisors. Later on, he became a member of the Aeronautical Research Council, then Chairman of Power Jets Limited, a Government owned concern developing jet propulsion, principally gas turbines, and became a Director of several companies, including H.W. Kearns of Altringham and Courtaulds.

He gathered many awards during his career - including a Knighthood in 1943, and a Fellowship of the Royal Society in 1944 (only the second locomotive engineer to do so, the other being Robert Stephenson) - and other forms of recognition - President of the Institution of Locomotive Engineers on two occasions and President of the Institution of Mechanical Engineers, being awarded medals by both bodies.

Sandham John Symes. Born in Tinahely, County Wicklow, on 25 February 1877 and died at his home in North London on 27 May 1970. Educated by private tuition before joining Kevin Street Technical School in 1894 at the same time as beginning an apprenticeship at the Inchicore Works of the Great Southern and Western Railway in Dublin. He qualified in 1899 and was employed in the company's drawing office as a junior draughtsman until 1903. He then secured employment as a locomotive draughtsman with the North British Locomotive Company in Glasgow, moving to the Midland Railway at Derby a year later.

After five years in their drawing office, he was promoted and placed in charge of all experimental work, and here he remained until 1913 when he was appointed Chief Locomotive Draughtsman.

In January 1923, he was again promoted and became Locomotive Works Manager at Derby, working in close co-operation with Fred Lemon at Crewe; one of his daughters marrying Symes' son, also called Sandham, in the process.

In 1928 Symes became Henry Fowler's personal assistant and then the company's Chief Stores Superintendent, in which role he occasionally stood in for the CME, William Stanier, often at crucial times in the locomotive building programme. He retired in 1943.

Arthur John Tassell. Born in Tonbridge on 12 September 1876 and died in Stoke on 16 December 1919. Educated at St Stephens then Sir Andrew Judd's School (Tonbridge), until 1892. He began a five year apprenticeship beginning at Tonbridge Running Shed before moving on to Ashford Works in 1894 to complete qualification. He spent the last part of his training in the Drawing Office there. From 1897 to 1899, he worked as a fitter at Ashford before being recalled to the Drawing Office as a draughtsman. In 1901, he transferred to Hyde Park Loco Works (Glasgow), and was then appointed as Chief Locomotive Draughtsman a year later to the NSR at Stoke. He held this post until 1916 and was then promoted to Loco Works Manager, holding this position until his sudden death in 1919.

David Chalmers Urie. Born 6 July 1884 in Glasgow and died in Watford on 3 August 1963. He was the son of a noted engineer – William Wallace Urie. He was educated at the Ardrossan Academy, Allen Glens in Glasgow and the Camberwell Grammar School. He was then privately educated and obtained a Board of Education pass in Pure Mathematics in 1906, followed by Associate Membership of the Institution of Civil Engineers in 1909. Whilst accomplishing this, he spent five years as an apprentice in the Locomotive Workshops of the London and South Western Railway at Nine Elms. On completion, he became a draughtsman, then leading draughtsman at Nine Elms, before transferring to Ireland in 1915 as Running Superintendent and Assistant Locomotive, Carriage and Wagon Superintendent. In Ireland, he had to run a 'gauntlet of fire' with the civil war raging there. After eight years, he returned to the mainland and was appointed Assistant Mechanical Engineer of the LMS's Northern Division. With James Anderson's enforced departure in 1932, Urie was appointed in his place. No other promotions came his way and he retired in the early post-war years.

EVOLUTION OF A DESIGN ENGINEER

In any career it is possible to trace the gradual emergence of talent. Signs and indications are usually there from the earliest days. Some children show artistic skills that continue to shine, others lean towards the natural world and others to all manner of sciences and history. If we nurture and support each seed of talent, this may simply lead to a lifetime of pleasurable interest or something more substantial that carries over to help produce careers of some substance and importance.

In Tom Coleman's case development of lasting interests began early in life – sport, engineering and the railways. Items such as scrapbooks, artwork, photographs and a few technical drawings still exist from that time to reveal a great deal about his genesis. And later this is supplemented by 'official' records and reports. All this allows us to see for ourselves in which direction his developing skills, growing experience and the random element of chance took him. And so his evolution began:

1885-1900
There is a clear Drummond theme amongst Tom's papers as his earliest surviving drawing of this 0-6-0 tank engine reveals (2-1);

apparently prepared in 1900 before his apprenticeship with Kerr, Stuart began. The skill used here suggests that he may have attended technical drawing classes or simply have been a very talented amateur.

1901-1925
This long period was defined by three things, a five-year apprenticeship, then his junior position as a draughtsman and the lack of records that have survived from this period. Whilst with Kerr, Stuart, it seems, he was involved in

the design of narrow gauge engines for use in Northern Ireland. And with the NSR he worked, in his early years, on plant and machinery plans, whilst occasionally assisting in the design of a variety of engines. However, despite the paucity of information from this period there are three well documented projects through which we can trace his growing skill as a designer.

Coleman's 'Endon Dip' as it was called. By 1917, with the ever-increasing need for raw material demanded by war, the more rapid

2-1

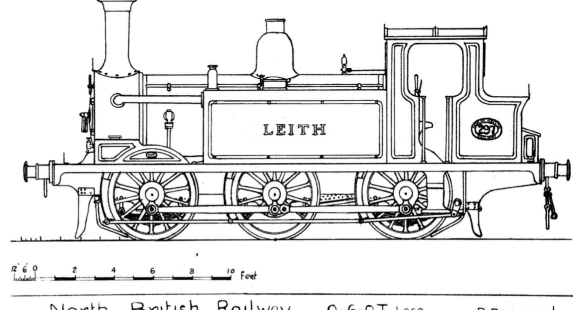

North British Railway. 0-6-0T. Loco. D. Drummond

2-2

2-3

movement of limestone from quarries in Staffordshire became essential. One stumbling block was the transfer of material from railways to canal at Caldon. Tom was assigned the task of designing an appropriate mechanism and, drawing upon his growing knowledge of plant and machinery, created the structure depicted in 2-2. Constructed within Stoke Works and then transferred, in kit form, to the canal it was a sound and effective solution that, by all accounts, increased capacity considerably.

Steam locomotives are of little use in certain types of industry or in enclosed spaces where danger of fire or explosions is high. In 1917, a requirement for a battery-powered shunting engine for the Oakamoor Copper Works was (2-3) Tom, in association

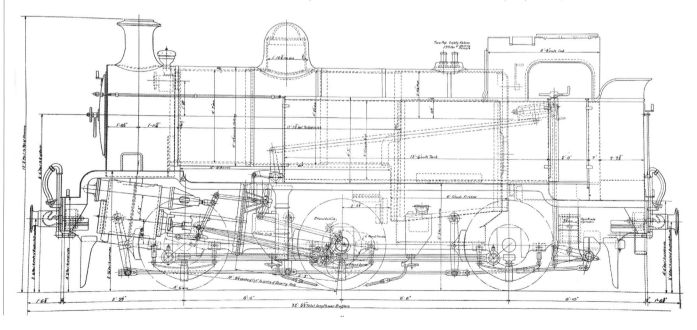

2-4

with one of the company's electrical engineers, Andrew Rock, designed and oversaw the construction of one 0-4-0 electric unit, which served until 1963. In concept, it was simply a converted truck, but was nevertheless a success. It is now preserved as part of the National Railway Museum's collection and sits close to 6229 *Duchess of Hamilton*, offering an interesting comparison of designs from the same drawing board.

In the early 1920s, under John Hookham's guiding hand, Tom cut his design teeth on a number of locomotive projects, as leading draughtsman, then Chief Draughtsman; a promotion that came about following John Tassell's death in 1919. The most notable of these, in terms of experimentation was the 0-6-0 tank engine (2-4), that appeared in 1922, with four cylinders – two inside and two outside. Such was its impact that Coleman wrote a short article for the Journal of the Institution of Locomotive Engineers.

1926-1934
Tom's promotion to Chief Draughtsman at Horwich Works opened the door to a much wider field of design and development. Work in the recently formed LMS being substantially greater than anything he faced whilst at Stoke. Three developments stand out in the first few years of his tenure, the first sponsored by George Hughes, the second by Sir Henry Fowler and the third by William Stanier. In the year before Tom arrived, planning for a new class 2-6-0 tender engine had been set in motion by Hughes. He would be 'in the chair', so

to speak, for the construction of all 245 engines, 5 of these being modified with Lentz cam operated poppet valves in 1931/32. By 1928 Tom had identified some design improvements to this class, but these were not activated until 1932 when Stanier took over as CME and sought authorisation for an additional forty 2-6-0s. But before this, in 1927, he had begun a project which for the first time was entirely his own responsibility from beginning to end – the design of a new 2F 0-6-0 dock tank engine. (2-5/2-6)

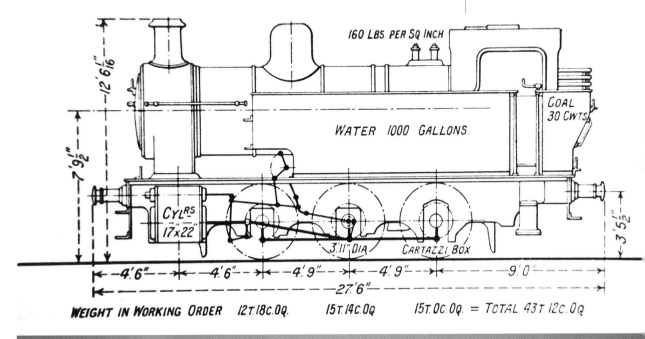

2-5

2-6

Initial diagram and photograph of the 2F. Later it would become known as 'Coleman's Baby'.
In shape, it bears a passing resemblance to the NSR's 4-cylinder 0-6-0 tank engine. Ten were built, all by 1929.

2-7

One of Stanier's first contributions to the LMS was a redesigned 2-6-0 mixed traffic engine. Under the new CME's guiding hand, Tom and the draughtsmen at Horwich produced a locomotive with a taper boiler and a simplicity and elegance

of line that would soon be passed onto many other classic Stanier/Coleman designs. They were all built at Crewe between 1933 and '34. (2-7/2-8)

A typical Stanier/Coleman cab on this unidentified locomotive. It contains all the sound ergonomic principles common to all Tom's work – uncluttered, spacious by comparison to many other types, well balanced and so on. (2-9)

By 1934 two other new designs had been introduced – the Princess Royal Class and the Jubilees – with their design being centred at Derby, under Herbert Chambers. The next in line was a mixed traffic Class 5 4-6-0 2-cylinder mixed traffic engine, that began life in Tom's hands after he had taken over the drawing office at Crewe, whilst retaining responsibility for Horwich. From the first this proved to be

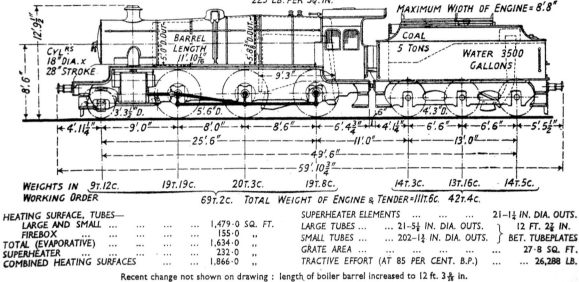

L. M. S. R.

"5F" Class (Taper boiler)

Recent change not shown on drawing : length of boiler barrel increased to 12 ft. 3 $\frac{9}{16}$ in.

HEATING SURFACE, TUBES—				
LARGE AND SMALL	1,479·0 SQ. FT.	SUPERHEATER ELEMENTS	21–1¼ IN. DIA. OUTS.
FIREBOX	155·0 ,,	LARGE TUBES ... 21–5¼ IN. DIA. OUTS.	12 FT. 2⅞ IN.
TOTAL (EVAPORATIVE)	1,634·0 ,,	SMALL TUBES ... 202–1¾ IN. DIA. OUTS.	BET. TUBEPLATES
SUPERHEATER	232·0 ,,	GRATE AREA	27·8 SQ. FT.
COMBINED HEATING SURFACES	1,866·0 ,,	TRACTIVE EFFORT (AT 85 PER CENT. B.P.)	26,288 LB.

2-8

2-9

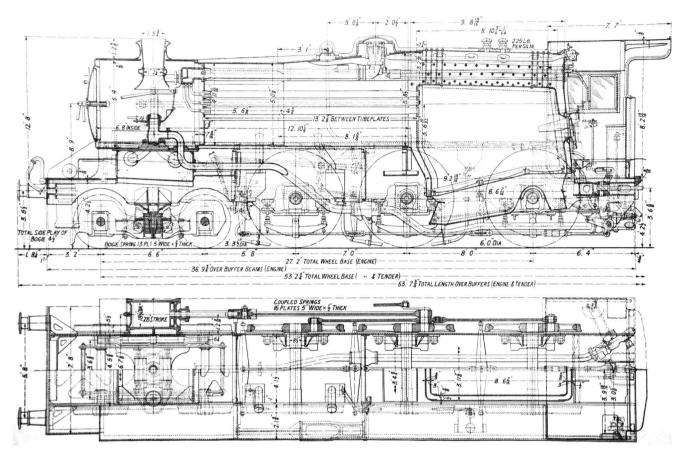

a highly successful and a classic design. 842 would be built, with construction running from 1934 to 1951 in various configurations; Timken roller bearings, Caprotti poppet valves, outside Stephenson link motion amongst them, all managed by Tom Coleman. (2-10)

1935-1939
In 1935, Tom replaced Chambers as the LMS's Chief Locomotive and Carriage Draughtsman and so began the most productive phase of his career. He would complete the design of the Black Fives and a new Class 8F 2-8-0 locomotive, take on the production of the next ten Princess Royals and complete the experimental turbine locomotive,

continue with the Jubilees and 2-6-2 Class 3P and 2-6-4 4P tank engines, redesign the failed experimental high pressure 4-6-0 locomotive and then top all this with the Princess Coronations. 1935 would also see the beginning of his collaboration with Frederick Johansen on streamlining high speed express engines.

(2.11/2.12) Tom Coleman's eventual streamlining solution for the Coronations, which tested effectively in the wind tunnel. He, it is recorded, coloured in the drawing and followed the ideas and colour used by Mitchell for his Supermarine seaplanes. It would be used by his successor when building a special high-speed Spitfire in 1939.

(2.13) The influence of the Art Deco movement on design was carried through on even the smallest items on board the streamlined Coronation.

(2.14/2.15) Five Coronations would be defrocked, ostensibly to compare the benefits of each type. This drawing of the front end of these new engines appeared in a booklet produced by the LMS for public consumption and is accompanied by this photo showing the reality of these changes.

'Fowler's Fury' as converted to 6170 *British Legion* by Tom and his team. It became the model for the modification of all seventy Royal Scots and eighteen Patriots. (2-16 to 2-17)

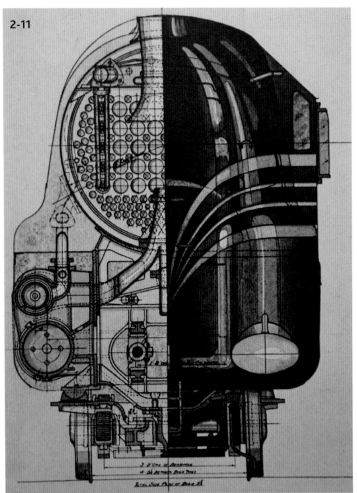

2-11

2-12

2-14

Even the fine detail of a Coronation locomotive reveals the influence of the Art Deco movement in Coleman's work.

2-13

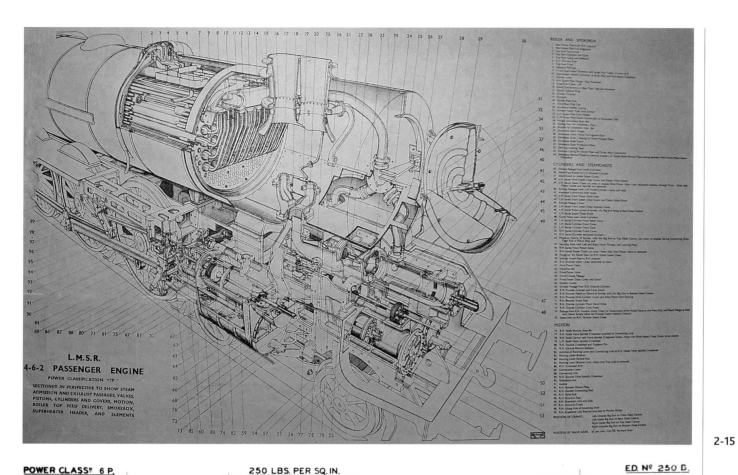

L.M.S.R.
4-6-2 PASSENGER ENGINE
POWER CLASSIFICATION "7P"

SECTIONED IN PERSPECTIVE TO SHOW STEAM
ADMISSION AND EXHAUST PASSAGES, VALVES,
PISTONS, CYLINDERS AND COVERS, MOTION,
BOILER TOP FEED DELIVERY, SMOKEBOX,
SUPERHEATER HEADER, AND ELEMENTS

2-15

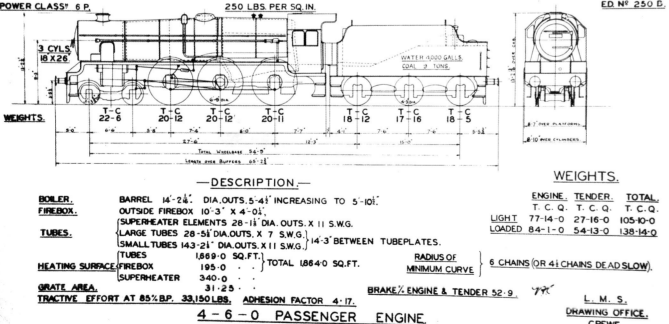

POWER CLASS" 6 P.   250 LBS. PER SQ. IN.   E.D. Nº 250 B.

3 CYLS.
18 X 26

WATER 4,000 GALLS.
COAL 9 TONS.

WEIGHTS.

T-C	T-C	T-C	T-C	T-C	T-C	T-C
22-6	20-12	20-12	20-11	18-12	17-16	18-5

Total Wheelbase 54-5
Length over Buffers 65-2½

—DESCRIPTION.—

BOILER. BARREL 14'-2⅛" DIA. OUTS. 5'-4½" INCREASING TO 5'-10½".

FIREBOX. OUTSIDE FIREBOX 10'-3" X 4'-0½",

TUBES. { SUPERHEATER ELEMENTS 28-1⅛" DIA. OUTS. X 11 S.W.G.
LARGE TUBES 28-5¼" DIA. OUTS. X 7 S.W.G.
SMALL TUBES 143-2⅛" DIA. OUTS. X 11 S.W.G. } 14'-3" BETWEEN TUBEPLATES.

HEATING SURFACE. { TUBES 1,669.0 SQ. FT.
FIREBOX 195.0 " " } TOTAL 1,864.0 SQ. FT.
SUPERHEATER 340.0 " "

GRATE AREA. 31.25 .

TRACTIVE EFFORT AT 85% B.P. 33,150 LBS. **ADHESION FACTOR** 4.17.

RADIUS OF
MINIMUM CURVE } 6 CHAINS (OR 4½ CHAINS DEAD SLOW).

BRAKE % ENGINE & TENDER 52.9

WEIGHTS.

	ENGINE.	TENDER.	TOTAL.
	T. C. Q.	T. C. Q.	T. C. Q.
LIGHT	77-14-0	27-16-0	105-10-0
LOADED	84-1-0	54-13-0	138-14-0

L. M. S.
DRAWING OFFICE.
CREWE

4-6-0 PASSENGER ENGINE.

2-16

2-17

2-18

Tom's involvement in carriage design is often overlooked in favour of his locomotive work. But whilst at Derby he took an active part in developing new concepts of interior as well as exterior design. He kept many records in his collection confirming his extreme interest and level of involvement. The Coronation Scot rake of coaches features large in these papers and this photograph, which defines certain elements of their design, was from a group he kept. (2-18)

The 2-8-0 8F was probably Tom's most successful and influential design, though not rushed into service, greater effort being expended by the LMS on producing 4-6-0 designs. Production began in 1935 and ran until 1946, with 852 eventually being constructed to become the mainstay of freight traffic across Great Britain and many battlefields. Construction was deemed so essential that it was undertaken by the LMS and the other three companies, under licence, plus North British and Beyer, Peacock. (2-19/2-20) So successful were his ideas on freight engines that Robert Riddles, by then attached to the Ministry of Supply, tried to enlist Coleman's secondment to the Department. This didn't happen but it seems likely that he did advise on the construction of War Department austerity 2-8-0 and 2-10-0 designs.

From the mid-1930s, Tom had been interested in the fledgling diesel programme being undertaken by the LMS, under the specialist eye of Tommy Hornbuckle. Stanier, aware of his Chief Draughtsman's interest in this field, attempted to pull him back from too close an association, ever conscious

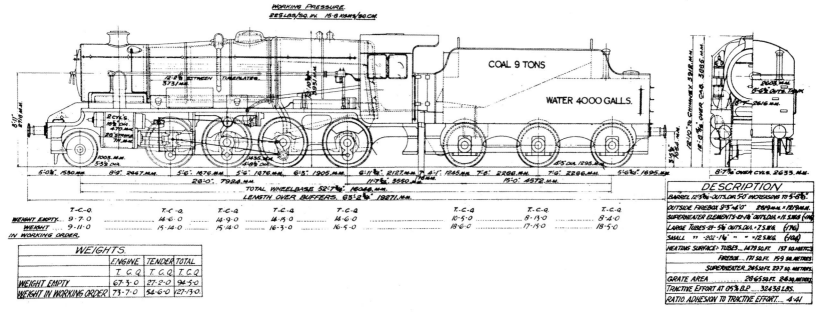

ENGINE DIAGRAM.

DESCRIPTION
BARREL 12'5⅜" OUTS.DIA.5'0" INCREASING TO 5'6"
OUTSIDE FIREBOX 9'3"x4'0" 2819M.M.x1219M.M.
SUPERHEATER ELEMENTS·21·1⅛" OUTS.DIA.x11.S.W.G (1⅛")
LARGE TUBES·21·5⅛" OUTS.DIA.x7 S.W.G. (176)
SMALL " -202·1⅝" " x12 S.W.G. (202)
HEATING SURFACE:- TUBES...1479 SQ.FT. 137 SQ.METRES
FIREBOX... 171 SQ.FT. 15·9 SQ.METRES
SUPERHEATER 265 SQ.FT. 22·7 SQ. METRES
GRATE AREA .... 28·65 SQ.FT. 8·6 SQ.METRES
TRACTIVE EFFORT AT 85% B.P. ...32438 LBS.
RATIO:ADHESION TO TRACTIVE EFFORT... 4·41

WEIGHTS.	ENGINE	TENDER	TOTAL
	T. C. Q	T. C. Q	T. C. Q
WEIGHT EMPTY	67·3·0	27·2·0	94·5·0
WEIGHT IN WORKING ORDER	73·7·0	54·6·0	127·13·0

2-19

2-20

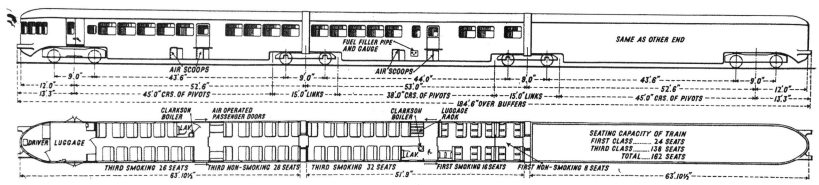

Diagram of 162-seater L.M.S.R. diesel train having a top speed of 75 m.p.h.

2-21

of his already heavy workload. Nevertheless, the drawing offices under his control were fully involved on a day to day basis so his interest was unlikely to have been curbed. One project held his interest more than the others though. In 1937, it was decided to build an experimental lightweight diesel multiple unit at Derby, using parts from twenty-six different manufacturers, to assess the value of such a design. It appeared in January 1938 and ran, with increasing success, until the coming of war curtailed any further work. Tom regarded this as a lost opportunity which would take many years to correct, whilst steam would continue on far longer than necessary and absorb precious resources for little gain. He remained a strong advocate of diesel designs until the end of his career. (2-21/2-22)

STREAMLINED DIESEL TRAIN.
L.M.S. Railway.

2-22

1940-1945

The war years were principally a time of make do and mend. The conflict absorbed people and resources at a precarious rate and the railways could do little but support the war with what they had. For the most part, new construction was limited to engines that best supported front line needs. A few Coronations appeared, a leftover of a pre-war programme that no one thought worth cancelling, but any new designs were primarily a paper exercise attempting to see beyond the battles into peace. Tom and Ernest Cox led on this work and produced a plan in 1942 that would see the LMS populated with some interesting designs.

In these proposals the Coronation was developed into a 4-6-4 design. (2-23) It was heavily influenced by work overseas. Though not constructed it is interesting to note that Tom still advocated the streamlining concept, continuing his support of these ideas for fast express services.

For fast freight a 4-8-4 non-streamlined engine was suggested. Locomotives of this capacity would probably have exceeded any predicted need at that time, but 2-8-0 configuration had probably reached its design limitations so the 4-8-4 may have seemed a natural evolution. As it was BR, and Riddles, would advocate a 2-10-0 instead. (2-24)

Development of tank engines continued throughout Tom's career, here with a modernised 2-6-4 4P tank, (2-25), which

2-23

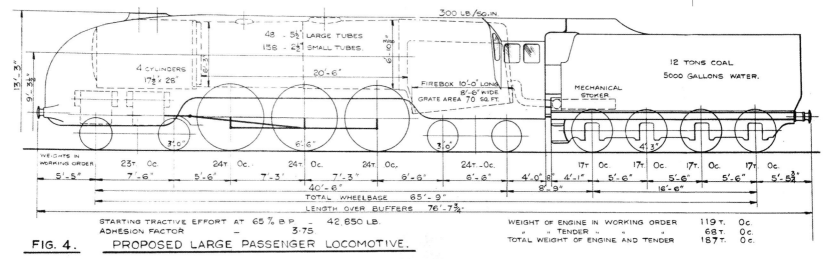

FIG. 4.   PROPOSED LARGE PASSENGER LOCOMOTIVE.

2-24

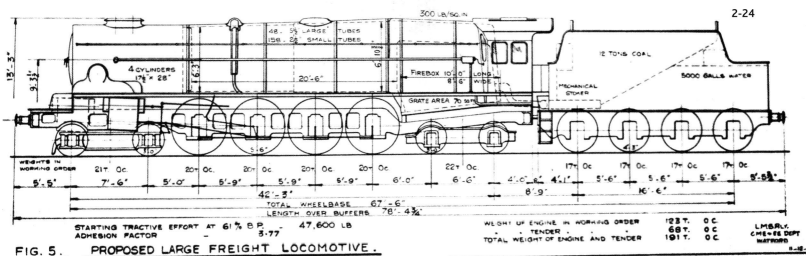

FIG. 5.   PROPOSED LARGE FREIGHT LOCOMOTIVE.

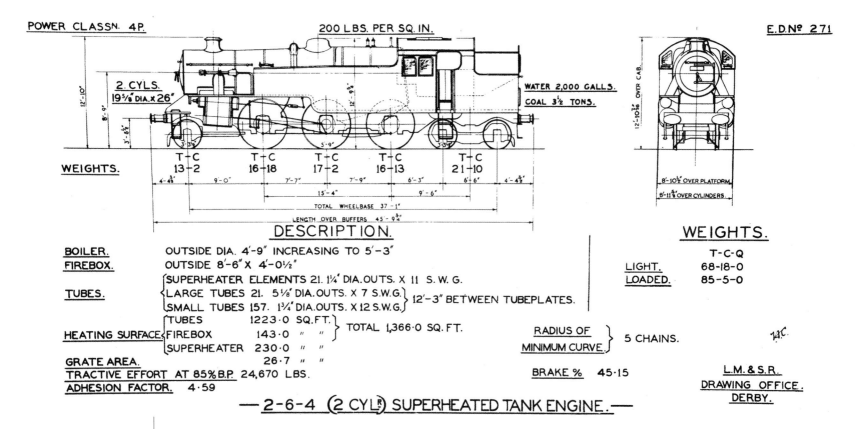

POWER CLASSN. 4P.　　200 LBS. PER SQ. IN.　　E.D. Nº 271

2. CYLS. 19⅝" DIA. X 26"

WATER 2,000 GALLS.
COAL 3½ TONS.

12'-10"
8'-9"
3'-6½"

WEIGHTS.

T-C	T-C	T-C	T-C	T-C
13-2	16-18	17-2	16-13	21-10

12'-10¾" OVER CAB.

8'-10½" OVER PLATFORM
8'-11⅝" OVER CYLINDERS

TOTAL WHEELBASE 37-1"
LENGTH OVER BUFFERS 45'-9¾"

DESCRIPTION.

BOILER.	OUTSIDE DIA. 4'-9" INCREASING TO 5'-3"
FIREBOX.	OUTSIDE 8'-6" X 4'-0½"
TUBES.	SUPERHEATER ELEMENTS 21. 1¼" DIA. OUTS. X 11 S.W.G.
	LARGE TUBES 21. 5⅛" DIA. OUTS. X 7 S.W.G.
	SMALL TUBES 157. 1¾" DIA. OUTS. X 12 S.W.G.

12'-3" BETWEEN TUBEPLATES.

HEATING SURFACE	TUBES	1223.0 SQ. FT.
	FIREBOX	143.0 " "
	SUPERHEATER	230.0 " "

TOTAL 1,366.0 SQ. FT.

GRATE AREA. 26.7 " "
TRACTIVE EFFORT AT 85% B.P. 24,670 LBS.
ADHESION FACTOR. 4.59

RADIUS OF MINIMUM CURVE. 5 CHAINS.

BRAKE % 45.15

WEIGHTS.

	T-C-Q
LIGHT.	68-18-0
LOADED.	85-5-0

L.M. & S.R.
DRAWING OFFICE.
DERBY.

—2-6-4 (2 CYLR) SUPERHEATED TANK ENGINE.—

2-25

was followed by a 2-6-2T Class 2 locomotive in 1946, sponsored by Ivatt. The tank classes proved to be effective workhorses, though their use and merits were largely unsung. It seems that Tom retained a special affection for these types from the earliest days of his career.

Tom's 1939 drawing of the Coronation Class that he himself kept modifying as the war progressed. (2-26) This work reflected his own and the company's thoughts on their future development. In this case he foresaw the design of the last two locomotives in the class (6256 and

6257 in 1947/48), one captured here late in her life. (2-27) It was a common feature of his work that he never lost the chance to draw and design himself, not simply issue instructions. He would even work on a drawing board at home to ensure he perfected ideas before passing them to his team

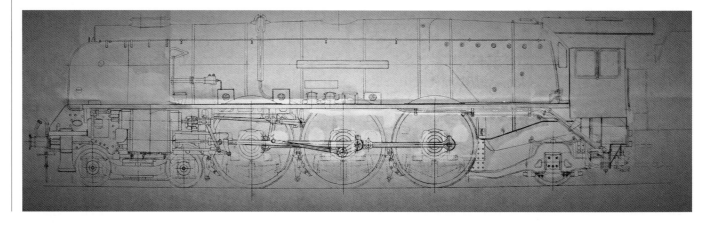

2-26

2-27 How the final Coronation appeared when in service.

2-28

for development. Eventually the familiar and classic lines of the post-war Coronation emerged as captured here in this classic picture of power and elegance. (2-28)

In 1942, the locomotive drawing office began laying down some designs for a main line diesel. This early proposal didn't advance too far, but reflects the thinking process of Tom and his team. The wheel base arrangement was an interesting one, suggesting one possible solution for producing drive and adhesion. (2-29)

But steam designs still dominated thinking as the war came to an end

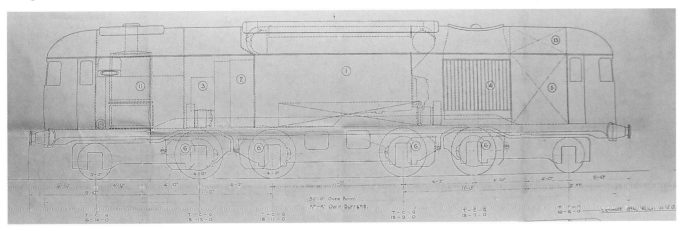

2-29

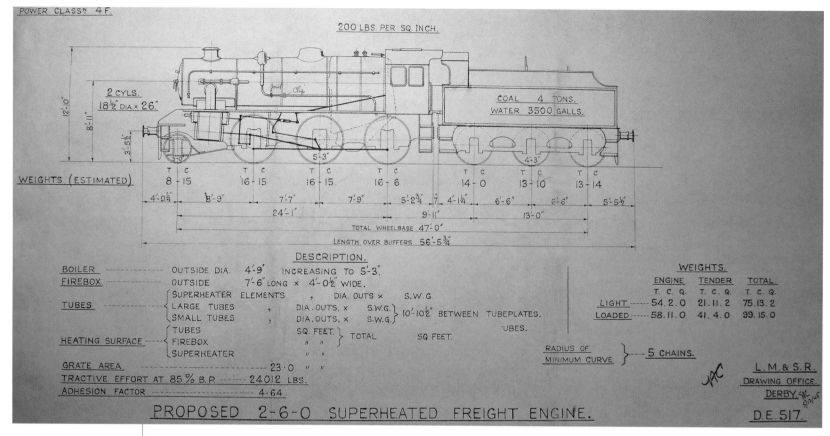

POWER CLASSᴺ 4F.

200 LBS. PER SQ. INCH.

2 CYLS.
18½″ DIA × 26″

COAL   4 TONS.
WATER 3500 GALLS.

WEIGHTS. (ESTIMATED)

T C	T C	T C	T C	T C	T C	T C
8 – 15	16 – 15	16 – 15	16 – 6	14 – 0	13 – 10	13 – 14

TOTAL WHEELBASE 47′-0″
LENGTH OVER BUFFERS 56′-5¾″

DESCRIPTION.

BOILER --------------- OUTSIDE DIA. 4′-9″ INCREASING TO 5′-3″.
FIREBOX ------------- OUTSIDE   7′-6″ LONG × 4′-0½″ WIDE.
TUBES ------ { SUPERHEATER ELEMENTS , DIA. OUTS × S.W.G.
             { LARGE TUBES   ,   DIA. OUTS. ×   S.W.G. } 10′-10½″ BETWEEN TUBEPLATES.
             { SMALL TUBES   ,   DIA. OUTS. ×   S.W.G.
HEATING SURFACE ----- { TUBES   SQ. FEET. } TOTAL   SQ. FEET. ᴜBES.
                       { FIREBOX   ″   ″   }
                       { SUPERHEATER   ″   ″
GRATE AREA ------------------------- 23·0 ″   ″
TRACTIVE EFFORT AT 85% B.P. ------- 24012 LBS.
ADHESION FACTOR ------------------- 4·64

WEIGHTS.

	ENGINE	TENDER	TOTAL.
	T. C. Q.	T. C. Q.	T. C. Q.
LIGHT ------	54. 2. 0	21. 11. 2	75. 13. 2
LOADED -----	58. 11. 0	41. 4. 0	99. 15. 0

RADIUS OF
MINIMUM CURVE } ----- 5 CHAINS.

L. M. & S. R.
DRAWING OFFICE.
DERBY.

PROPOSED 2-6-0 SUPERHEATED FREIGHT ENGINE.

D.E. 517.

and Ivatt proposed new 2F and 4F 2-6-0s, which the drawing office duly produced; construction of 290 engines of both classes began in 1946 and '47 respectively and continued into 1953. In contrast to the Stanier/Coleman engines these were definitely ugly sisters, although they were designed for ease of maintenance not looks. In both cases their performance was deemed good and sufficient for need. (2-30)

1946-1949

The post-war years were about restoration and change on the railways. Nationalisation was waiting in the wings, but whilst the companies awaited the 'chop' they continued designing and building good engines, amongst them the last Coronations and the first main line diesels. When BR was formed, in January 1948, the focus would be on steam and a new range of standard locomotives. These would be constructed alongside the best the 'Big Four' could offer, many of which would continue to be manufactured into the 1950s. Pre-nationalisation work on diesels would be abated and held in abeyance for some years. 'Another lost opportunity', in Tom's words

The LMS main line diesel emerged in the drawing office in 1947 and would be unveiled in December at the same time as Coronation 6256. Designated 10000, the new diesel was advanced for its age and contained many elements that would continue

to find favour in locomotive design to the present day. (2-31/2-32)

There were other attempts made by the LMS to construct effective diesel engines that continued into BR days and Tom played a part in their evolution as his career came to end. The first of these was an 0-4-4-0 type locomotive (numbered 10800), for secondary services, which was built in collaboration with NBR. It appeared in 1950 and then proved of mediocre design and was eventually withdrawn in 1959, though lessons had been learnt that would inform later diesel designs. (2-33)

The second design was a joint venture between the LMS and Fell Development Ltd, which created a single 4-8-4 locomotive (numbered 10100). Like 10800,

2-30

2-31

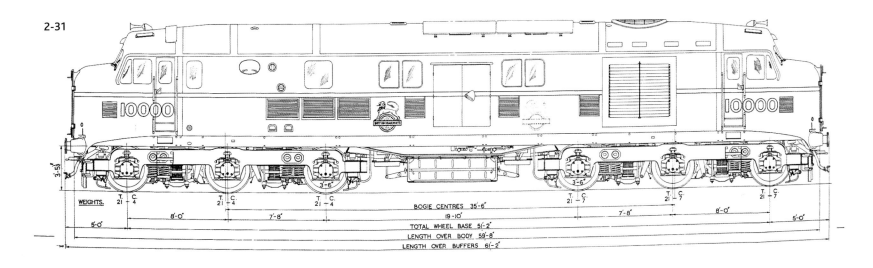

2-32

2-33

it appeared in 1950 and was withdrawn in 1958 having covered more than 100,000 miles (2-34 and 2-35).

The last steam design that Tom can be said to have played a part in is that of the standard Class 7 and 6 Pacifics. These were initiated in 1948 and assigned to the Derby drawing office for development, presumably because of their success in producing the superlative Coronations and, one assumes, because they had an outstanding designer in Tom there. A number of preliminary schemes were produced under his guiding hand. The drawing here shows a revised scheme that appeared in 1948.

2-34

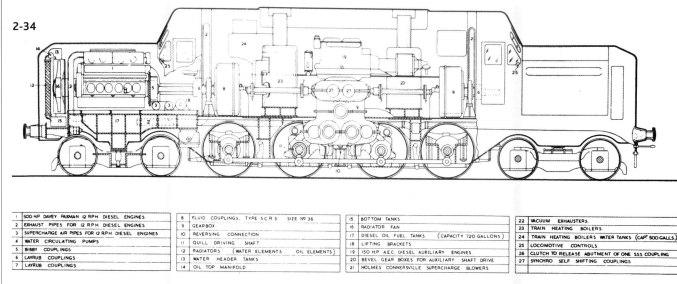

1	500 H.P. DAVEY PAXMAN 12 RPH DIESEL ENGINES	8	FLUID COUPLINGS, TYPE S.C.R.5 SIZE Nº 36	15	BOTTOM TANKS	22	VACUUM EXHAUSTERS
2	EXHAUST PIPES FOR 12 RPH DIESEL ENGINES	9	GEARBOX	16	RADIATOR FAN	23	TRAIN HEATING BOILERS
3	SUPERCHARGE AIR PIPES FOR 12 RPH DIESEL ENGINES	10	REVERSING CONNECTION	17	DIESEL OIL FUEL TANKS (CAPACITY 720 GALLONS)	24	TRAIN HEATING BOILERS WATER TANKS (CAPᵀ 500 GALLS.)
4	WATER CIRCULATING PUMPS	11	QUILL DRIVING SHAFT	18	LIFTING BRACKETS	25	LOCOMOTIVE CONTROLS
5	BIBBY COUPLINGS	12	RADIATORS (WATER ELEMENTS OIL ELEMENTS)	19	150 H.P. A.E.C. DIESEL AUXILIARY ENGINES	26	CLUTCH TO RELEASE ABUTMENT OF ONE S.S.S COUPLING
6	LAYRUB COUPLINGS	13	WATER HEADER TANKS	20	BEVEL GEAR BOXES FOR AUXILIARY SHAFT DRIVE	27	SYNCHRO SELF SHIFTING COUPLINGS
7	LAYRUB COUPLINGS	14	OIL TOP MANIFOLD	21	HOLMES CONNERSVILLE SUPERCHARGE BLOWERS		

50'-0" OVER BUFFERS

The final Class 7 design appeared shortly after Tom's retirement. (2-36). The first engine, 70000 *Britannia,* rolled off the production line at Crewe in January 1951. Tom was invited to attend but declined, but he and Fred Lemon did visit Crewe twice to see this locomotive under construction. A year later he would ride behind her and, as usual, kept notes of her performance. Old habits die hard.

A preserved Britannia Class engine in all its glory (70013). (2-37)

Old and new together. Both a fitting tribute to a master of locomotive design. (2-38)

2-35

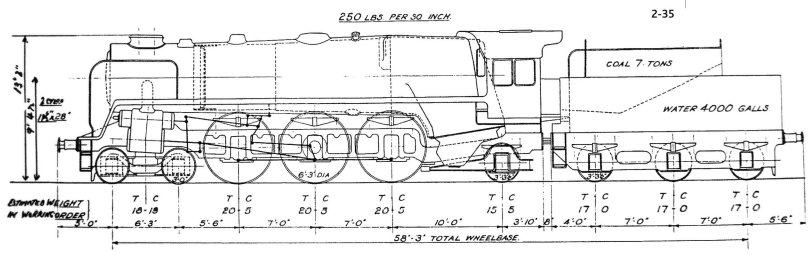

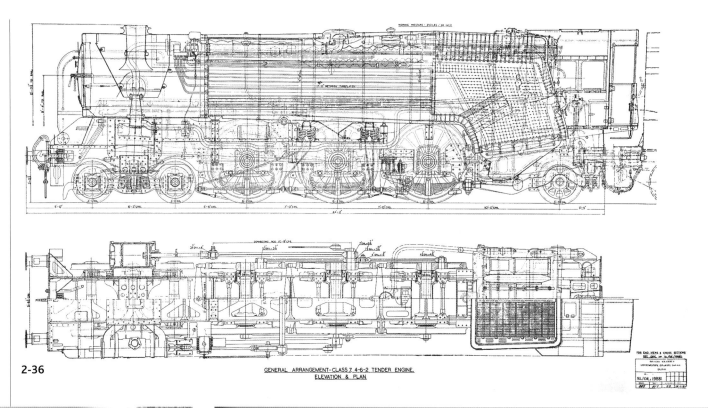

2-36

GENERAL ARRANGEMENT-CLASS 7, 4-6-2 TENDER ENGINE.
ELEVATION & PLAN

2-37

Past and present come together making an interesting comparison between the two classes of Pacifics in which Tom had a hand.

2-38

Appendix 3

THE CORONATION CLASS – DESIGN, CONSTRUCTION AND EVOLUTION

As with any scientific development, the Coronation Class didn't simply come straight from the drawing board, the product of original thought without history. There are few truly unique developments that embrace such singular beginnings. In reality, design builds on established ideas mixed with untried or unrefined inventions, occasionally drawing inspiration from the collectivism of scientists often working in unrelated fields of science. The clever, the astute and the open minded seek a variety of solutions and have the analytical skills to absorb and understand when lesser people are made rigid by their lack of imagination or their conservatism. 'It's always been done that way', is the cry of these hidebound, conventional minds. Tom Coleman and a few others couldn't be counted amongst their number. He was a scientist of vision and great skill.

By the time Tom reached the pinnacle of his career there was very little left of significance to discover about steam locomotives. Bigger, faster, stronger and more economical seemed the only possibilities of this aging science. But in the years left to him, he took what was on offer and led in creating the ultimate engines, before new science and changing needs eclipsed these soon to depart relics of a passing world. The Coronations were a worthy 'last fling' and in their development showed Tom Coleman's perception and the need to embrace change and seek perfection. They were masterpieces that had a slow birth, but kept evolving to meet changing circumstances.

In 1937, the LMS issued a broad description of the first five locomotives to the press, which in time was sold as a booklet for public consumption. It provides a concise, but effective summary of the key features of the new class and sets out very clearly the complexity of the designer's work (a draft of this paper is included in Tom Coleman's papers, suggesting that he played an active part in its preparation):

Boiler and Firebox Details

The boiler shell is constructed of nickel steel, and the inner firebox

A **coronation** boiler complete and ready for installation.

of copper. The firebox stays are of steel, with the exception of the outer and top rows which are of Monel metal; the throat plate stays are also of this material. The firebox is extended into the barrel to form a combustion chamber with the object of allowing the gases to complete their combustion before entering the tubes. The large flues are screwed into the firebox before being expanded. The firedoor is of the sliding type, carefully designed to direct the incoming secondary air down on to the fire.

A Davies and Metcalfe exhaust steam injector with 13 mm cones

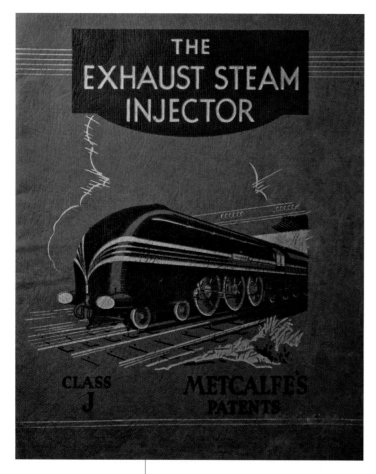

Metcalfe's make full use of the advertising potential connected with their work on the Coronation Class.

gases contained in the water may become disengaged; de-aerated water is finally discharged through pipes below the water level. The superheater has 40 flue tubes, all containing triple elements 1 in outside diameter, so that the steam passing to the cylinders is split up into 120 paths. The regulator, of the grid type, is located in the steam dome. Baffle plates are provided beneath the dome to prevent water from lifting and entering the steam pipe. To facilitate the removal of ashes, particular care has been taken in designing the smokebox so to arrange the steam and exhaust pipes that the smokebox bottom is free as far as possible from all obstructions.

The boiler is fitted with four pop safety valves 2 ½ in diameter. Steam for the various fittings is taken from a manifold on the top of the firebox backplate in the cab. The fittings are of the company's standard type. The boiler is provided with a sand gun of the railway company's standard type, which enables the tubes to be cleaned during a run.

Frames, Cylinders and Motion

The frames, cylinders and motion from above.

The frames are 1 1/3 in thick, and are of high tensile steel. At each

is fitted on the fireman's side, and on the left hand or driver's side is a live steam injector with 13 mm cones; both injectors are of the flooded type. The injectors deliver to the boiler through top feed clack valves which discharge into trays within the steam space, wherein any

side of the hind end two separate frame plates are spliced to the main frame, and carried through to the hind buffer beam. The outer frames are splayed outwards, and the inner frames inwards to take the side bearers for the trailing two-wheeled truck. There are 4 cylinders, of 16 ½ in diameter x 28 in stroke. The piston valves are 9 in diameter with a maximum travel of 7 1/32 in. There are two sets of Walschaert gear, situated outside the frames, which drive the outside piston valves direct and the inside ones by means of rocking levers; the whole arrangement is specially designed to allow the removal of both sets of valves for examination with the minimum amount of trouble. The valve motion is provided with Hoffman needle bearings, except the big ends of the eccentric rods which are fitted with SFK self-aligning ball bearings. Lubrication of the needle bearings is by means of a grease gun.

Inside and outside cylinder arrangements

The exhaust passages in the cylinders have been carefully designed to give free exit to the steam without providing an excessive volume which would act as a reservoir. The exhaust from the inside cylinders and from the two outside cylinders are combined in the saddle casting, so

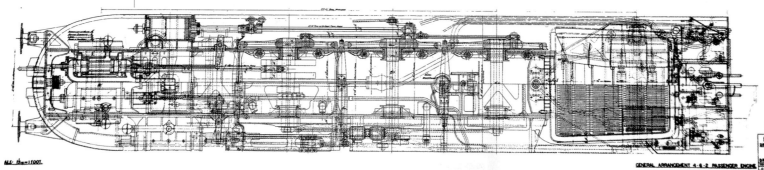

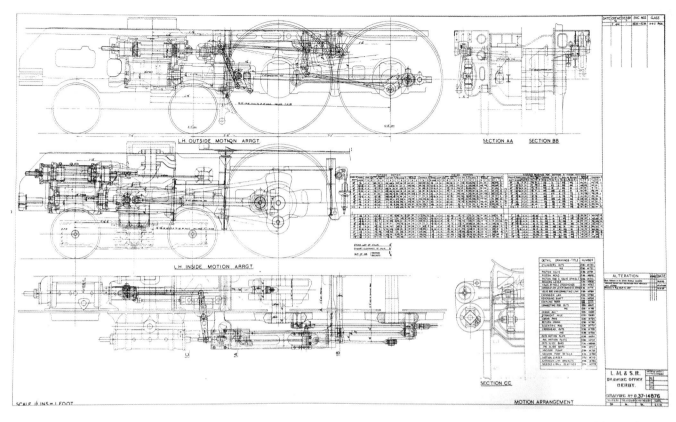

that the blastpipe is a simple straight pipe. The piston valves are designed for lightness, and are fitted with six narrow rings to ensure steam tightness. The pistons are of the box type, screwed on to the piston rods, and are provided with three narrow rings. Mechanical lubrication is provided for the cylinders, and the oil to the piston valve liners is atomised by being mixed with a jet of saturated steam taken from an independent supply on the boiler, so that the atomised oil is supplied continuously while the engine is running, either with the regulator open or shut.

The crossheads are of the two bar type and are steel castings with bronze slippers, having the surfaces which make contact with the slidebars white-metalled. The gudgeon pin is prevented from turning in the crosshead by two keys, and is secured by a split cone and nut. The coupling and connecting rods are of Vibrac steel, and are designed to withstand the inertia stresses due to high speeds. The tyres are secured by the Gibson ring type of fastening, and the wheel rims are of triangular section. The balance weights are such that 50% of the reciprocating weights are balanced, equally divided between the coupled wheels. The whole of the revolving parts are balanced in each wheel.

Axles, Wheels and Springing

These axleboxes are steel castings with pressed-in brasses completely lined with white-metal on the bearing surface. There are no oil grooves in the crown of the box to disturb the continuity of the oil film, but the oil from the mechanical lubricator is introduced through a row of holes on the horizontal centre line of the axle. Hollow axles are used throughout, the internal diameters being 4 ½ in for the coupled wheels, 3 in for the trailing wheels and 2 in for those of the leading bogie. In addition to mechanical lubrication, every axlebox underkeep is fitted with an efficient oil pad arranged to be easily withdrawn for examination. A dust shield is also provided on the inside faces of the intermediate and trailing coupled axleboxes. The supply of oil from the mechanical lubricator is taken through a spring loaded back pressure valve fixed at the top of the axlebox, the function of which is to keep the oil pipes full of oil while the engine is standing,

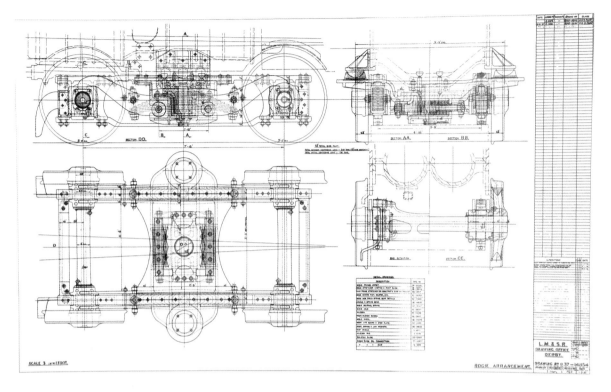

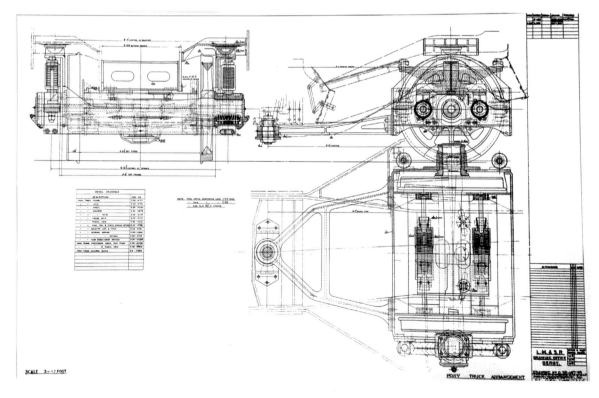

so that delivery to the journal will begin immediately the engine moves. The sides of the axleboxes are fitted with bronze slippers, making contact with the faces of the axlebox guides.

Design of leading and trailing trucks

Side bolsters transmit the load from the main frames to the leading bogie. The bearing springs are of the inverted laminated type, with screw adjustment. The trailing two-wheeled truck is of the Bissel type, and the bogie arm is anchored to the engine cross stretcher immediately in front of the throat plate. As in the case of the leading bogie, the weight from the main frames is taken through side bolsters.

All the laminated bearings springs for the engine and tender are made of silico-manganese steel; the plates are of a ribbed section with cotter type of fixing in the buckle. The spring links are screwed to permit of adjustment. Rubber damper springs are also provided between the spring link heads and the frame brackets for the coupled wheels. The brake gear is compensated to give equal pressure on each brake block. The driver's brake valve controls proportionately the application of the steam brake on the engine and the vacuum brake on the train. Separate steam valves are used for controlling the steam to the large and small ejectors. A vacuum pump, driven from one of the crossheads, is also provided.'

The series of drawings and photographs reproduced here follow the development of these engines from 1935 to 1947:

3-1

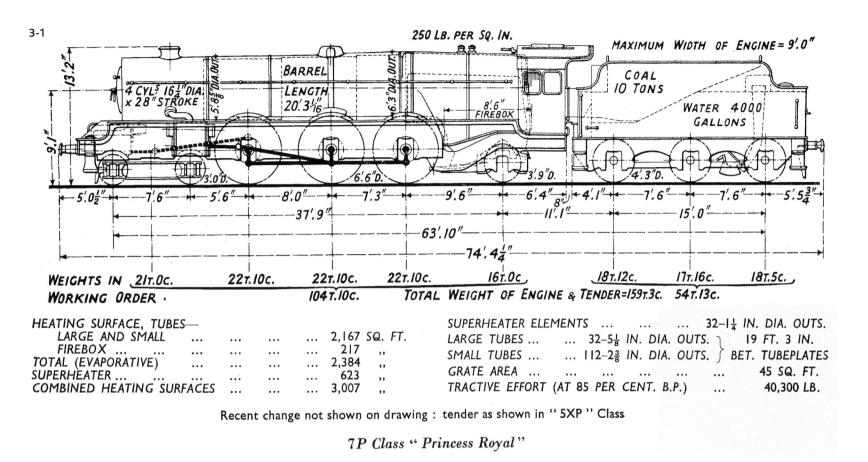

250 LB. PER SQ. IN.

MAXIMUM WIDTH OF ENGINE = 9'.0"

13'.2"

4 CYL^S 16¼" DIA. x 28" STROKE

5'.8⅝" DIA. OUT.

BARREL LENGTH 20'.3¹¹⁄₁₆

6'.3" DIA. OUT.

8'.6" FIREBOX

COAL 10 TONS

WATER 4000 GALLONS

9'.1"

3'.0" D.

6'.6" D.

3'.9" D.

4'.3" D.

5'.0½" 7'.6" 5'.6" 8'.0" 7'.3" 9'.6" 6'.4" 8" 4'.1" 7'.6" 7'.6" 5'.5¾"

37'.9"

11'.1"

15'.0"

63'.10"

74'.4¼"

WEIGHTS IN WORKING ORDER ·

| 21T.0C. | 22T.10C. | 22T.10C. | 22T.10C. | 16T.0C. | 18T.12C. | 17T.16C. | 18T.5C. |

104T.10C.   TOTAL WEIGHT OF ENGINE & TENDER = 159T.3C.   54T.13C.

HEATING SURFACE, TUBES—		
LARGE AND SMALL ... ... 2,167 SQ. FT.		
FIREBOX ... ... 217 ,,		
TOTAL (EVAPORATIVE) ... ... 2,384 ,,		
SUPERHEATER ... ... 623 ,,		
COMBINED HEATING SURFACES ... ... 3,007 ,,		

SUPERHEATER ELEMENTS ... ... 32–1¼ IN. DIA. OUTS.	
LARGE TUBES ... ... 32–5⅛ IN. DIA. OUTS. } 19 FT. 3 IN.	
SMALL TUBES ... ... 112–2⅜ IN. DIA. OUTS. } BET. TUBEPLATES	
GRATE AREA ... ... 45 SQ. FT.	
TRACTIVE EFFORT (AT 85 PER CENT. B.P.) ... 40,300 LB.	

Recent change not shown on drawing : tender as shown in " 5XP " Class

7P Class " Princess Royal "

3-2

POWER CLASS^N 7P

ED N° 259 A

250 LBS PER SQ IN

13'-2"

4 CYLRS. 16¼ DIA x 28"

9'-4"

WATER 4000 GAL^S COAL 10 TONS

3'-0"

6'-6"

5'-9"

4'-3"

WEIGHTS

| T. C. 20–15 | T. C. 22–7 | T. C. 22–7 | T. C. 22–7 | T. C. 18–0 | T. C. 18–14 | T. C. 19–8 | T. C. 18–4 |

5'-0½" 7'-6" 5'-6" 7'-3" 7'-3" 9'-6" 6'-1" 8" 4'-1" 7'-6" 7'-6" 5'-5¼"

37'-0"

10'-10"

15'-0"

TOTAL WHEELBASE 62'-10"

LENGTH OVER BUFFERS 73'-4¼"

WEIGHT PER FT RUN OVER BUFFERS 2·2 TONS

TOTAL WHEELBASE 2·579 TONS

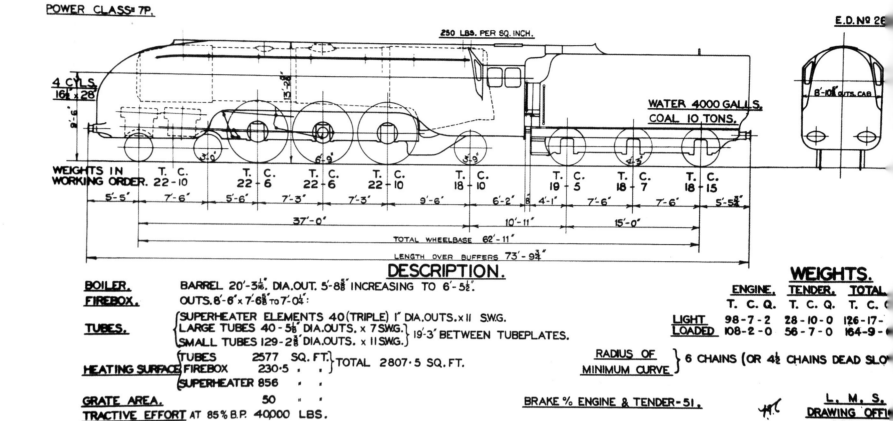

POWER CLASS: 7P.

250 LBS. PER SQ. INCH.

E.D. N⁰ 26

4 CYLS
16¼ x 28

WATER 4000 GALLS.
COAL 10 TONS.

8'-10⅞" OUTS. CAB.

WEIGHTS IN WORKING ORDER.

T. C.	T. C.	T. C.	T. C.	T. C.	T. C.	T. C.	T. C.
22-10	22-6	22-6	22-10	18-10	19-5	18-7	18-15

5'-5'   7'-6'   5'-6'   7'-3'   7'-3'   9'-6'   6'-2'   4'-1'   7'-6'   7'-6'   5'-5¾'

37'-0'   10'-11'   15'-0'

TOTAL WHEELBASE 62'-11'

LENGTH OVER BUFFERS 73'-9¾'

DESCRIPTION.

BOILER. BARREL 20'-3¹⁄₁₆" DIA.OUT. 5'-8⅝" INCREASING TO 6'-5½".

FIREBOX. OUTS. 8'-6" x 7'-6⅝" TO 7'-0¼":

TUBES.
{ SUPERHEATER ELEMENTS 40 (TRIPLE) 1" DIA.OUTS. x 11 S.W.G.
{ LARGE TUBES 40-5⅛" DIA.OUTS. x 7 S.W.G. } 19-3' BETWEEN TUBEPLATES.
{ SMALL TUBES 129-2⅜" DIA.OUTS. x 11 S.W.G.

HEATING SURFACE
{ TUBES   2577 SQ. FT. } TOTAL 2807·5 SQ. FT.
{ FIREBOX   230·5 " "
{ SUPERHEATER   856   " "

GRATE AREA.   50 " "

TRACTIVE EFFORT AT 85% B.P. 40,000 LBS.

ADHESION FACTOR   3·73

RADIUS OF MINIMUM CURVE } 6 CHAINS (OR 4½ CHAINS DEAD SLOW)

BRAKE % ENGINE & TENDER-51.

WEIGHTS.

	ENGINE.	TENDER.	TOTAL
	T. C. Q.	T. C. Q.	T. C. Q.
LIGHT	98-7-2	28-10-0	126-17-
LOADED	108-2-0	56-7-0	164-9-

L. M. S.
DRAWING OFFICE
DERBY.

4-6-2 PASSENGER ENGINE. (STREAMLINED.)

3-3

3-1 The Princess Royal Class in their 1935 form, when ten more appeared. The first two engines, constructed in 1933, had a number of teething problems, amongst them the low degree of superheat provided (a feature common to other early Stanier designs, but with a more noticeable effect on the high speed express engines). When, under Coleman's guiding hand, they were modified with 32 element superheaters their performance improved. But he had other concerns about the design which he wished to address if and when more were authorised.

3-2. The next phase in the development of the class, including a shorter wheelbase and sturdier frames, lower axle loading, the cylinders set further forward and the other improvements Tom had made to the earlier engines. When five more Princesses were authorised for construction in 1937 this would have been their likely configuration. But Tom wished to go further and Hartley, through Johansen's advocacy, wanted to develop the streamlining concept that had proved a success on the LNER, so the next five took on a completely different form.

3-3. The Princess Coronation as it appeared in 1937, as directed by Tom in Stanier's absence on duty in India. An almost entirely different locomotive, with more potential and better performance. The changes included 6'9' driving wheels, streamlined casing for loco and tender, lower axle loading, shorter wheelbase, 40 element superheater, larger boiler barrel, cylinders set further forward and so on.

The new design in detail: general arrangement drawing of Princess Coronation Class as built.

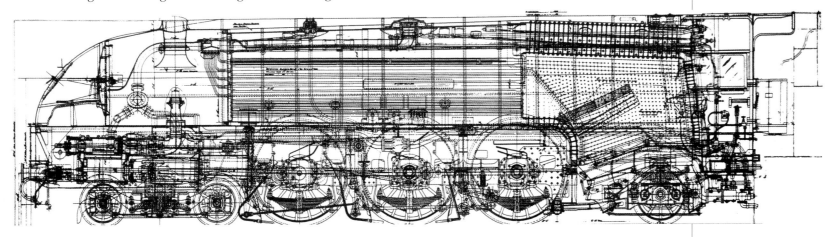

Photo showing the driving wheel, outside cylinder, brakes and motion arrangement of a streamlined Coronation. The picture also reveals how casing plates were removed to give access during maintenance.

Drawing showing the design of the new engine's front end and the reality.

A boiler is lowered into its frames.

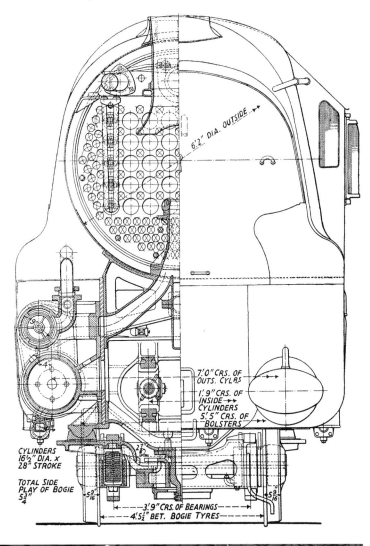

The smokebox showing its single blast pipe arrangement. In 1939 a double blast pipe was fitted to 6234 and significantly improved performance.

Cab arrangements.

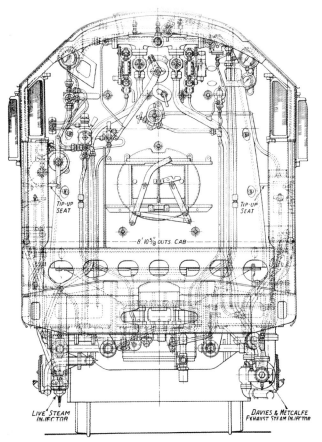

Streamlined tender design and two units under construction at Crewe.

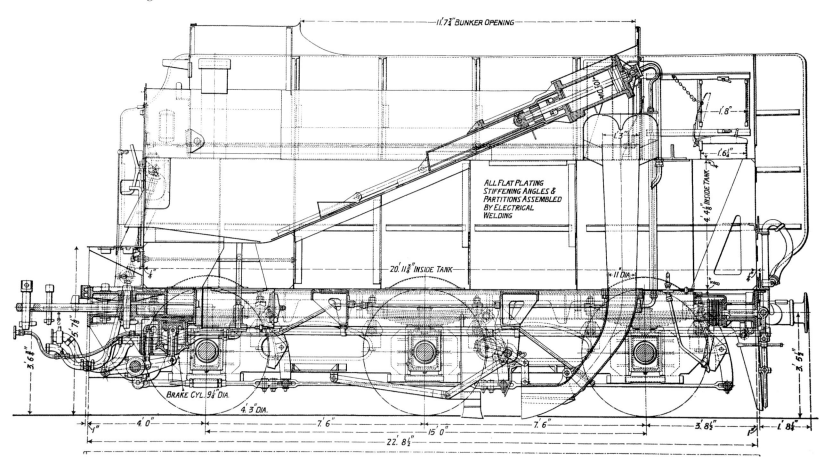

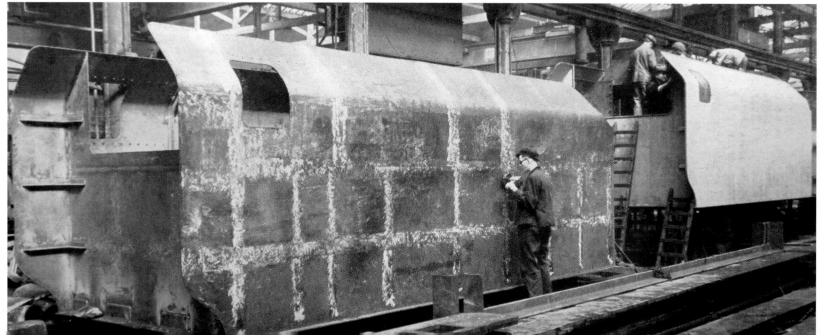

A Coronation boiler under construction and test. The boiler was held vertically so that riveting could take place.

Frames completed and the lower sections of streamlined casing are in place.

The locomotive is carefully lowered onto its leading truck.

Two engines on the production line in different stages of streamlining.

The 6' 9' main driving wheels of a Coronation under test before fitting, showing the crankshaft that would be connected to the inside cylinders.

3-4. The evolution continues. It seems that Stanier was not a strong advocate of streamlining and obtained permission to build five (6230 to 6234) in a defrocked state.

Diagram EDN 261, initialled by Tom Coleman, defined the shape and dimensions. They received de-streamlined tenders so the engines didn't have a mixed state

look, unlike the next batch of conventional engines which carried streamlined tenders when they appeared later in 1944.

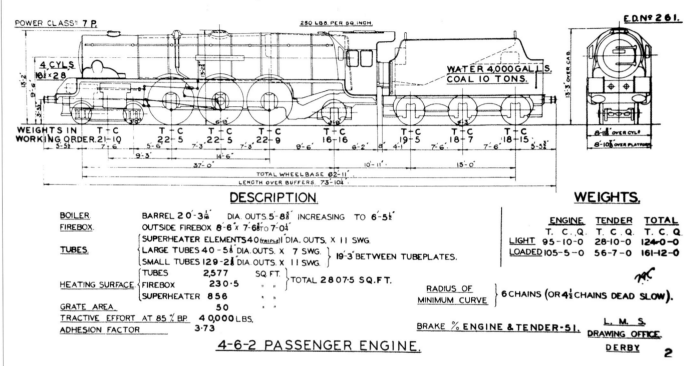

POWER CLASS: 7 P.   250 LBS. PER SQ. INCH.   E.D.N° 261.

WEIGHTS IN WORKING ORDER.

DESCRIPTION

BOILER.	BARREL 2 0'-3¹⁄₁₆" DIA. OUTS. 5'-8⅜" INCREASING TO 6'-5½"	
FIREBOX.	OUTSIDE FIREBOX 8'-6" x 7'-6⅝" TO 7'-0⅛"	
TUBES.	SUPERHEATER ELEMENTS 40 (TRIPLE) 1" DIA. OUTS. X 11 SWG.	
	LARGE TUBES 40 - 5⅛" DIA. OUTS. X 7 SWG.	19'-3" BETWEEN TUBEPLATES.
	SMALL TUBES 129-2⅛" DIA. OUTS. X 11 SWG.	
HEATING SURFACE	TUBES 2,577 SQ. FT.	TOTAL 2807.5 SQ. FT.
	FIREBOX 230.5 " "	
	SUPERHEATER 856 " "	
GRATE AREA.	50 " "	
TRACTIVE EFFORT AT 85 % B.P.	40,000 LBS.	
ADHESION FACTOR	3.73	

WATER 4,000 GALLS.
COAL 10 TONS.

WEIGHTS.

	ENGINE	TENDER	TOTAL
	T. C. Q.	T. C. Q.	T. C. Q.
LIGHT	95 - 10 - 0	28 - 10 - 0	124 - 0 - 0
LOADED	105 - 5 - 0	56 - 7 - 0	161 - 12 - 0

RADIUS OF MINIMUM CURVE } 6 CHAINS (OR 4½ CHAINS DEAD SLOW).

BRAKE % ENGINE & TENDER - 51.

L. M. S. DRAWING OFFICE. DERBY   2

4-6-2 PASSENGER ENGINE.

6231 *Duchess of Atholl* as she appeared in 1944. This shape, which was similar to the Princess Royals, appealed to many and some felt it should have continued on, even without smoke deflectors, to cover the entire class. As with anything, looks are always in the eye of the beholder and each shape had its supporters.

The second batch of non-streamlined Coronations (6249 to 6252) as they appeared in 1944. The streamlined tender looked a little odd to some, but they were built and available, so provided a practical solution.

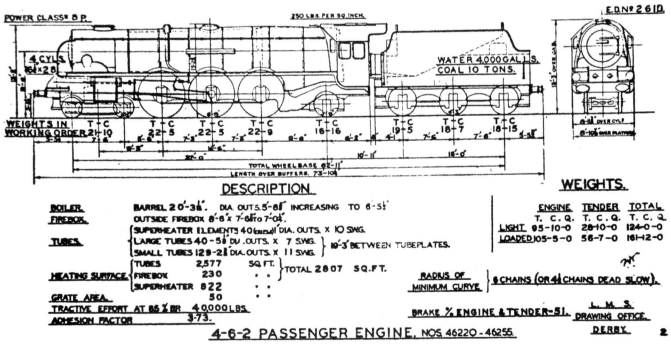

3-5. Tom's thoughts on the eventual configuration of the Class, predicting the removal of the streamlined casing and fitting of smoke deflectors. This drawing, also initialled by the Chief Draughtsman, defines what many consider to be the classic shape of these engines.

The double blast pipe arrangement that improved an already exceptional locomotive.

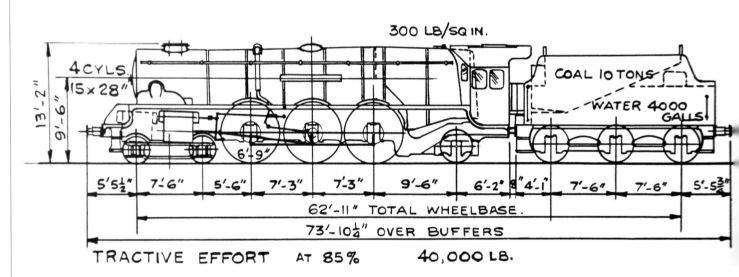

3-6. As part of the wartime Coronation building programme a proposal to build two experimental engines was considered and this is one proposal. Nothing came of this work, although some consider the last two engines of the class fulfilled such a role.

Two views of how the locomotives looked post-war through to the 1950s – no streamlining and smoke deflectors fitted - some with cut outs above the gap in the running plate to allow easier access to the motion.

3-7. The final design. Tom began work on these improvements during the war and these came to fruition under Ivatt as part of the company's search for economy in operation and easier maintenance. It seems they were also constructed as 'ultimate' steam engines, containing as they did many of the latest ideas on steam development, to compare with the new LMS main line diesels. Nationalisation put paid to work on both designs.

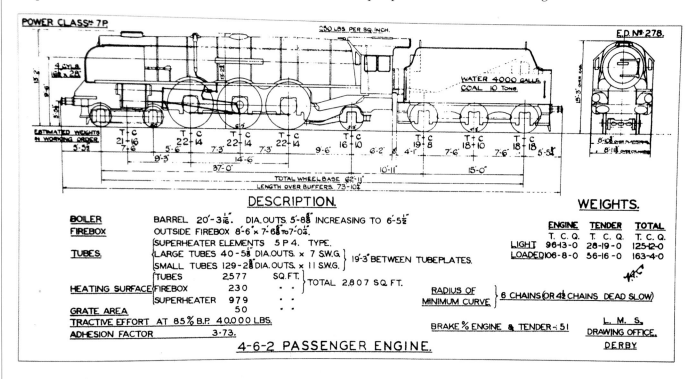

The cut down cab and new trailing truck arrangement were the obvious differences between 46256/46257 and the remainder of the class.

Final views of Tom's greatest creation in their working glory. Even when covered with dirt and grime, their thoroughbred origin and nature couldn't be hidden.

REFERENCES SOURCES

The National Railway Museum (Search Engine)
Records Consulted –
Loco/Expt/1.
Test/LMS/21.
Test/Expt/1.
Tech/LMS/ 1 to 4.
The E.A. Langridge Collection.
The E.S. Cox Collection.
The R. Riddles Collection.
The W. Starvis Collection.
The Tommy Hornbuckle Collection.

The National Archives (On Line Discovery Programme)
Frederick Johansen's papers contained in the Rail series of records held by the National Archives.

Staffordshire County Records Office
School and Education records.
Railway Records.
Local newspapers.

Derbyshire County Records Office
Railway Records.
Local newspapers.

Institution of Mechanical Engineers
Proceedings and Journals.
Solent Sky Museum
Items relating to R.J. Mitchell and the development of the Spitfire.

Private Collections
T. Coleman.
R. Hillier.
M. Lemon.
A. Ewer.
F. Johansen.
B. Graves.

The Churchill Centre, Cambridge
The papers of Sir Harold Brewer Hartley.

Books and Other Publications Consulted
BENNETT, A.: *Clayhanger*, Egmont Books, 1910.
BOND, R.: *A Lifetime With Locomotives*, Goose & Son, 1975.
BULLIED, H.A.V.: *Master Builders of Steam*, Ian Allan, 1965.
CHACKSFIELD, J.E.: *Sir William Stanier*, Oakwood Press, 2001.
COX, E.S.: *Locomotive Panorama*, Ian Allan, 1965/66.
COX, E.S.: *Chronicles of Steam*, Ian Allan, 1967.
COX, E.S.: *Speaking of Steam*, Littlehampton Books, 1971.
JAMES, F. et al: *LMS Locomotive Profile No 11 The Coronation Class*, Wild Swan, 2008.
LANGRIDGE, E.A.: *Under 10 CMEs* (2 volumes) Oakwood Press, 2011.
MITCHELL, G. – *R.J. Mitchell: Schoolboy to Spitfire*, Nelson and Saunders, 1986.
NOCK, O.S.: *William Stanier – An Engineering Biography*, Ian Allan, 1964.
POWELL, A. J.: *Stanier Pacifics at Work*, Ian Allan, 1986.
ROGERS, H.C.B.: *The Last Steam Locomotive Engineer – R.A. Riddles*, Ian Allan, 1970.
RIMMER, A.: *Testing Times at Derby*, Oakwood Press, 2004.
SIXSMITH, I.: *The Book of the Coronation Pacifics*, Irwell Press, 1998.
The Journal of the Institution of Locomotive Engineers (Various editions).
Meccano Magazine (1935 – 1940).
The Engineer (1935 – 1940).
Backtrack (Various editions).
The Railway Magazine (Various issues).
The Railway Gazette (Various editions).

Photographic Sources

The photographs reproduced in this book come from many sources and are credited as follows:

Roland Bond (RB), Tom Francis Coleman (TFC), Ernest Cox (EC), Alfred Ewer (AE), Bernard Graves (BG), Ronald Hillier (RH), Tim Hillier-Graves

(THG), Ron Jarvis (RJ), Frederick Johansen (FJ), Mike Lemon (ML), Robert Riddles (RR) and Bishop Eric Treacy (ET).

Photo Credits (by page):

RB – 140, 154 and 168.
TFC/ML – 8–9, 11, 17–19, 22, 24, 26–30, 33–4, 37–44, 47–51, 57–61, 63–4, 66, 68, 70–1, 73–4, 77, 82–4, 88, 90, 94–5, 98, 102–104, 106–107, 109–10, 112, 114, 116, 120–2, 124–7, 136–8, 142, 146–53, 155–6, 158–62, 164, 166–7, 171–4, 178–82, 186–7, 189, 193–4, 197–202, 207, 209–10, 216, 219, 236, 254–7, 260, 268–87
EC – 141
AE – 12–14, 65, 72, 75, 80–1, 117–18, 128–31, 143, 151, 163, 166, 175–6
BG – 183–5
RH – 16, 31, 46, 52–6, 64, 67, 76, 79, 89, 91, 97–9, 115–16, 120–1, 132, 135, 140, 144–5, 148, 165, 168, 170, 188, 190–1, 195–6, 203, 208, 211, 235, 238, 265, 267
THG – 5, 7, 9–10, 14–15, 17, 21, 25–6, 35–6, 45, 66, 69, 71, 78, 83, 86–7, 92–3, 96, 105, 107, 113, 122, 125, 129, 133, 139, 149, 154–5, 173, 192–3, 204–207, 212–42, 261–2, 265, 270
RJ – 157, 169
FJ – 101, 178
RR – 132, 135, 144–5
ET – 170

INDEX